Amish Enterprise

CENTER BOOKS IN ANABAPTIST STUDIES

Donald B. Kraybill
Consulting Editor

George F. Thompson
Series Founder and Director

Published in cooperation with the Center for American Places,
Santa Fe, New Mexico, and Staunton, Virginia

Second Edition

From Plows

Amish Enterprise

to Profits

Donald B. Kraybill
Steven M. Nolt

THE JOHNS HOPKINS UNIVERSITY PRESS
Baltimore & London

© 1995, 2004 The Johns Hopkins University Press
All rights reserved. Published 2004
Printed in the United States of America on acid-free paper
9 8 7 6 5 4 3 2 1

The Johns Hopkins University Press
2715 North Charles Street
Baltimore, Maryland 21218-4363
www.press.jhu.edu

Photography credits: p. 235 by Karen Johnson-Weiner; pp. 150 and 230 by
Daniel Rodriguez; p. 240 by Doyle Yoder; all other photographs by
Dennis L. Hughes

Graphics credits: p. 236 by Amish.net; pp. 9, 14, 24, 28, 37, and 117 by Linda
Eberly; p. 147 by Lancaster County Barns

Book design: Teresa Bonner

Library of Congress Cataloging-in-Publication Data

Kraybill, Donald B.
   Amish enterprise : from plows to profits / Donald B. Kraybill, Steven M.
Nolt.—2nd ed.
        p.   cm. — (Center books in Anabaptist studies)
Includes bibliographical references and index.
   ISBN 0-8018-7804-7 (alk. paper)—ISBN 0-8018-7805-5 (pbk. : alk. paper)
   1. Economics—Religious aspects—Amish—History of doctrines—20th
century. 2. Amish—Pennsylvania—Lancaster Co.—History—20th century.
3. Lancaster County (Pa.)—Church history—20th century. 4. Lancaster
County (Pa.)—Economic conditions. I. Nolt, Steven M.   II. Title.
III. Series.
   BX8128.E36K73 2004
   305.6'87074815—dc21

                                                         2003010637

A catalog record for this book is available from the British Library.

CONTENTS

PREFACE

In recent years, *Fortune 500, Forbes,* the *Wall Street Journal,* and the *New York Times* have profiled the success of Amish entrepreneurs—the one-time barefoot farmers who have learned to turn a tidy profit in business.* The Amish have been a people of the plow for more than three centuries. Their agrarian tradition and love of the land have shaped their distinctive faith and culture in many ways. They remain a rural people, but their rapid entry into the world of business is bringing dramatic changes to their traditional way of life.

This book tells the story of the Amish of Lancaster County, Pennsylvania, who have abandoned their plows for the pursuit of profit. It is, in short, the story of a mini-industrial revolution—the transformation of Amish society in virtually one generation. A case study of one Amish community cannot be generalized to all Amish everywhere, but the story of Lancaster's Amish may be a harbinger of things to come in other settlements that also face encroaching urbanization.

Numerous changes in the last ten years called for a revised edition of this book—greater use of the Internet to market Amish products, growing entanglements with technology, the sale of some large Amish businesses to non-Amish buyers, the creation of an Amish industrial park, continued growth in the number and size of Amish enterprises, more aggressive advertising of Amish products, and greater recognition of the productivity of Amish shops by media.

*These stories appeared in *Fortune 500,* June 1995; *Forbes,* 9 March 1998; *Wall Street Journal,* 8 February 1996; and *New York Times,* 28 November 1997. A major story on Amish businesses, distributed by the Associated Press on 9 March 1998, was printed in numerous newspapers across the country. Even the English edition of the *Daily Yomiuri,* a Japanese newspaper, carried a story of Amish business success in 7 July 1998.

This revised edition of *Amish Enterprise* reflects the continuing growth and changes of Amish businesses in the Lancaster area. New data from a sample of 800 adults in ten church districts suggests that some 1,600 Amish businesses are flourishing in the Lancaster settlement. One in five adults now owns a business, and all signs point to financial success. Chapter 14 is a new addition that overviews the rise and implications of nonfarm work in other Amish settlements across the country.

Throughout the text we employ the image of plow and profit in both a literal and metaphorical fashion. Today hundreds of Amish people who grew up on farms manage successful businesses. They have literally left their plows for the pursuit of profit. In some cases a second generation that knows little about farming is assuming business ownership from their parents. This dramatic shift has triggered many consequences in the life of this traditional people. It brings not only work-related changes but also implications for education, technology, child-rearing practices, gender roles, community structure, and relations with the outside world.

Deep cultural changes also lurk beneath the surface of this transition from plows to profits. The plow is more than an occupational tool; in many ways it also symbolizes a worldview. Indeed, the traditional horse-drawn plow articulates a preindustrial understanding of reality—a worldview dominated by nature and supernatural forces. The plow was part of a social order in which the community—not the individual—was the supreme unit of reality. It was a community where neighbors gathered together in seasonal rituals to harvest crops and to battle the unpredictable vagaries of fire, storm, and flood.

In the past, the weather and the seasonal cycles regulated the rhythms of Amish life. Because the hand of providence bestowed the terms of life, rural peasants could do little to control their surroundings or to take charge of things. The patterns of community life, the shape of religious practice, and the structure of family ritual were simply accepted as the divine order of things—embedded in the universe and handed down by past generations. The rationality, efficiency, and technology of modern times had not penetrated this traditional world that was regulated by the hand of God. Strategic goals, specialization, and marketing were unknown. But all of this would change with the abandonment of the plow.

Amish farming of bygone days was not a commercial enterprise devoted to the pursuit of profit; it was a worldview and a way of life. Unlike a career in business, farming was a calling, a way of life shaped by the wisdom of the centuries. It was a way of living that was accepted, not planned; bestowed, not strategized—a way of being that wove individuals into a seamless fabric of tradition, church, family, and community.

The abandonment of the plow in Amish life and the boon of commercial enterprise signal the entry of this sectarian community into a different world. It is a world where entrepreneurs take charge of things, test markets, create new products, and seek the most efficient means to boost productivity. It is a world where individuals engage in advertising and shoulder responsibility for the failure and success of their efforts. It is, in short, a world where individualism, efficiency, control, planning, and specialization—all foreign to the economy of the plow—are essential tools for making a living. In the commercial setting, work is no longer a way of life bestowed by the hand of God; it is an endeavor one creates, controls, and manages in order to turn a profit. Thus, the shift from plows to profits reflects a fundamental transformation of worldviews—a transition between two different cultural worlds.

The rationalized worldview is not confined to shops; it penetrates Amish agriculture as well. In the Lancaster area, dozens of farmers employ agricultural consultants to test their soils and crops in order to apply the proper fertilizer and pesticide. Many farmers keep extensive records to chart the productivity of their dairy herds. Such behavior also signals a commitment to efficiency and profit. Thus, although we use plow and profit in a symbolic fashion to signal two different cultural worlds, we must draw the line cautiously, because the pursuit of profit also guides the literal plows of some Amish farmers.

Although Lancaster's Amish are abandoning their plows, they have not completely conceded their cultural souls to the pursuit of profit. Indeed, a major contribution of this book is our analysis of the many ways their religious subculture harnesses the impulses of entrepreneurship. Although the Amish church has many resources that empower entrepreneurship, its moral boundaries also curb business endeavors. But despite the cultural constraints, Amish entrepreneurs have created an astonishing story of success. Although small businesses often fail, few of these ethnic enterprises have stumbled. Moreover, they have been able to achieve their economic success without the typical trappings of technology and education.

Five major questions guide our analysis: (1) Why did microenterprises arise at this particular juncture in Amish life? (2) In what ways does Amish culture regulate entrepreneurial activity? (3) How are these enterprises distinctive? (4) Why are they successful? And, most important, (5) How will they influence the future of Amish society? Thus, although ethnic business is the focus of our investigation, this is not primarily an economic study or an analysis of commercial activity. Rather, it is a cultural study of the formation and regulation of entrepreneurship in a traditional community. We are particularly interested in exploring the ways in which the resources of a religious subculture are used both to bolster and to restrain economic pursuits.

The story we tell is the saga of a traditional people struggling to save their cultural souls while turning their backs on the pastures of their past. It is the story of a people in transition, perched between the worlds of nature and of commerce. Reluctant to leave the farms that have nurtured their sectarian heritage, and fearing the outside world of the factory, the Lancaster Amish have staked out a middle ground that straddles the boundaries of modern and traditional ways. In this sense, the hundreds of Amish industries scattered across Lancaster's landscape represent negotiated cultural bargains that blend the historic strands of a religious subculture with the commercial patterns of the modern world.

Finally, a word about cultural sensitivities. Responding to concerns for anonymity, we have not identified many of the entrepreneurs who are quoted throughout the text. However, in those cases where Amish names have been previously published in newspaper or magazine articles, we have used their names in the text. Dennis L. Hughes, who snapped many of the photographs, was sensitive to Amish concerns about not posing for photographs; thus, few persons appear in his many splendid illustrations. The Amish typically refer to out-group people as *English* because outsiders speak English instead of the Pennsylvania German dialect. Except for direct quotations, we have chosen, for stylistic reasons, to use the term *non-Amish* for those outside the Amish community.

ACKNOWLEDGMENTS

We are grateful to the many persons whose cooperation and assistance made this project possible. We owe a special debt to the more than 170 entrepreneurs who generously shared ideas and opinions as well as time from their busy schedules. Various non-Amish business leaders, consultants, and municipal officials also provided valuable insights and assistance. Gertrude Huntington and four Amish leaders (three entrepreneurs and a historian) gave helpful feedback on the text of the first edition.

The research for the first edition was made possible in part by a grant from the Center for Rural Pennsylvania. Our colleagues, Steven M. Smith and Jill L. Findeis, provided helpful guidance and counsel throughout the research phase of the project. The Young Center for Anabaptist and Pietist Studies at Elizabethtown College provided generous assistance and support for both editions of the book.

Interviewers for the first edition included Jean-Paul Benowitz, Martin Franke, Lester Hoover, Conrad Kanagy, and Jerold Stahly. Michele Kozimore and Conrad Kanagy performed the computer analysis of our survey data. Jodi L. Brandon, Erin Keefe, Sherry Troutman, and Brenda Spiker provided valuable editorial assistance in the preparation of the first edition. Terri Hopkins at Messiah College and Sandy Metzler at Elizabethtown College keystroked the manuscript for the revised edition. It was a special pleasure to work with Dennis L. Hughes, who took most of the photographs with keen sensitivity to the concerns of the various shop owners. Linda Eberly prepared the graphic artwork. As always, we found it delightful to work with George F. Thompson, president of the Center for American Places and founder and director of the series in which this book appears. Editors Elizabeth Yoder and Courtney Bond provided superb editorial counsel throughout the project. It was a pleasure to work with all these colleagues who have contributed in many significant ways to our efforts. And finally, we have enjoyed working with each other in a constructive and pleasant partnership.

PART ONE

The Cultural Context

1. The Roots of Amish Life

It's not best for Amish people to leave the farm.

— AMISH BISHOP

Leaving the Farm

Hidden from the bustle of modern life, Amish farms nestle in the gently rolling hills of Lancaster County, Pennsylvania. To the casual observer, the Amish appear aloof from the larger world about them. Televisions, computers, and video games—the pride of technological progress—find no place in Amish homes. Amish children attend one-room private schools through the eighth grade and then waive formal education in high school and college. Using horse-and-buggy transportation, wearing plain clothing, and burning gas lamps, the Amish stand apart from modern life.

At first blush, the rural ways of Amish life seem tied to the perpetual cycles of seed time and harvest. But a deeper look belies this bucolic image, for the Lancaster Amish have been leaving their farms in record numbers. Within one generation, they have established hundreds of enterprises with stunning success. Unable to secure more farmland, they have entered trades, crafts, and merchandising in surprising numbers. Amish manufacturing establishments boast sophisticated machinery and quality artisanship. Many firms ship orders across the country, and a few even trade in global markets. Energetic entrepreneurs have created hundreds of shops that serve their own community as well as outsiders and curious tourists.

Why have a people who have worked the land for generations suddenly discarded their plows for the pursuit of profits? And, having moved into the world of commerce, how have they managed to become successful entrepreneurs in a single generation? What enables young farmers without a high school education to become successful managers of prosperous companies posting million-dollar sales? And how do enterprising Amish women balance their traditional responsibilities as wives, mothers, and homemakers with the demands of business? Moreover, how are small shops—bridled by Amish taboos on vehicles and electricity—able to compete with high-tech manufacturers?

Without computers, splashy advertising, or personally owned vehicles—the tools any CEO would consider essential—the Amish have built an impressive array of robust operations. Their foray into business, however, poses many questions for a people of the land. How will this abrupt turn from farming transform their historic way of life? Will they retain their symbolic separation from the world as they grow more comfortable in the marketplace? Will the ethnic rhythms of church and community, long shaped by seasonal cycles, fade in the face of commercial success? Having survived religious persecution and the forces of assimilation for some three hundred years, will the Amish be able to withstand the pernicious snares of wealth?

The story of Amish entrepreneurship poses questions for the larger world as well. How can work support and fortify family life? Is it possible for work to bring satisfaction without consuming personal identity? Do small-scale enterprises bring greater satisfaction and fulfillment? Can the cultural texture of an ethnic community guide business without hampering productivity? And does apprenticeship provide an optimal form of training for entrepreneurship?

Ironically, the Amish venture into business offers suggestive clues about the ingredients of successful entrepreneurship—lessons that in many ways overturn cherished assumptions. The story of Amish entrepreneurship is especially intriguing because it unfolded suddenly after nearly three hundred years of plowing the soil. The Amish have a rich heritage that stretches back to Europe—a saga we will briefly explore before tracing the rise of Amish enterprises.

The Anabaptist Legacy

The Amish church grew out of the Anabaptist movement of sixteenth-century Europe.[1] In 1517, Martin Luther's criticism of the practices and teachings of the Roman Catholic Church spawned the Protestant Reformation. Within a short time, other prominent church leaders, such as Ulrich Zwingli, in Zurich, Switzerland, were spearheading similar efforts of their own. Like Luther, Zwingli relied on state sanctions and the consent of the Zurich city council to implement his religious reforms.

Some of Zwingli's associates thought the Reformation was proceeding too slowly. These young students, craftspeople, and merchants argued that the Bible alone, not political expediency, should guide the church. Moreover, they wanted to discard the rituals of infant baptism and the Mass, which in their view lacked biblical foundation. Disillusioned by Zwingli's cooperation with government leaders, the young radicals soon began meeting privately for Bible study and discussion. When Zurich city officials ordered the group to disband, the young mavericks broke with the state church and rebaptized each other in a private home on 21 January 1525. This simple ceremony triggered a harsh confrontation with civil authorities.

The dissenters called for a radical commitment to the teachings of Jesus. Moreover, they argued that only persons who were old enough to understand the implications of Christian faith should receive baptism. Because the young reformers had already been baptized as infants in the Catholic Church, they were often labeled Anabaptists, meaning "rebaptizers." The Anabaptists sought a separation of church and state that threatened to erode the authority of civil magistrates over religious affairs.

Breaking with both Catholic and Protestant thought, the radical reformers established a church based on voluntary choice, one whose members were accountable to one another and were expected to live apart from the worldly society. Many Anabaptists emphasized the importance of following the teachings of Jesus in their daily lives and thus rejected all violence, including military participation. Following the biblical injunction, many Anabaptists would not swear civil oaths or bring suits in court. Like Jesus their savior, they were willing to absorb hostility and suffer even unto death.[2]

The Anabaptist challenge to the long-standing unity of church and state did not go unanswered. The church and the state quickly joined hands to eradicate the heretics that threatened to fracture the very underpinnings of social order. Within months, authorities had arrested many Anabaptists. When argumentation and imprisonment did little to quell the movement, the state turned to execution. Anabaptists were hunted, jailed, tortured, and killed. The decades following 1525 saw several thousand rebaptizers beheaded, drowned, or burned at the stake. The harsh stories of persecution remain alive among the Amish even today and reinforce their cultural separation from the world. Hundreds of stories of suffering are recorded in the *Martyrs Mirror,* a book of some twelve hundred pages that is commonly found in Amish homes.[3]

Persecution drove the Swiss and south German Anabaptists into remote areas and more tolerant sections of Europe. In the Netherlands, where Anabaptist ideas had circulated since 1530, a Catholic priest named Menno Simons emerged as an articulate Anabaptist leader. Breaking with Rome in 1536, Menno Simons spent the next twenty-five years shepherding

Anabaptist congregations across northern Europe. His writing, wisdom, and winsome leadership earned him wide recognition both within and beyond his church, so that many Anabaptists soon became known as Mennonites.[4]

Amish Beginnings

The Amish and the Mennonites share the same Anabaptist heritage, but in 1693 they formed two separate groups. Persecuted for decades after 1525, many Swiss Anabaptists found safe havens in mountainous regions, where they frequently rented marginal land for farming. Despite these hardships, many Anabaptists became known for their agricultural husbandry. Often exhausted in spirit, the once fiery Anabaptists turned more and more to the daily pursuits of making a living and passing on their faith to their children. After 1648, groups of Swiss Anabaptists periodically moved northward into the Palatinate and Alsace regions of present-day Germany and France, located east and west of the Rhine River. Although the new daughter settlements in these regions maintained contact and fellowship with their maternal church in the Alps, some differences soon began to emerge.[5]

In the late 1600s, controversy began to swirl around the activities and teachings of a reform-minded Anabaptist elder, Jakob Ammann. A recent convert to Anabaptism, Ammann migrated from Switzerland to Alsace, where he led several Anabaptist congregations. Concerned about lax church discipline and a weak spiritual life, Ammann instituted a series of reforms. He urged congregations to celebrate communion twice a year, instead of once, and to carefully discipline erring members. Additionally, Ammann forbade people from secretly joining Anabaptist congregations while still holding membership in the state church.

Most important, Ammann taught that when wayward members were excommunicated, other members should shun them in daily life as well. This social avoidance, earlier practiced by some Dutch Anabaptists, emphasized the purity of the church and the seriousness of sin, and it also encouraged excommunicated members to repent and return to the church.[6] Different understandings of social avoidance soon drove a wedge between Ammann and other Anabaptist leaders. After heated meetings in 1693 and 1694, two separate groups—Amish and Mennonite—emerged over the course of several months. Most of the congregations that followed Ammann eventually took the name Amish. Many of the other Anabaptists eventually used the name Mennonite.[7]

In addition to strict discipline, Ammann stressed simple, unadorned living. In time, untrimmed beards, simple clothing, and the use of hook-

◆

This shop on an Amish farm builds Victorian-style playhouses for children. The
playhouses are sold to non-Amish buyers through distributors in several states.

and-eye fasteners instead of buttons became trademarks of Amish life. A
conservative flank of Anabaptism, the Amish maintained a distinct identity from their Mennonite cousins as they emigrated and settled in the
Americas.[8] The last Amish congregation in Europe dissolved in 1937.

Economic problems, incessant warfare, and political instability drove
many Europeans to risk their lives crossing the Atlantic in hopes of finding a more stable life in North America. For the Mennonites and the
Amish, the promise of religious tolerance was an added lure. Already in
1683, ten years before the Mennonite-Amish schism, Mennonites had begun settling near Philadelphia, Pennsylvania. Along with other persecuted religious minorities, the Mennonites chose land in Penn's Woods,
the colony governed by the English Quaker William Penn. Offering freedom of worship and religious practice, Pennsylvania became a haven for
the Amish as well.[9]

Several Amish families may have arrived on American shores before
1730, but sizable communities began to form only after 1737. Amish families continued to arrive in Pennsylvania throughout the 1770s, settling in
both southern Berks County and north-central Lancaster County. Defec-

tion to other churches, Indian raids, and the lure of better land eventually dispersed the original communities. By 1760, a permanent Amish settlement congregated near the Berks-Lancaster border, and by 1790 another community had formed in eastern Lancaster County.[10]

The communities grew slowly; by 1900 Lancaster's Amish settlement included a mere six congregations. The twentieth century, however, witnessed phenomenal growth, as the Lancaster settlement grew to more than a hundred congregations. Today across North America, the Amish population of adults and children exceeds 180,000. Members reside in twenty-eight states and the province of Ontario, with about 65 percent in Ohio, Pennsylvania, and Indiana.[11] During the twentieth century, the Amish population has doubled about every twenty years, bringing a diversity of lifestyles and practices among the more than 330 different geographical settlements.[12]

The Texture of Amish Society

Amish society has several distinctive features. It is small, informal, local, compact, and fairly homogeneous.[13] From egos to organizational units, the Amish prefer small-scale things. They fear that bigness will lead to pride and the abuse of power. Small-scale life encourages informality and flexibility. The bureaucratic organizations and procedures of modern societies are completely missing in Amish life. Horse-and-buggy transportation and large families living close together encourage face-to-face interaction. Social networks overlap because the same persons are fused together by residence, kin, ethnicity, work, education, leisure, and worship—yielding a dense and compact social structure. Historically, Amish involvement in farming produced a homogeneous occupational structure, though that is changing with the rise of business.

The Amish church is organized congregationally. Commonly known as a *district,* an Amish congregation includes all the families living in the immediate geographic area. There are more than 1,400 congregations in North America. Some twenty to forty households comprise a district. Congregations do not use church buildings but gather for worship in the homes of their members. When a district grows too large to hold services in a home, it divides into two. The small size of the typical district facilitates a close-knit, intimate fellowship in which members come to know each other very well.

The church districts in a given geographic area comprise a *settlement.* As many as one hundred districts, or as few as one, may be found in a single settlement. Lancaster's Amish community ranks second only to Holmes and adjacent counties in Ohio, which host the largest settlement in North

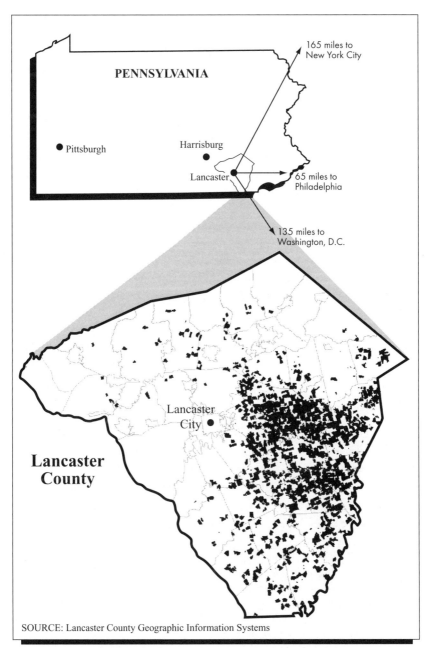

PENNSYLVANIA

165 miles to
New York City

● Pittsburgh   Harrisburg
                    ●
                 Lancaster
                           65 miles to
                           Philadelphia

                 135 miles to
                 Washington, D.C.

Lancaster
City ●

Lancaster
County

SOURCE: Lancaster County Geographic Information Systems

Figure 1.1 Farmland Owned by the Amish in Lancaster County

America. The Lancaster settlement has about 150 districts. Since 1970, various migrations out of Lancaster County have seeded nearly thirty new settlements in other parts of Pennsylvania as well as in Indiana, Kentucky, Missouri, New York, and Wisconsin. Nevertheless, over the years only a small proportion of families have left the Lancaster area.

Amish church districts that share similar religious practices consider themselves "in fellowship" with one another and constitute an *affiliation.* Districts in an affiliation usually permit their ministers to speak in one another's worship services. In Lancaster County, the Old Order Amish are the largest affiliation. The more progressive New Order Amish and the Beachy Amish are two small affiliations that have two and five congregations respectively.[14]

Each Old Order congregation gathers for worship every other Sunday. A bishop, two ministers, and a deacon preside over the three-hour gathering and serve the church without pay or formal theological training. Leaders exert considerable influence. Bishops preach and teach as well as administer the rites of baptism, communion, marriage, discipline, and excommunication. They also are expected to model the virtues of an obedient Christian life to which the church calls all its members.

The practices, teachings, and taboos of the church are known as the *Ordnung,* a word without a simple English equivalent.[15] The Ordnung defines the expected conduct of members. The "understandings" of the Ordnung include general principles, such as modesty and nonviolence, as well as specific applications, including prohibiting television and wearing prescribed styles of clothing. Generally unwritten and passed on by oral tradition, the Ordnung is a body of communal regulations that cultivate group identity, cohesion, and order. The Ordnung articulates the moral order of the community, and its practice defines the very essence of Amish identity:

Examples of practices prescribed by the Ordnung:	*Examples of practices prohibited by the Ordnung:*
the color and style of clothing	tractors for fieldwork
men's hat styles	ownership and operation of automobiles
the color and style of buggies	electricity from public power lines
horses or mules for fieldwork	filing a lawsuit
steel wheels on machinery	entering military service
the Pennsylvania German dialect	owning computers and televisions
worship services in homes	pipeline milking equipment
unison singing without instruments	high school education
the menu of the congregational meal	jewelry, wedding rings, and wrist watches
marriage to church members	divorce

Slowly changing over the years, the Ordnung is the social glue and guiding principle of the Amish community. Church leaders, especially bishops, play a major role in persuading members to follow the Ordnung in their daily lives. The general contours of the Ordnung—horse-and-buggy travel, distinctive costume, the Pennsylvania German dialect, the taboos on electricity and high school—are followed in all church districts in the Lancaster settlement. Some other practices, however, vary from district to district—access to telephones, the size of businesses, the use of power lawnmowers, and the style of furnishing in homes. Ordained leaders in the Lancaster area confer twice a year, hoping to promote a common Ordnung as much as possible.

When baptized members overstep the boundaries of the Ordnung—by buying a car or wearing jewelry, for example—they encounter the discipline of the church. Excommunication faces all those who persist in flouting the guidance of the Ordnung. Excommunicated members who refuse to change their ways are shunned. Members may not eat or conduct business with former members who are under the ban of the church. Restoration is always possible for those who are willing to humble themselves and return to the church, but for the unrepentant, shunning continues until death.[16]

The Quiltwork of Amish Culture

The core of Amish culture is embedded in the German word *Gelassenheit*.[17] Roughly translated, it means "submission"—yielding to a higher authority. A rather elastic concept, it carries many specific meanings: self-surrender, resignation to God's will, yielding to God and others, willingness to suffer, self-denial, contentment, and a calm spirit. Although the term *Gelassenheit* is not typically used in everyday speech, many words in the Amish vocabulary capture its meaning—obedience, humility, submission, simplicity, and plainness.

Gelassenheit stands in sharp contrast to the proud, aggressive spirit of individualism afloat in modern culture. The meek stance of Gelassenheit unfolds as individuals yield to higher authorities: the will of God, the Ordnung of the church, ordained leaders, parents, and teachers. As the core value of this ethnic culture, Gelassenheit collides with the heartbeat of modernity—individual achievement. Whereas moderns cheer self-fulfillment and individual rights, the Amish cherish subdued and humble persons who are willing to give up some personal freedom in return for a durable and visible ethnic identity.

Gelassenheit penetrates many dimensions of Amish life—its values, symbols, rituals, personalities, and social organization. The practice of Gelassenheit entails a modest way of walking, talking, and dressing. Gelassenheit brings self-effacing comments and defers to others. It forbids the use of force and thus prohibits members of the church from joining the military, holding political office, or filing lawsuits. The lowly spirit of Gelassenheit uses silence and avoidance to deal with conflict, denies ostentatious display, and champions the virtues of simplicity, humility, smallness, and quietness. The graces of Gelassenheit place the welfare of the community and respect for its traditions above the whims of individual preference.

Gelassenheit also reflects a worldview that in many ways is premodern; it not only suppresses individualism but patiently waits for things to happen. Rather than taking charge of things in modern fashion and trying to control human life at every turn, this mind-set patiently accepts whatever flows from providential hands. It is a religious worldview, but not one that emphasizes personal salvation, personal evangelism, and personal interpretations of scripture—all of which reflect the values of individualism. Instead of controlling eternal outcomes, the Amish seek to yield to the will of God in what may seem to modern minds like a religious fatalism of sorts. This view of reality has been cultivated and reinforced by an agrarian tradition that requires one to yield to vagaries of the weather and its seasonal rhythms.

The social scientist Max Weber has argued that rationalization is the hallmark of the modern world—a rationality that expresses itself in calculating minds and in the formalized structures of bureaucracy.[18] The primary manifestations of rationality include efficiency, calculation, and control. The press for efficiency transforms the meaning of time and is symbolized, of course, by the presence of clocks everywhere. Strategic goals, a pervasive emphasis on planning, and the quantification of virtually everything reveal the modern penchant for calculation. Indeed, lack of planning has become the cardinal sin of modernity. Technology serves as the handmaiden of modernity by enabling humans to control and master both physical and social environments—or at least to live by the illusion of such control.

The absence of bureaucracy in Amish life is perhaps the most compelling evidence of their rejection of a rationalized view of the world. Traditional Amish culture has eschewed efficiency, calculation, and control. The pace of life is rather slow in traditional Amish homesteads—not sliced into short segments by wrist watches, digital clocks, radios, and television ads. The calculating mind-set of modern life is foreign to Amish culture, which lacks five-year plans, strategic goals, and career planning. And, of course, the taboos on DVD players, computers, electricity, and vehicle ownership reflect the Amish reluctance to use technology to control things. In

♦

Several Amish auction companies hold public auctions for Amish and non-Amish clients. The attire prescribed by the Ordnung of the church marks ethnic boundaries in public settings.

contrast to moderns, the Amish have been more interested in controlling technology itself than in using it to control their own environment.

But all of this is changing. The rise of microenterprises signals the social transformation of a traditional culture. The embrace of entrepreneurship encourages individualism as well as a rationalized approach to life with its accessories of efficiency, calculation, and control. The Amish, however, have not completely capitulated to modern ways; indeed, the story of Amish entrepreneurship can be called "a war against progress."[19] The Amish encounter with the world of commerce is indeed a struggle between the quiet and modest habits of Gelassenheit and the efficient, high-tech ways of modernity.

An Interactive Model of Culture and Entrepreneurship

Our analysis of Amish enterprise explores the cultural factors that regulate ethnic entrepreneurship—forces that both empower and retard entrepreneurial activity.[20] We trace the ways in which an ethnic culture has both facilitated and impeded the rise of microenterprises in the face of pressures that jeopardize its centuries-old agrarian tradition. A cultural heritage

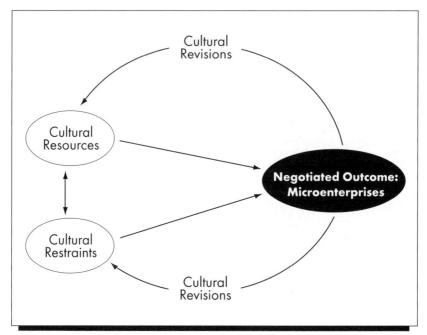

Figure 1.2 An Interactive Model of Culture and Entrepreneurship

carries both *resources* and *restraints* for the development of entrepreneurial activity (fig. 1.2). In the pages that follow, we explore how Amish culture marshaled its resources and restraints, often in opposition to each other, to create hundreds of small businesses.

Cultural resources include the values, norms, customs, and skills as well as the kinship and community arrangements that are available to empower prospective entrepreneurs.[21] All of these resources provide potential cultural and social capital for underwriting new commercial ventures. Cultural resources for entrepreneurship in the Amish community include a vigorous work ethic, managerial skills forged on the farm, frugality, strong kinship networks, large and stable family units, and a religious asceticism that rejects consumerism. A long-standing emphasis on practical education—especially apprenticeship—also facilitates the development of microenterprises. All of these resources, floating in the ethnic reservoir, provide cultural and social capital for the formation of Amish business.

Not all the commodities in a cultural tradition are beneficial for entrepreneurial development, however. Indeed, Amish culture holds many restraints that impede entrepreneurial activity. These *cultural restraints* stowed away in the heritage of the community include historic values, norms, taboos, customs, and practices. The church's long-standing prohibitions against litigation, politics, individualism, commercial insurance, and higher education, and its restraints on free interaction with the outside world all hinder the development of business.[22] Moreover, restrictions on technology—motor vehicles, telephones, computers, and electricity—also levy constraints on entrepreneurial activity. The esteemed virtues of Gelassenheit—modesty and humility—as well as age-old taboos on pride, restrain advertising and promotional efforts. Many of these cultural constraints on entrepreneurship counterbalance the resources that can empower business activity. Thus, the rise of Amish enterprises often involved a delicate negotiation between the cultural resources and restraints within their ethnic community.[23]

The development of Amish enterprises was a negotiated social process that entailed both ethnic *facilitation* and *resistance.*[24] That is the real story of this book—an exploration of the ways in which an ethnic culture both facilitates and resists the emergence of entrepreneurship. *Ethnic facilitation* refers to the various ways in which cultural resources mobilize and build business enterprise. In the 1980s the Amish marshaled their social, material, and financial resources in an enormous burst of entrepreneurial activity. The community deployed the values of hard work and frugality, as well as entrepreneurial skills honed over the centuries in farming, in burgeoning commercial enterprises. Family and kinship networks sprang into action and provided capital, counsel, mentoring, and labor for hundreds of fledgling businesses. In addition to the public market, the growing Amish population itself welcomed the new products and services that were spilling out of the commercial ventures.

In all these ways, the cultural resources of the ethnic community facilitated the growth of entrepreneurship by providing the necessary social and cultural capital to underwrite hundreds of new enterprises. But the mobilization of resources for commercial activity was only half of the story; the ethnic community also hindered the growth of entrepreneurship. Indeed, this is one of the unique features of the Amish saga. Most ethnic cultures have resources of one sort or another to deploy for entrepreneurship, but few have the heavy restraints of Amish culture that impede business development.

Cultural restraints within the Amish tradition hampered, or at least constrained, the growth of business. The process of *ethnic resistance* thwarted entrepreneurial activity in several ways. The values of Gelassenheit, humility, and nonresistance hampered entrepreneurs from engaging in the type of assertive behavior often required for successful commercial competition. Aggressive advertising was frowned upon, and filing a lawsuit was cause for excommunication. Moreover, the church's restrictions on the use of technology clearly obstructed commercial activity. Other aspects of Amish culture also bridled entrepreneurial impulses. The taboo on high school blocked access to credentials and to advanced technical training, thus impeding upward social mobility. The moral boundaries of Amish culture also blocked business involvements in entertainment, leisure, travel, liquor, and certain forms of technology—cars, televisions, videos, and computers. In all of these ways and more, the process of ethnic resistance imposed cultural constraints on entrepreneurial activity.

Thus, Amish enterprises can be viewed as *negotiated outcomes*—cultural compromises produced by the countervailing forces of both ethnic facilitation and ethnic resistance.[25] Shaped by both the resources and restraints of their cultural heritage, the burgeoning shops reflect a process of cultural bargaining within the ethnic community. But they have been shaped by external bargaining as well—for they also embody numerous compromises with the larger culture. The Amish have long stressed the importance of separation from the outside world, but now they are doing business with the world—a world that once persecuted them—and in the process, the larger world is transforming them and their values in new ways.

Consequently, the rise of Amish industry has produced *cultural revisions* in the traditional patterns of Amish life. Business involvements are reshaping old cultural values and social arrangements, and these changes will inextricably alter the face of Amish society in the years to come. The shops and stores that developed because of certain deeply held Amish beliefs are now acting back upon—indeed, revising—the very cultural values that gave rise to them in the first place. Signs of modernity—growing individualism, control, efficiency, rationality, mobility, technology, and occupational specialization—abound more and more. The growth of Amish businesses is, in short, transforming the traditional values of Amish society in new and more modern directions.

PART TWO

Cultural Resources
for Entrepreneurship

2. From Plows to Profits

*It's like a parting of the Red Sea again, only this time Moses led us
into different occupations.*

— AMISH SHOP OWNER

The Garden Spot

The transformation of Amish work unfolded in the
garden spot of Lancaster County, Pennsylvania. The
county's fertile soil and robust economy provide a
pleasant habitat for both plows and profits. Lancaster's multifaceted economy, anchored in agriculture, industry, and tourism, insulates the area from
the erratic cycles of business that plague some single-industry towns and
has remained remarkably stable over the years.[1] In the words of an Amish
contractor, "Lancaster's economy is so diverse. We have one of everything.
When things get bad it doesn't hit us as hard, because we don't have one
big employer. I've often said Lancaster is really isolated from 'the real
world.' We hardly know how good we have it."

Today the county's 955 square miles provide a home for more than
475,000 people. Located within several hours of Philadelphia, New York,
Baltimore, and Washington, D.C., Lancaster sits on the edge of the sprawling eastern megalopolis stretching from Boston, Massachusetts, southward
to Norfolk, Virginia. One of the fastest-growing metropolitan areas in
Pennsylvania, the county population climbed some 30 percent between
1980 and 2000.[2] Business and industry continue to thrive, with more than
eleven thousand firms in the Lancaster area. A dependable workforce, low
unemployment, sustainable growth, and easy access to eastern metropolitan markets have made the county a commercial paradise for new businesses, all of which fuel the region's prosperity. The county, in fact, ranks
in the top twenty-five regions of the country for entrepreneurial growth.
U.S. News and World Report acclaimed Lancaster as one of America's seven
"new boomtowns" in the late 1990s because of its rapid growth.[3]

Despite the commercial growth, agriculture remains an important sector of the local economy. The output from Lancaster's 4,500 farms ranks it first in the U.S. for agricultural sales among nonirrigated counties. The county's combined output of corn, hay, tobacco, soybeans, and other crops tops the state of Pennsylvania. Lancaster's 340,000 beef and dairy cattle, 62 million laying hens and broilers, and 325,000 hogs produce more than $875 million worth of products a year. Lancaster cows feed nearly 11 million people a year, and its chickens provide eggs for 4.3 million.[4] Moreover, one in five jobs in Lancaster County are tied to agriculture.

Testimony to agriculture's importance is the high level of emotion generated by public discussions of farmland preservation, manure storage, and the maintenance of family farms in the face of development. Lancaster ranks first in the nation for farmland preservation, with more than 51,000 acres preserved.[5] However, with 2,500 acres lost each year to development, the battle between preservationists and developers continues.

Lancaster's unique mix of rural and urban flavors draws an estimated seven million visitors a year, including a growing number of international visitors. Hundreds of outlet stores and business establishments—some operated by the Amish themselves—profit handsomely from the annual influx of visitors. Tourists spend some $1.6 billion annually, which produces $238 million in tax revenues, and more than twenty-five thousand tourist-related jobs.[6]

The county hosts the oldest and second-largest Amish settlement in North American. Indeed, about half of Pennsylvania's 50,000 Amish live in the Lancaster area. Although the best known of Lancaster's residents, the Amish are by no means in the majority. With some 25,000 adults and children, they comprise about 5 percent of the county's populace. Even in the heart of their settlement, where the Amish may own 90 percent of the land, they are outnumbered by non-Amish neighbors living in small towns and along rural roads. The Amish remain a religious minority as well; for Roman Catholics, United Methodists, and several other denominations in the county outrank the Amish in membership.[7]

A People of the Plow

The Amish have always been a people of the land. Ever since European persecution pushed them into rural isolation, they have been tillers of the soil, and good ones.[8] The land has nurtured their common life. They have been stewards of the land—plowing, harrowing, fertilizing, and cultivating it with care. The rich limestone soil of Lancaster County, like a magnetic force, holds their community together and binds them to their history.[9] They have tenaciously clung to the soil and have purchased more

◆

Tour buses by the hundreds bring visitors to Lancaster County. Amish-made
furniture, crafts, quilts, and food are popular products with tourists.

acreage at every opportunity. An Amish leader expressed the traditional view in these words: "A long-standing tradition is that a consistent Amish family will be on the farm or attached close to the soil, and a father will provide a farm for his boys.[10]

"Agriculture," according to one leader, "is a religious tenet, a branch of Christian duty." The divine injunction to Adam to till the ground from which he came provides a religious mandate for the Amish. They believe that the Bible instructs them to earn their living by the sweat of their brown. Tilling the soil induces sacramental meanings, for it ushers them into the presence of God. "I don't know what will happen if we get away from the soil," an Amish farmer said. "I can see where it's not a very good thing. You get away from working with the soil, and you get away from nature, and then you are getting away from the Lord's handiwork."

Another Amishman argues that the Amish were unable to establish a stable and permanent community life in North American until they found the rich soils of Lancaster County, where they could "live together, worship together, and work together." Even an Amish business leader traces the vitality of the Amish community to the quality of the local soil, but he fears that their new prosperity will, in the long run, ruin the church with luxury.

Although the Amish delight in working it, the soil is not an end in itself: it is the seedbed for family life. A persistent theme extolled by Amish elders is that the farm is the best place to raise children. Even the owners of booming Amish industries repeat the litany of praise for the family farm. Despite success in their thriving enterprises, entrepreneurs worry about the fate of their grandchildren, growing up without roots in the soil.

In the past, the farm provided a habitat for raising sturdy families. Daily chores taught children the value of personal responsibility. More important, they learned the virtue of hard work, a value praised for keeping them out of trouble. Parents were always nearby—directing, supervising, advising, or reprimanding. As a family, they were pitted together against the forces of nature—a challenge that forged a strong sense of identity and group cohesion. Moreover, the demands of farmwork kept young people at home and limited their interaction with the outside world. Thus, the family farm was the cradle of Amish socialization—a cradle that until recently held the very essence of their way of life.

A Demographic Squeeze

The agrarian tradition that had cradled Amish ways for many years became endangered in the mid-twentieth century when a confluence of forces precipitated a major crisis. During the 1950s, the social contours of Lancaster County began to change. Fueled by the postwar baby boom and an influx of newcomers from urban centers, the county's population flourished. New industries moved to Lancaster, transferring large labor forces. Suburban housing developments spread into rural areas and enveloped Lancaster City. By 1954, construction crews were completing more than one hundred new homes a month. And in the years that followed, many retail businesses departed from Lancaster City for the sprawling shopping malls of suburbia.[11]

The postwar years also witnessed the rise of tourism. Better roads and faster vehicles, coupled with growing amounts of leisure time and income, encouraged tourist travel. Organized in 1957, the Lancaster Tourism Committee solicited and welcomed visitors to the vistas of Lancaster County.[12] Tourist-related businesses, with their accompanying motels and restaurants, soon opened on the fringes of the historic Amish settlement.[13] Several Amish contractors and work crews participated in the building boom of the 1950s. Amish carpenters completed homes in suburban subdivisions and also constructed commercial properties for tourist-related enterprises. Still, the overwhelming majority of Amish families continued to plow the land.

Meanwhile, in the 1960s, cropland continued to dwindle. Many Amish families were forced to divide their farms in half; but a farm could only be divided once. The county's surging population and industrial growth slowly encroached on prime acres and spiked the price of land beyond the reach of average farmers.[14] The cropland loss and suburban sprawl persisted throughout the twentieth century.

As farms were sold for development, land values began to surge. Land in the heart of the Amish settlement, which in the 1940s had sold for $300 to $400 per acre, soared to $4,500 by the early 1980s. The cheap land of the Depression years had turned to gold in a few decades. A sixty-acre farm bought for $21,000 in 1940 would sell for $273,000 by 1981. In 1984 an Amishman bought a fifty-four-acre farm in the center of the settlement for $7,593 per acre, totaling $410,022. In the late 1980s one Amishman paid $820,000 for a single farm. Said one Amish farmer in the early 1990s: "It used to be that when we'd hear that someone had paid $100,000 for a farm, we'd say, 'He'll never make it. He's in over his head.' Now $100,000 is nothing! No one's paid a million yet, but that's probably coming." And, indeed, it was, as some farms sold for more than $10,000 an acre by the dawn of the twenty-first century.

The Amish were not the only people snatching up land. In the 1960s, Lancaster County was the fastest growing region in Pennsylvania, as expanding suburbs nibbled away at prime farmland. The county was an enticing area for industry because of its dependable, antiunion labor force as well as its proximity to eastern seaboard markets. Indeed, some 40 percent of the nation's buying power lived within 500 miles of Lancaster. During the 1960s, some thirty-six new industries entered the county. They, of course, needed land and attracted employees, who required housing. The estimated number of tourists jumped from one and a half million in 1963 to nearly 7 million by 2000. Tourist sites as well as motels and restaurants also needed land. All of these factors tightened the squeeze on farmland.

For those fortunate enough to obtain farmland, the start-up costs for farming were also on the rise. Said an older Amishman, "When my grandparents were married, they bought a wheelbarrow and a plow, two or three cows, and some chickens. That was all you needed and you grew from there. Today, just to start you need at least $100,000, and that's not the farm; it's just for your herd and equipment, and then land prices, well, the way they are you can't crop farm and make it. With a business you can start small and grow, but nowadays with a farm you can't even start small."

The growing industrialization and suburbanization of Lancaster County prodded the shrinking availability of farmland and the exorbitant prices. New technological changes in the larger society also added pressure. With farm equipment manufacturers no longer producing horse-drawn machinery, Amish farmers were forced to build some of their own equipment as well as to adapt modern machinery for horse use—thus encouraging the formation of dozens of small machine shops.

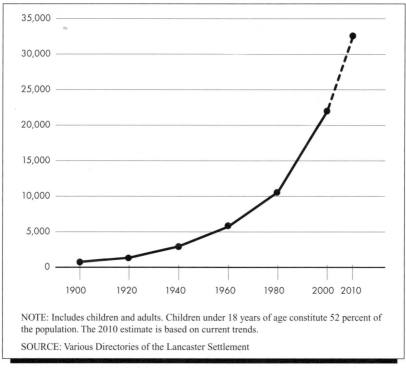

NOTE: Includes children and adults. Children under 18 years of age constitute 52 percent of the population. The 2010 estimate is based on current trends.

SOURCE: Various Directories of the Lancaster Settlement

Figure 2.1 Amish Population Growth in the Lancaster Settlement, 1900–2010

Other external factors provided new markets for Amish products. The growing number of tourists visiting Lancaster County brought a new market that was literally knocking on Amish doors. Moreover, Amish prestige was riding high in the public consciousness, as national media gave positive press to Amish ways. The growing acclaim in public taste for country fashions and crafts sped the rise of Amish enterprise. These external forces provided a mixture of push-and-pull forces that fueled the growth of Amish industry, but there were internal prods as well.

The demographic vise was also being tightened by changes inside the Amish community. Fueled by a high birthrate and strong retention, the Amish population had doubled between 1940 and 1960 and virtually doubled again by 1980 (fig. 2.1). In the early part of the century, large families had provided a hedge against fatal diseases and attrition to other groups. Improved medicines, which the Amish began using, helped to lower infant mortality and increase longevity. Thus, as they entered the last quarter of the twentieth century, the Amish were squeezed by their own growth. Birthrates remained high as infant mortality continued to drop, producing sizable families of seven children on average. Moreover, the Amish were persuading more than 90 percent of their children to join the church, despite teeming temptations from without. The joint effect of large families and low attrition produced a rapidly growing population. Planting new communities in other states and a trickle of migration out of Lancaster County did little to check the burgeoning Amish growth.

The expanding Amish community was steadily buying much of the salable farmland in the eastern and southern portions of Lancaster County.[15] In fact, one public official reported that between 1920 and 1940, the Amish had bought every farm near the center of their settlement that had been put up for auction except one, which was sold on a Sunday.[16] The pressure peaked one year in the late 1960s, when eighty young couples started housekeeping but only ten farms were sold on the open market.[17] Thus, even if commercial development had frozen, the growth of the Amish community itself would have created a crisis, producing too many babies for too few farms. The expanding Amish population also provided an ethnic market for the products that would soon roll out of Amish shops. These internal changes in Amish society added to the external ones that were producing the pending crisis.

The Lunch Pail Threat

Despite the pressures, farming remained the preferred and honored way of life throughout the 1960s and 1970s. So strong was the church's conviction that congregations usually did not consider nonfarmers as candidates for ordination and church leadership. Indeed, mere employment in factories had been a cause for excommunication as late as the 1940s.[18] After the middle of the century, however, as farmland dwindled, some Amish began working in non-Amish factories.

In the mid-1960s, several mobile-home factories sprang up on the edge of the Amish settlement. Attracted by the work ethic and antiunion stance of local Amish and Mennonites, the industries hoped to draw a reliable workforce. Lured by high wages and the fear that the farm shortage would render the next generation landless, dozens of Amishmen dropped their plows for factory employment. By the early 1970s, Amish employees accounted for a sizable portion of the labor force in the new manufactured housing industry. The workforce in one plant was more than three-quarters Amish.[19]

But Amish leaders were unhappy with the move toward the factory. "Past experiences have proven that it's not best for the Amish people to leave the farm," one bishop warned in 1975. "If they get away from the farm they soon get away from the church, at least after the first generation." Another bishop feared that if one generation grew up off the farm, "their sons won't want to farm."[20] Other church leaders said, "The lunch pail is the biggest threat to our way of life."

Church leaders had good reason to be wary of lunch pails.[21] The factory system split the Amish family by removing the father from the home. Whereas traditional farming united the family in a cooperative effort, the factory turned the father into an isolated breadwinner and the mother into a solitary housewife and demeaned the economic contribution of children and grandparents. Taking work away from the home separated the family and placed the burden of raising and disciplining children on the shoulders of Amish women. Spouses working away from home also faced an array of worldly temptations.

The bishops' fears were confirmed when some factory workers became involved in a sports betting pool arranged by their non-Amish co-workers. More subtle were the temptations in the benefit packages of factory employment. The pensions, health care, and life insurance provided by large companies would erode dependency on the church for care and support. The practice of mutual aid would weaken if members found economic security in their jobs instead of in their ethnic community. The factory system worked against Amish solidarity in other ways as well. Wage earners were not as free to participate in community work frolics or barn raisings. Factory work schedules could not be juggled as easily as those of self-employed farmers. Holidays posed another problem because Amish celebrations did not always fit the secular calendar. In addition, Amish weddings, traditionally held on Tuesdays and Thursdays in late autumn, clashed with company production schedules. Although some firms made concessions to the Amish calendar, others did not.

Despite the dangers posed by factory work, church leaders did little to stop the flow of farmers to the trailer plants in the early 1970s. In the end, however, the elders of the church were helped by the economy. A recession in the mid-1970s closed several of the plants and shrank the workforce of others. As one Amishman after another faced unemployment, the church was hard-pressed to support the idled workers and their families. A few Amish even resorted to collecting unemployment insurance—previously unheard of, and testimony to their desperate situation. Chastened by the harsh lessons of recession, the lure of factory employment diminished after 1975. Yet the problem of how to earn a living persisted and intensified with each passing year as Amish ranks spiraled upward.

Sizing Up the Options

The convergence of external and internal forces produced a demographic crisis as the community struggled with the fate of its future. Was there no middle ground between the farm and the factory? At least seven options offered possible safety valves to the mounting social pressures: (1) migration, (2) subdivision of farms, (3) purchase of new farmland, (4) non-Amish employment, (5) use of artificial birth control, (6) higher education, and (7) microenterprises (fig. 2.2).

Migration to rural counties within the state as well as to other states provided one option. During the 1970s, some families left the Lancaster area to begin daughter communities in other parts of Pennsylvania. Indeed, between 1960 and 1978 nearly a dozen daughter settlements were established in other counties of Pennsylvania. About 15 percent of the Lancaster settlement pulled up stakes and moved to these new communities; nevertheless, the demographic vise continued to tighten. Indeed, between 1978 and 1988, in the heat of the crisis, migration dwindled, underscoring the importance of other choices.

In the late 1980s and early 1990s, other families headed for new settlements in Indiana, Kentucky, and Wisconsin; but these newer, more distant ventures drew few migrants. Strong family and community ties have kept the Amish tethered near their place of birth. "If all of our friends moved away, I would want to move, too," one Amish mother explained. "But not enough leave to make me want to pack up." Although the outlying settlements drew some families, it was not enough to ease the demographic pinch.

Subdividing farms so that they could support two families apiece provided another option in the 1970s. But farms could only be subdivided once and remain viable for a dairy operation. Some farms were small to begin with, and other farmers needed their full acreage, all of which limited the subdivision option. Thus, although many farms were split, this tactic only delayed the crisis.

Purchasing new farmland from non-Amish farmers provided another short-term solution. But although the Amish frequently bought farms at public auctions, they could not compete with major developers. Moreover, the number of farms coming on the auction block did not begin to match the growing number of Amish babies. By the mid-1980s, only one-third of the married men in some church districts were farming full time.[22]

Working for non-Amish employers provided still another option. Although some Amishmen worked for non-Amish contractors, this was not always satisfactory, for they lost control of their working conditions. They also found the demands of full-time jobs difficult to reconcile with residual farmwork and the rituals of community life. Employment, especially in tourist restaurants and motels, did often provide income for single women, but it was not an attractive alternative for men. Although a small number of Amish people over the years worked in small non-Amish busi-

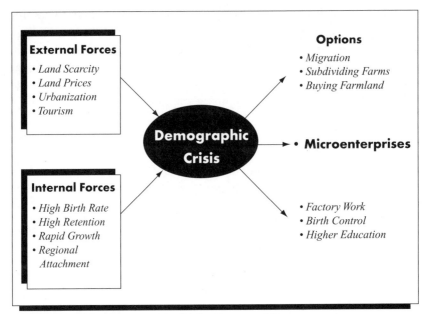

Figure 2.2 The Demographic Crisis: Causes and Responses

nesses, leaders always feared that such work would bring temptations and undercut the influence of the church. And, of course, elders continued to oppose factory employment.

The church might have bridled population growth by lifting its traditional taboo on artificial birth control, but population control was unthinkable. The Amish view artificial birth control as interference with God's will, an unforgivable attempt to play the role of God. Although some couples undoubtedly used various forms of birth control, church leaders continued to frown on artificial means of contraception.

A detour might have also been found if the church had lifted its taboo on high school and college education. Such a move would have enabled Amish youth to enter new technical and professional occupations otherwise beyond their reach. As a matter of fact, however, the number of Amish eight-grade schools grew rapidly during the 1970s.[23] These schools underscored the church's unwavering opposition to high school and eliminated education as a track to other jobs and thus, as a possible relief valve.

The seventh alternative, which quickly became the favored choice, funneled occupational activity into small businesses and cottage industries. It was a negotiated compromise, to be sure.[24] The Amish were conceding their three-hundred-year agricultural tradition. Yes, they would leave the farm; but no, they would not enter large factories or work as day laborers for non-Amish employers.[25] Instead, they would create hundreds of small businesses—a cultural compromise—that would enable them to control the terms and conditions of their work in the context of family and ethnic community. Many tried to cling to their plows for at least a generation by developing seasonal and part-time enterprises, but an irrevocable bargain had nevertheless been struck. By the turn of the twenty-first century, fewer than 30 percent were farming in many church districts.

The options surrounding the crisis represented strategic choices, for they held the fate of the Amish community. The church did not engage in a formal decision-making process. Rather, the choices were sorted informally, somewhat by default, but always in the context of ethnic wisdom accumulated over the centuries. And although the choice to develop small businesses was prodded by outside factors and permitted by default for a decade or so, it was nonetheless a choice.[26] The Amish could have elected to migrate, as some families did, to the rural backwaters of other states. But most chose to stay in the midst of a rapidly urbanizing Lancaster County and negotiate with modernity by establishing a host of microenterprises. The embrace of small business was a strategic choice that brought monumental consequences—the abandonment of an agrarian tradition and the opening of Amish society to the world of commerce with all its dubious ramifications.

The Growth of Amish Shops

A few Amish shops and carpentry crews had existed in Lancaster County before 1950, but the sharp turn to business in the late 1970s was unprecedented. From a small handful of shops in the 1960s, entrepreneurship ballooned into a thousand ventures by the 1990s. Amish-owned enterprises became the primary strategy for dealing with the economic forces that were badgering Amish life in the late twentieth century.[27]

Nonfarm work among the Amish evolved in three phases after the Depression. In the first stage, as cars gained widespread acceptance and horse travel declined, the Amish developed their own carriage and harness shops and began shoeing their own horses. In the second phase, as tractors gained popularity among non-Amish farmers, Amish shops began repairing and modifying horse-drawn machinery. The third stage evolved in the 1970s as a multitude of new shops, stores, and services appeared on the scene.[28]

The first Amish enterprises in the Lancaster area were closely tied to agriculture. A few blacksmiths and harness makers had operated small shops for many years, and a few Amish carpenters had earned their living away from the farm as well. Other Amish businesses provided goods and services such as carriage construction, blacksmithing, or manufacturing

◆

*This was one of the first Amish machine shops to adapt modern farm
implements for horse-drawn use on Amish farms. Located along the Old
Leacock Road, it was established by Gideon Fisher, an Amish farmer.*

Amish hats. But for all practical purposes, Amish life in North America
from 1750 to 1950 revolved around the farm.

Horse-drawn equipment became increasingly scarce after 1940 as more
American farmers began using tractors. Consequently, several Amish mechanics opened machine shops to refurbish horse-drawn implements. By
the mid-1960s it was difficult to buy horse-drawn machinery, so Amish
welders and mechanics began producing component parts in order to
repair horse-drawn equipment. Taking a major turn, they also began buying field implements designed for tractors and adapting them for horses.
For example, they mounted engines on modern hay balers so horses
instead of tractors could pull them. Thus, somewhat ironically, the Amish
were nudged into business in order to preserve their horse farming in the
face of a booming agri-business enamored with tractors.

One church leader described the rise of shops in his church district from
1963 to 1993. The congregation had twenty-one working households, not
counting retired persons, at each time period. But the geographic size of
the district shrank in half by 1993 because half the households had nonfarm enterprises. In 1963, the district had one shop; by 1993, this number
had grown to ten, and only half of the adult men were farming.

During the explosive growth of Amish business in the 1980s, entrepreneurs moved into a wide variety of new ventures. Some opened retail stores for their own people, selling shoes, lighting fixtures, kitchen appliances, batteries, hardware supplies, furniture, and all sorts of food. New firms also targeted non-Amish customers with furniture, dry goods, greenhouse products, camping gear, and building supplies. Others plied the tourist trade, selling quilts, lawn furniture, and other crafts to visitors as well as to wholesale dealers. In the twenty-first century, Amish entrepreneurs continue to develop new products and enter new markets. The proliferation of these ethnic enterprises has created a variety of arrangements with the larger economy.

Types of Ethnic Enterprise

Amish enterprises vary in their linkage to the larger economy and the ethnic community.[29] Those that are tightly entwined in the ethnic community we call *segregated enterprises,* and those that are coupled more directly with the outside economy we call *integrated enterprises*. As shown in table 2.1, ethnic businesses range across a continuum from segregated to integrated, depending on the extent of their linkage with the external economy. The thickness of their ethnicity reflects their use of various ethnic resources: ownership, employees, ethos, location, capital, technology, production, products, customers, suppliers, and distributors. Both segregated and integrated types are ethnic enterprises, because members of the ethnic community own them and their primary labor force is ethnic. Their degree of ethnicity reflects how much they interface with the larger society. In other words, segregated enterprises tap the social and cultural capital of Amish society more than integrated ones.

In its pure form, a segregated enterprise is completely enmeshed in the ethnic community and weakly connected to the larger, outside economy. Consider an Amish shop that makes fiberglass bodies for Amish buggies. The owner and one employee are Amish, and the culture of the shop—its values, norms, identity, and customs—exude an Amish ethos. The Pennsylvania German dialect is spoken among employees as well as to Amish suppliers, dealers, and customers. The shop is located in the hub of the Amish community, and thus ethnic holidays and community activities are easily woven into its flow of work.

Although fiberglass is the raw material, traditional patterns of Amish artisanship are used to produce the buggies, which are, of course, purchased by ethnic customers. Several Amish shops provide the component parts, which are then assembled into the complete carriage at another Amish shop. Electricity, telephones, computers, and motor vehicles are

TABLE 2.1

Types of Ethnic Enterprise, by Use of Ethnic Resources

Ethnic Resources	Segregated Enterprises	Hybrid Enterprises	Integrated Enterprises
Ownership	high	high	high
Employees	high	high	mid
Ethos	high	high	mid
Location	high	high	low
Capital	high	mid	low
Technology	high	mid	low
Production	high	mid	low
Products	high	mid	low
Customers	high	mid	low
Suppliers	high	mid	low
Distributors	high	mid	low

missing from the shop. Capital resources and much of the technological know-how is garnered from the ethnic community. But even a buggy shop is not completely segregated. Some of the raw materials and the initial expertise for fabricating fiberglass came from the outside world.

At the opposite end of the spectrum stand integrated enterprises, which in their pure form are ethnic only because the owners and some of the employees are ethnic. Apart from this distinction, integrated enterprises are fully entangled in the outside economy. The ethnic ethos varies with the ethnic self-consciousness of the employees and the owner. An Amish entrepreneur who operates a vegetable stand in a farmers' market in Philadelphia typifies an integrated enterprise. A non-Amish employee transports owner, employees, and produce for the twice-a-week, sixty-mile trip. Located beyond Amish turf, the operation has a weak ethnic ethos. The products—fresh vegetables and meats—carry no distinctive ethnic imprint. English is spoken to the customers. The retail space is rented from a nonethnic owner, and this enables the Amish stand holder to use electrical lights, which are provided with the space. There is little linkage to suppliers or dealers, and the capital requirements are slim. The enterprise is clearly oriented to the public economy, yet it retains an ethnic identity because of its ownership and the distinctive dress of its Amish employees.

The bulk of Amish enterprises transcend the neat categories of segregated and integrated and fall into hybrids of one sort or another. An overwhelming majority are distinctively Amish in their ownership, employees, ethos, and location; but they vary widely in their use of other ethnic resources—products, customers, suppliers, capital, and technology. Many firms manufacture a mixture of both ethnic and nonethnic products—doghouses, rocking chairs, kitchen cabinets, cattle feeders, and gazebos—that are sold to ethnic and nonethnic customers alike. The commercial network encompassing a particular shop often includes a mixture of Amish and non-Amish suppliers, subcontractors, dealers, and wholesalers.

An Amish shop that repairs electrical alternators for automobiles typifies a hybrid enterprise. The owners, employees, ethos, and location are clearly ethnic, but the services of the shop are directed toward the non-Amish community. The enterprise began by repairing alternators for the diesel engines that provide power for many Amish farms and shops. Similar alternators are used to charge batteries in cars. Responding to the requests of their non-Amish neighbors, the shop gradually began repairing alternators on automobiles. The non-Amish clientele grew, so that today most of the customers come from outside the ethnic community.

A multitude of patterns mix ethnic and nonethnic products, customers, suppliers, dealers, capital, and technology in different proportions across the spectrum of Amish enterprises. Although the segregated and integrated models symbolize pure types, the bulk of Amish enterprises are hybrids of one sort or another that cluster around the center of the spectrum.

◆

A self-employed Amish craftsman and his son make fiberglass bottoms for buggies in this shop. The buggies are assembled in another Amish shop. This shop illustrates a segregated ethnic enterprise that primarily serves the Amish community.

Cultural Bargaining

The creation of microenterprises was, in many ways, an ingenious negotiation with modernity.[30] The Amish have repeatedly dickered with the larger society at the cultural bargaining table over the years. Both sides grant concessions, make allowances, and defend nonnegotiables. The negotiation model helps to clarify the often puzzling patterns of interaction between the Amish and the surrounding society. The ever-changing lines of separation are continually redrawn as the two sides informally fashion a common existence. The negotiated agreements have enabled the Amish to maintain their ethnic identity and cultural values while also enjoying many of the fruits of progress.

Cultural bargaining has enabled the Amish to flourish in modern life. The church has acquiesced to nonfarm employment, some household conveniences, and the use of modern medicine. Meanwhile, the larger society has exempted the Amish from high school, military service, and Social Security taxes. The Amish have negotiated "agreements" on many technological issues, choosing to use—in a limited way—the scientific advances of the twentieth century but without fully endorsing modern gadgetry. Through a delicate and largely informal process of cultural negotiation, both sides are able to preserve their key interests as they craft creative and viable modes of coexistence.

Our cultural analysis assumes a dialectical interaction between material conditions and human values. In the Amish story, a changing economic environment—declining farmland, exorbitant land prices, and a growing Amish population—forced a crisis of major proportions. The traditional values of Amish culture mediated the community's response by blocking employment in large factories, forbidding the use of birth control, and rejecting higher education. But ethnic values also bolstered the rise of microenterprises that mirrored long-held Amish virtues of family, smallness, artisanship, and cultural separatism from the larger society. Thus, the moral order of Amish culture shaped the nature of the Amish response to the farmland crisis.

But this was not the last word in the Amish saga, for the entry into microenterprises, endorsed by traditional values, is now reshaping the ethos of Amish culture. The new material realities—the microenterprises endorsed by Amish values—are now, in turn, revising long-held religious beliefs related to individualism, status, rationality, social equality, gender roles, the use of the courts, and separation from the larger society. Thus, the very ideological factors that steered the Amish toward microenterprises in the first place are now being revised by the emergence of these new commercial realities, demonstrating the reciprocal relations between cultural ideas and material conditions.

The transformation of Amish work was a monumental bargain between a tenacious people and the forces of a modern, rationalized social order. The Amish were willing to experiment with new occupations, products, and markets if they could control their newly created world of work. Farming remained highly regarded. Indeed, many novice entrepreneurs tried to maintain the patterns and virtues of farm life in their new commercial context. Moreover, some remembered the lessons from their aborted foray into factory employment in the 1970s. Thus, the ethnic enterprises burgeoning in the 1980s were located at or near home as much as possible. Home work preserved family values by blending spouses and children into the world of business. Parents working alongside their children could pass on the virtues of Amish life in the context of work, albeit at the edge, not the center, of the farm.

This astute compromise enabled the Amish to harness their work within an ethnic subculture. Employment within the context of kin and church reinforced Amish values, fortified the Pennsylvania German dialect, and accommodated the calendar of ethnic holidays and celebrations. Finally, and most importantly, the implicit terms of the agreement enabled the Amish to work within the moral boundaries of their faith. They could now easily avoid Sunday sales, fringe benefits, and other dubious influences—blaring music, profane language, and organized labor—that sometimes accompany factory employment.

The decision of many Lancaster Amish to leave their plows for profitable ventures was a negotiated cultural settlement. Forced out of farming, adverse to the factory, and hoping to retain family ties in Lancaster County, many farmers conceded their love affair with the soil. But they did not completely abandon their cultural soul. They opted for meaningful work—within ethnic networks and the moral order of the church—where they could control the terms and conditions of their employment. Those who could continue farming did, and some took their plows to other states. But the vast majority entered the world of business.

3. A Profile of Amish Enterprises

You would flip out if you knew how much product is being pumped out of all these little shops.

— AMISH ENTREPRENEUR

A Surge of Small Shops

The rapid rise of Amish enterprises is surely the most significant social transformation in the history of the Lancaster settlement. Although a few Amish-owned firms existed before 1970, some 1500 shops were established in the next three decades. This dramatic development continues today. Each month new firms move into new markets, offer new products, develop new product lines, and increase their sales.[1] Figure 3.1 plots the rapid growth of microenterprises in the Lancaster settlement in recent years.[2]

By 2003 the Lancaster settlement had nearly 1,600 Amish-owned businesses with an average of 11 per church district. The enterprises are not spread evenly across the settlement. The older, more densely populated portions of the settlement, with the greatest land and population pressures, have the most enterprises. Near the heart of the settlement, about half of the households own a business. On the other hand, in the more rural, southern flank of Lancaster County, fewer are involved in business.

About one-third of the firms are part-time or seasonal operations. These sideline businesses provide extra household income. Two-thirds of the businesses are full-time enterprises that provide regular employment for the owner and employees. Some firms employ up to twenty people, although four to six employees is more common. All totaled, Amish businesses provide nearly two thousand full-time and some fourteen hundred part-time or seasonal jobs. The financial scope of Amish commerce varies as well. Although typical firms are small, many sport annual sales of several million dollars.

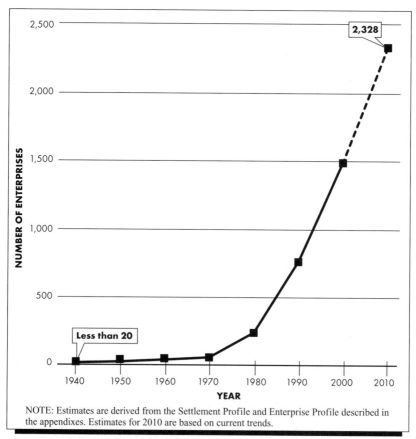

Figure 3.1 Estimated Number of Amish Enterprises in the Lancaster Settlement, 1940–2010

One shop owner described the rise of enterprises in these words. "[The old cabinet makers] would start with a pile of 1 x 12 white pine boards, a small gas-powered table saw, a box of cigars, and lots of muscle. Nowadays over twenty large shops produce 800 storage sheds and thirty gazebos a week. This yields some 40,000 items a year in only one of many product lines. About fifty Amish cabinet shops each produce fifteen to a hundred new kitchens every year. No longer restricted to the corner of an old tobacco shed, the larger businesses occupy 20,000- to 30,000-square foot areas in spanking new facilities."[3]

The array of entrepreneurial activity is shown in table 3.1. Amish shops produce an amazing variety of products and services. "You would flip out if you knew how much product is being pumped out of all these little shops," one Amishman chortled. Woodworking trades comprise the largest clus-

TABLE 3.1

Amish Enterprises in the Lancaster Settlement

Type of Enterprise	Percentage of Total
Contractors and builders	8.5
Retail shops (local interest)	7.6
Furniture manufacturing and sales	6.8
Harness shops	6.8
Lawn furniture manufacturing and sales	6.8
Retail shops (quilts and crafts)	6.8
Agricultural equipment sales	5.1
General woodworking	5.1
Greenhouse and nursery sales	5.1
Roadside produce stands	4.2
Bakeries	3.4
Cabinetmaking	3.4
Storage barn and gazebo construction	3.4
Welding shops	3.4
Animal sales	2.5
Blacksmith shops	2.5
Farmers' market stands	2.5
Metal fabrication shops	2.5
Carriage and wheelwright shops	1.7
Machine shops	1.7
Silo building	1.7
Tax accounting	1.7
Toy manufacturing and sales	1.7
Other	5.0

Source: Enterprise Profile (*N* = 118).
Note: This estimated distribution of enterprises in the Lancaster settlement is based on the sample of businesses in the Enterprise Profile.

tering of enterprises—furniture building, cabinetmaking, and storage barn and gazebo construction, as well as more general woodworking activity. Smaller wood products such as doghouses, birdhouses, cupolas, picnic tables, and lawn furniture also flow from Amish shops. The small storage sheds widely distributed in several states are another popular product of carpentry shops. One Amish observer estimates that more than seven hundred "little red barns" are shipped out of the county each week during peak production. One shop alone makes about four thousand storage sheds a year.[4]

Residential and commercial construction, the largest sector, accounts for nearly 10 percent of business activity. Amish contractors do general contracting, framing, roofing, painting, masonry, and even landscaping. Another sizable group of firms is engaged in retail sales. Many stores cater to the needs of local Amish and non-Amish residents alike, providing groceries, hardware, or fabrics. Others offer goods to local tourists. Quilts and handcrafted items from Amish shops find ready markets among Lancaster County's many visitors.

Amish quilts, of course, have garnered considerable attention in recent years. Although sometimes portrayed as the wintertime handiwork of one woman, Amish quilt making has become a rather complex project that may involve several operations at different locations. Similar to the "putting out" labor system of preindustrial America, some women cut pieces for the decorative top of the quilt and do the piecing—sewing the pieces together and adding a border. Others cut the batting and back to fit the top of the quilt. Still other women may do the actual quilting—stitching the three layers together—at another location. And the final step—a narrow binding, which hides the raw edges of the three layers and completes the quilt—may be done by yet another person. The finished quilts may be sold to an Amish wholesale dealer who sells them to retail shops across the nation. Various functions of the "outwork" system in Amish quilt making are sometimes done in Amish communities in other counties and states.[5]

Although most enterprises operate independently from the agrarian economy, some are tied to farming. Machine shops that manufacture and repair farm equipment as well as blacksmith and harness shops, while not serving farm needs exclusively, are linked to the agricultural economy. Some metal fabrication shops produce farm equipment for non-Amish farmers. Entrepreneurs who construct silos and manufacture farm implements, of course, cater exclusively to agricultural markets. Families who operate roadside stands often sell raw or processed farm products, as do many others who rent market stands in cities some distance from their homes. Despite traditional ties to farming and the presence of some farm-related enterprises, however, most Amish-owned businesses are not directly linked to agriculture. The growing involvement in business is gradually pulling the community's roots away from the soil.

Types of Enterprise

The spectrum of business activity has taken Amish firms into scores of new markets and product lines. Despite diversity in size, function, and location, four broad types of enterprise have flourished: sidelines, cottage industries, manufacturing establishments, and construction crews.

Sidelines, as they are called by the Amish, provide supplemental income to farmers, homemakers, or retired persons. Often seasonal, the sidelines do not provide full-time employment. Many, however, eventually grow into full-time enterprises. Home-based businesses operate from a family dwelling, farm building, or small-scale facility adjacent to a house. At times, old storage barns or unused tobacco sheds are converted into workshops or retail spaces. Families selling vegetables or crafts may construct a small, enclosed roadside stand. Many cottage industries are farm-based, although numerous nonfarm families have also created home businesses. Bakeshops, hardware stores, greenhouses, craft shops, shoe stores, carpenter shops, and small-engine repair shops are among the hundreds of enterprises commonly located at home. These enterprises may employ up to a half dozen individuals but typically remain small, family-centered establishments.

Cottage industries thrive on family labor, and most involve members of both the nuclear and the extended family. Children might help to pick vegetables for a produce stand, wait on customers in a bulk food store, or sweep up scraps in a small, at-home harness shop. Often involving both husbands and wives, cottage industries resemble the mom-and-pop grocery stores of yesteryear. Cottage industries are clearly under the family's control, making them especially attractive to Amish households. The opportunity to work together as a family and to define the conditions, terms, and methods of their work is highly valued.

Larger machine shops and manufacturing establishments constitute the third segment of business endeavors. Generally based in new facilities outfitted for their use, these enterprises often sit on the edge of a farm or on a small plot adjacent to a home. In some cases, an Amish manufacturer may lease space in a local industrial park. One of the newest developments is the formation of an industrial park in the late 1990s near New Holland that has attracted numerous Amish businesses. By 2003, a second phase of the park was under construction.

The larger shops may have as many as twenty employees, but the norm hovers around five. Although family members are involved, some employees typically come from outside the entrepreneur's household. Several Amish neighbors may work together in the larger shops, and it is not unusual to have one or more non-Amish employees as well.

Machine shops that repair or build horse-drawn equipment serve an almost exclusively Amish clientele. Some shops produce component parts and supplies for other Amish manufacturers. Cabinet shops, household appliance businesses, and manufacturers of storage barns supply both Amish and non-Amish customers. Some wood and metal shops operate almost exclusively on contracts with large non-Amish firms or distribute their products through a national network of wholesale dealers.

Mobile work crews represent a fourth type of Amish business. Contractors involved in building, roofing, masonry, and painting crisscross the Lancaster settlement, constructing new houses and remodeling existing ones. Some firms also travel outside the county to neighboring communities and states. The Amish have had a longtime affinity with carpentry.

Today woodworking and construction rank next to farming as the occupations of choice among the Amish. Working away from home in a non-Amish setting, Amish contractors are permitted to use state-of-the-art tools powered by portable electric generators or on-site electricity. Carpenters construct both residential and commercial buildings and in some cases fit them with Amish-produced cabinetry. To transport their mobile crews, some contractors hire trucks and vans, with non-Amish drivers, on a daily basis. Others contract with a non-Amish employee to provide transportation to and from work sites.

Another type of mobile work involves selling produce in urban farmers' markets. Located in Philadelphia, Reading, Baltimore, and other eastern cities in Pennsylvania, New Jersey, Maryland, and Delaware, these popular markets offer produce, meats, baked goods, deli items, crafts, and other goods to urban residents. An Amish family might grow or buy vegetables and then clean and prepare them at their home before transporting them in rented vehicles to an urban market. Amish stand holders purchase meats, produce, and deli items from various suppliers and transport them to their market. Farmers' markets typically operate two or three days a week, allowing stand holders time to prepare their goods during the off days.

Market stand holders resemble mobile crews because they work away from home in a somewhat foreign cultural setting. Families hire vehicles on a daily basis and immerse themselves in the larger non-Amish world. Like contractors, stand holders are free to use electrical gadgets because they rent the retail space. But produce sellers also differ from construction crews. Market tending typically involves various family members, whereas construction primarily attracts males from various households. Market stands also offer more stability because of their permanent location, while contractors shift from job to job.

As businesses grow, they tend to diversify their products. Three-quarters of Amish entrepreneurs report that they began their business with a single product line. Presently almost half of them offer at least two product lines or services, and 6 percent claim four or more offerings. One Amishwoman began a dry goods store, and within several years, she added shoes, ready-made clothing, greeting cards, housewares, and groceries. Not all new product lines were successful. Her attempt to market hardware fell flat. "You have to go into what you know," she discovered. "Hardware is a man's thing. I knew housewares, but not hardware."

Other entrepreneurs receive special orders that lead them to new products. At age eighteen an Amishman on the northeastern edge of the settlement opened a small welding shop. He relied on repair jobs from local customers and farmers. After fifteen years of solo labor, he was asked to build

TABLE 3.2

Sales Volume of Amish Enterprises

Annual Sales	Percentage of Enterprises
Under $10,000	21
$10,000 through $49,999	20
$50,000 through $99,999	21
$100,000 through $499,999	24
$500,000 through $1,000,000	7
Over $1,000,000	7

Source: Enterprise Profile (*N* = 118).

an industrial-size garbage receptacle. His finished product and reasonable price won the admiration of dozens of businesses. Several years later, he was producing some five hundred receptacles a year.

Along with product diversity, the sales volume of Amish firms has also flourished. Fewer than one in ten had annual sales above $100,000 in their first year of business. But by the early 1990s, 38 percent exceeded that figure (see table 3.2). More than 7 percent of Amish firms have sales above a million dollars a year. Part-time or seasonal efforts tend to garner modest sales, but the annual sales of more than half of the full-time businesses top $100,000. Indeed, one-third of the firms with two or more employees have sales above $500,000. A banker who works closely with Amish businesses estimates that the top firms have annual sales of $8 to $12 million and net at least 10 percent in profit. One thing is clear: Amish enterprises have grown far beyond making homemade root beer and brooms as a seasonal hobby.

Patterns of Ownership

Business ownership in the American economy typically falls into three broad categories: sole proprietorships, partnerships, and corporations. Amish firms reflect these patterns as well. Proprietorships, owned and operated by a single individual or married couple, require little start-up capital and face fewer state regulations. Some 71 percent of American firms are organized as proprietorships.[6] Among Amish enterprises in Lancaster County, many began as proprietorships, but over time, some have incorporated or created partnerships. Nevertheless, about three-fourths are proprietorships. Amish farmers typically operated as sole proprietors and often transferred this single-owner approach to business. The Amish, although valuing cooperation and mutual aid, support the independence of sole proprietorships.

The second form of organization is the partnership. Partnerships involve two or more people who share responsibility of ownership, debt, decision making, and profit. Like proprietorships, partnerships are easy to establish and rather flexible. Additionally, partnerships can pool experience and start-up capital. Although partnerships account for only about one in ten American businesses, they represent about a fifth of Amish enterprises. Amish partnerships are popular for several reasons. Because the Amish are leery of the legal and regulatory entanglements of incorporation, many partnerships remain in effect long after non-Amish businesses would have discarded them. Moreover, the family orientation of the Amish buoys their interest in partnerships because many of these arrangements involve family members. In many Amish partnerships all the partners are family members. Occasionally partnerships include non-Amish persons as well. Trying to explain the composition of one firm, a non-Amish partner said, "Well, there are four of us in the partnership—two Amish and two white guys."

Historically, a special circumstance also encouraged partnerships. In 1965 the federal government exempted self-employed Amish farmers and businesspeople from paying Social Security taxes. The Amish reject government insurance on religious grounds and refuse to draw benefits from the state, preferring to rely on mutual aid from within their community in time of need.[7] Because the exemption only covered the self-employed, some new businesses were organized as partnerships. Each employee was legally considered a self-employed partner and thus qualified for an exemption. The original owner-founder typically retained a controlling interest as the senior partner.[8]

In 1988 Congress exempted from Social Security Amish persons who were employed by Amish employers. This led to a decline in partnerships. Some partnerships reverted to sole proprietorships, while others remained partnerships but with only the owners as partners.

The third organizational model is the corporation. Twenty percent of U.S. businesses are organized as corporations, but among the Amish there are few. Less than five percent of Amish firms have evolved into corporations, and few began that way. Those that legally incorporate typically form limited liability corporations. These legal vehicles provide legal protection but do not have to pay corporate taxes, only individual income taxes.

Corporations are unattractive to the Amish for several reasons. First, the Amish are wary of the regulations that constrain corporate America. Moreover, the financial security provided by church and family reduces the fear of financial liability that often prods incorporation in the larger society. The few businesses that have incorporated have often done so when their growth pushes them beyond the limits of Amish propriety. A corporate charter establishes a legal separation between the owners and the business, which at times enables an Amish owner to live personally by the rules of the church, while the enterprise steps outside boundaries. An Amish-owned enterprise in need of computerization, for example, might incorporate and then sublease a portion of the business to a non-Amish shareholder who would install desktop computers. Or the incorporated enterprise might lease a vehicle. The possibility of such arrangements sometimes encourages incorporating.

"Starting Right In"

Because many Amish firms are first generation, few entrepreneurs bring business experience to their work. Although the skills and values important in farming—hard work, independence, and ingenuity—transfer easily to commercial endeavors, most business owners have waded into the marketplace with little else but a willingness to work and learn. Amish entrepreneurs, for the most part, have bypassed courses in management and marketing. Most have consulted family members, neighbors, or other Amish business owners; but few, if any, consider formal education a prerequisite for success. As one grandfather counseled, "If you want to start a business, don't read about it, just start right in. Don't talk about it, just start right in and get to work."

Dozens of entrepreneurs tell stories of beginning a small business with patience, persistence, family support, and hard work. Many did not plan to establish a full-time enterprise but ended up with a flourishing business that became self-supporting. In the mid-1960s, Levi Esh, an Amish farmer living in the heart of the settlement, began buying spare parts for Coleman gas lamps—the type of lighting device used by many Amish in lieu of electrical fixtures. Before this time, families with broken or damaged lamps had to order parts from the manufacturer and wait for shipments to arrive by mail. By stocking commonly requested parts, Esh offered a valuable service to his community. The family kept the inventory in an old milk house on their farm. Eventually, they opened a small store with other Coleman products, later adding gas appliances. When the Coleman company stopped producing the lamp, Esh struck an agreement with the company allowing him to produce the lamp himself. He also improved its design and durability.[9]

All the while, the family continued to operate their dairy, but farm and business soon began to vie for time and resources. Esh tried limiting the store hours to several evenings a week, but the business suffered. Indeed, an employee noted, "When someone comes in to buy a three-thousand-dollar stove and you smell like manure, well, that just doesn't go well"— surely not with the non-Amish families who come to the farm-based store

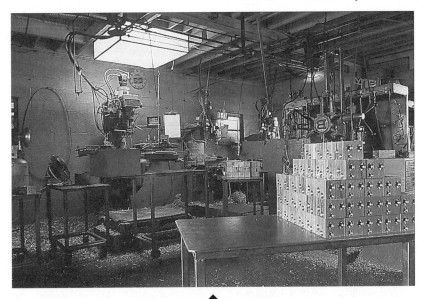

◆

Among other products, this machine shop manufactures high-precision valves that are used in large hydraulic lifts. The skylight provides illumination without electricity. The wall clock is battery powered. Pressurized air and oil (hydraulic) power the shop equipment.

for gas, coal, and wood stoves. By 1981, annual sales had soared to $2.5 million. Finally, the family sold its dairy and focused on manufacturing and retail sales, which were supplemented by a growing mail-order business. Eventually the business was sold to a non-Amish owner—a practice that occurs frequently when businesses grow beyond the boundaries of Amish propriety.[10]

Other business ventures begin on farms and remain a secondary stream of income. In the mid-1980s, a young Amish couple with time to spare on their dairy farm during winter months searched for a hobby to spike their income. Chatting with friends one day, they struck upon the idea of making decorative wall plaques—neatly lettered poems or mottoes, glued and lacquered on stained wooden frames. Using a saw he already owned, the farmer began to produce decorative wooden frames. In an empty bedroom, his wife took the frames and attached poems and pictures that they bought from a local printer. Finally, the couple laminated the pictures. Their work found ready buyers in local flea markets and nearby stores.

Within several years, they had remodeled an outdoor building to accommodate their business and purchased an automatic glue press and a wider assortment of prints. Their niece created some original pieces, including a decorated zip code directory of Amish addresses. Within several years, half of their pictures were going to dealers out of state, and special requests for laminated-picture clocks, sports-team photos, and completed jigsaw puzzles filled their now busy winter season. The couple hopes to keep their business small so they can also keep their dairy herd and not need to employ anyone outside their family. "Farming is something we can do together as a family," the father explained.

Still other businesses begin with the hope of providing all of the family's income. In the early 1990s, following the birth of their first child, one couple began a cottage business so that both parents could work at home. Located along a heavy tourist route, they began selling quilts and handcrafts from their house. The young mother made as many quilts as possible and also accepted consignments to fill the rest of the shop. The most difficult part in the early days, said the young businesswoman, "was knowing what patterns and colors to stock." Gaining practical experience with each new year, the eager entrepreneur hoped to erase the guesswork from inventory within several seasons.

Meanwhile, her husband began tapping another market by working with ceramics. His popular products—ceramic kitchen containers, canisters, trivets, wall plaques, and decorative dishes—are common Amish wedding gifts. The young man molds and paints each piece himself and then fires them in a gas kiln. His small cottage industry, which provides full-time self-employment, meshes smoothly with his wife's in-home quilt shop. Although the ceramics operation required more start-up capital, the quilt and craft shop and didn't have to borrow a thing," the husband said with a smile. "It's debt free except for the mortgage on the house, which we'd have even if we didn't have a shop." With careful decision making and minimal investment, these business ventures will likely support the family for years to come.

Securing Start-up Capital

Most Amish entrepreneurs begin on shoestring budgets, making use of personal savings and limited amounts of borrowed money. Others obtain commercial loans before opening their doors. Traditionally within the Amish community, private and family loans have financed new operations. Parents, other relatives, or fellow church members extend credit to newly married couples or young families. Those buying a farm can count on obtaining a portion of their funding from relatives and other church members at modest interest.[11] At the same time, the Amish have always turned to commercial lenders for supplemental financing. When approaching new business ventures, entrepreneurs often tap both private and commercial loans.

The moral order of Amish culture, however, prohibits the use of government subsidies that are sometimes offered to fledgling businesses.

Many firms, especially those created to supplement farm earnings or to provide retirement income, start with sparse personal savings. Other firms, intent on becoming full-time establishments, typically need a larger pool of funds. Many owners turn first to private loans. Amish entrepreneurs disagree, however, about the value and source of borrowed capital. A few argue against debt at all costs. They believe that borrowing may be necessary at the outset but contend that further indebtedness is a dangerous liability. "Debt will kill a business," a small proprietor warned. Indeed, some sizable Amish enterprises have operated for years without debt.

Most entrepreneurs, however, view borrowing as a practical necessity in today's market but warn against foolish borrowing or over-extending debt. Said one welding shop owner: "A little borrowed money is healthy. It keeps you on your toes." A fencing contractor agreed: "I feel debt's right. That's what gives you a go. That's the challenge." Many larger manufacturers and contractors operate with approved lines of credit from commercial banks, taking out seasonal or inventory loans. One Amish contractor, absorbing attitudes from the larger world, strongly encourages commercial loans. In his words, "Never use your own money . . . I only work on a line of credit. You can write it off at the end of the year. It works out best that way."

Borrowing from banks instead of private lenders has stirred some discussion in the Amish community. Larger operators, drawing on conventional wisdom, favor lending institutions. "I would always choose a bank loan if I were borrowing. That's what they're here for," said a storage barn builder. The owner of a sizable harness shop appreciates the vigorous examination lending officers conduct. He views their work as a helpful review of his own planning. "If the bank would say no, I would take that seriously," he counsels. "They've probably found a hitch that you didn't think of." Other businesspeople prefer commercial loans because they "don't want to get other people involved personally." Explained one contractor, "In case something wouldn't work out, every time you see Mr. Jones, you think, 'I took him across.'" A few businesspeople insist on using private loans, but many are comfortable with tapping commercial banks for day-to-day financing.

Regardless of their view of debt, Amish entrepreneurs share a common understanding of the ingredients of stable growth: slow expansion, coupled with demanding work. They dismiss any get-rich-quick schemes as well as shortcuts to success. Experience in farming has taught them to invest time and energy up front and then wait for the harvest. Said one

◆

This large Amish retail store sells bulk food to both Amish and non-Amish
customers. Skylights illuminate the aisles and shelves.

businesswoman characteristically: "You have to watch your money steps.
You crawl up the ladder. You can't start at the top." Pointing to the disas-
trous experience of a nearby non-Amish neighbor who started a lumber
business that failed, an Amish storeowner underscored the mistakes. "He
went out and bought a computer, phone system, fax, and wood kilns right
off the bat. His work ethic was his downfall. It's that simple—you've got
to work up slowly." The Amish preference for starting small and building
gradually has enabled them to start with surprisingly small investments.

In order to minimize capital requirements, many firms have opened
their doors in already existing buildings. Forty-five percent of the enterprises were initially located in a home or in a farm building. As they grew
and prospered, many moved into new facilities built to house them. Currently only half of the firms that began in a farm building remain there.
Likewise, only one-third of those that started in or attached to a dwelling
remain there. Some growing enterprises have relocated to small plots away
from the entrepreneur's home, but the separation of work and home is not
the norm. The Amish have struggled to keep family and work together,
signaling not only Amish practicality but also the centrality of the family.

Finding a Corner of the Market

Many Amish entrepreneurs display a remarkable market savvy. Providing customer service, carefully choosing retail space, and expanding distribution networks are among the ways Amish enterprises operate within the bounds of conventional marketing. Understanding the targeted clientele is important, business owners emphasize. Choosing a market—Amish, non-Amish, wholesale, or tourist—and then serving that sector well is also critical. Said a gas appliance storeowner: "Customers today want service. They want quick service, and they want good service. It's the way you have to be to be competitive these days." A contractor agreed that service as well as building a favorable reputation is the key to keeping ahead in today's competitive market: "Our theory was satisfy the customer and then let him spread the word." A grocery storeowner stresses the importance of bargains to stimulate sales: "The demand is there for a bargain," he discovered. "In an area like Lancaster County where there's a lot of hardworking people, a dollar means a lot to them. They want to stretch that dollar and make it work for them because they earned it."

Amish entrepreneurs consider marketing implications when choosing business locations if they hope to sell to tourists or non-Amish retail customers. One businesswoman rejected space along a busy highway because it lacked other retail stores and connecting sidewalks. "If I pay rent for a place, I need to make sure that it has a lot of walk-in traffic," she said. Another storeowner recalled finding a building for lease on a well-traveled intersection: "I thought, 'That shouldn't be empty. Right there on the corner—that's a busy corner. Someone should be in there doing something.' . . . I watch the corners." Although most businesses remain at or near home, a number that target specific consumer groups—such as tourists or local non-Amish buyers—have moved to "corners" that enhance their sales.

Some entrepreneurs have also created marketing networks reaching far beyond the local community. Some Amish businesses remain local in scope and focus, but many stretch beyond Lancaster's borders. As shown in table 3.3, about 20 percent of the owners report that most of their sales go beyond Lancaster County. Using limited but specialized advertising, some farm machinery manufacturers are distributing products from Maine to Florida. Many have distributors in other states. One firm that makes small-scale farm implements for hobby farmers has eighty dealers in twenty states and two Canadian provinces.

By pricing competitively, Amish firms can wedge into new markets. Non-Amish farmers in upstate New York, for example, can buy replacement parts for silos from an Amish business in Lancaster for 15 percent

TABLE 3.3

Sales Activity of Amish Enterprises

Type of Sales	Percentage of Enterprises
Distance	
Over 90% inside Lancaster County	31
Over 90% outside Lancaster County	22
Mixture of inside and outside	47
Retail/Wholesale	
Over 90% retail	52
Over 90% wholesale	20
Mixture of retail and wholesale	28
Tourist Related	
Over 90% tourist related	7
Over 90% nontourist related	81
Mixture of tourist and nontourist	12
Ethnic Related	
Over 90% of retail sales to Amish	18
Over 90% of retail sales to non-Amish	43
Mixture of retail sales to Amish and non-Amish	39

Source: Enterprise Profile (N = 118).

below New York prices. Other manufacturers and craft producers ship merchandise by the truckload to stores and wholesalers in other parts of the country. Attracted by the price and quality of Amish goods, distributors often beat a path to Amish doors. An Amishwoman who paints pastoral scenes on wooden buckets made by other family members offers wholesale discounts exceeding 50 percent. Such discounts allow her to sell wholesale lots of five hundred buckets to first-time buyers.

Amish-owned enterprises work within a number of market sectors: fellow ethnics, local non-Amish, wholesalers, and tourists Many businesses cater to Amish customers for at least part of their business. One-fifth of the firms report that a majority of their retail sales go to Amish customers. Amish blacksmiths work almost exclusively with Amish clients. An Amish shoe store, bonnet shop, or hat shop typically sells only to fellow church members, although some Old Order Mennonites also frequent such businesses. Self-taught Amish tax accountants and bookkeepers work with a largely Amish clientele. Amish horse dealers primarily provide animals for fellow church members. Smaller harness shops sell mostly to other Amish neighbors, although some larger ones cater to non-Amish customers.

Non-Amish customers also form a large market for Amish firms. As shown in table 3.3, nearly half of Amish enterprises sell over 90 percent of their retail items to non-Amish customers. Four out of ten establishments have a sizable mixture of Amish and non-Amish customers. An Amish paint store or hardware store will sell to fellow Amish and non-Amish alike. Stand holders, in farmers' markets in distant locations, however, sell to an entirely non-Amish clientele. Many Amish contractors work primarily for non-Amish customers. Selling to outsiders can sometimes be difficult for people who are unfamiliar with the styles and tastes of the larger society. One dry goods storeowner noted that different kinds of fabrics are required to please her non-Amish customers. For example, the material for Amish men's vests does not sell in her shop, which caters to non-Amish customers. Likewise, farm machinery manufacturers often offer two lines of equipment—steel wheeled and rubber tired—if they wish to entice non-Amish as well as Amish customers. A partly Amish-owned silo construction business builds larger silos for its non-Amish clients and smaller ones for Amish farmers.

Other markets unwittingly cross cultural boundaries. Having rejected power lawn mowers, Amish families have continued to use old-fashioned, push-type reel mowers. When non-Amish hardware stores discontinued reel mower service, some Amish entrepreneurs started part-time businesses selling new and used push mowers as well as sharpening mower blades. At nearly the same time, some residents of Lancaster City returned to reel mowers for their small yards in order to save fuel costs, increase exercise, and comply with noise ordinances. Unable to find service in conventional mower shops, the urbanites discovered Amish dealers in the countryside. Word spread, and now some Amish mower shops—much to their surprise—have a majority of non-Amish customers.

Carriage shop owner Abner Lapp found that his skills in coach repair were coveted by collectors of antique carriages across America. After working on Amish buggies for some twenty years, Lapp began restoring rare nineteenth-century coaches. Although a sense of personal diffidence led him to never attach a signature plate to his finished work, his superb artisanship built a reputation that spread rapidly among collectors. A second generation is now continuing the sterling tradition of restoration. Today the Amish shop delivers finished carriages to the private Rockefeller family collection, the Smithsonian Institute, and other prestigious collectors and museums. Employing three other people, the carriage maker is well know among nationally recognized collectors. In addition to repairing carriages, his shop sells small children's wagons and other wooden items—largely to tourists.[12]

Other Amish entrepreneurs have entered the wholesale marketplace (see table 3.3). One out of five enterprises sells more than 90 percent of its products on a wholesale basis. Many of these enterprises have accounts across the United States, and a few do business with Canadian or overseas firms as well. One wood products manufacturer creates simple pine furniture for national distribution. He also creates wooden items for home-decorating projects such as holiday wreath making. His shop supplies craft stores and chain outlets far beyond Lancaster County. Most of the wooden creations he produces are his own designs. Continually generating new ideas is a challenge he enjoys. "The craft industry is very trendy," he acknowledges. "While the competition is copying what I just did, I'm moving on to something new. I try to keep one step ahead."

Another manufacturer builds merchandise display racks for a national chain of auto parts stores. Amish metal fabricators send machinery, steel window frames, and cattle stanchions and feeders up and down the East Coast through their distributors. Some entrepreneurs have sought out sales representatives, but many have been approached by eager dealers hoping to offer the reasonably priced, quality merchandise flowing out of Amish shops.

Closer to home, some Amish have targeted the county's tourist market. About 7 percent of Amish firms report that over 90 percent of their sales go to tourists (see table 3.3). About one-fifth of the enterprises report at least some sales to tourists. Quilt and craft shops are especially tied to Lancaster County's multibillion-dollar-a-year hospitality industry.[13] Retail craft sales can be as difficult to predict as wholesale trends. Said one businesswoman and quilt store owner, "You have to keep your eyes open to what's new. You can't be selling last year's stuff." Staying on the lookout for new items has driven some Amish shop owners to regional off-season craft shows, where they scout the competition and get new ideas for the coming years.

Entrepreneurs who target tourist dollars have a built-in advantage because county visitors, on hand to see the Amish community, are eager to buy Amish products. Additionally, tourists hold Amish merchandise in high regard. Our Product Perception Survey found that 88 percent of area visitors rated the artisanship of Amish products higher or much higher than similar non-Amish merchandise. When asked to judge their overall value, an amazing 91 percent of the respondents considered Amish products to be higher or much higher in value. The positive image that Amish merchandise commands in the public mind serves Amish enterprise well, especially in the local tourist economy.[14]

The Amish Difference

Several distinctive features characterize Amish microenterprises. First, their social structure is remarkably flat. Because the shops are small, they exhibit little hierarchy and few social distinctions between labor and management. Although the entrepreneur is clearly in charge, most owners work alongside their employees. The boss's makeshift office is typically

◆

This small traditional shop makes decorative buckets for the tourist market.

empty—used mainly for early morning bookkeeping. Only a few of the larger businesses have a middle layer of management. In the congenial ethos of cottage industries, as well as in larger shops and on mobile work crews, managers are immersed in the actual work of their business. The owners are hands-on managers, and their hands are dirty. A machinery manufacturer spends his days painting finished pieces and checking quality control alongside his employees, who are turning out the product. Working together, owners interact with employees in ways that build camaraderie and enhance communication. The adversarial stance that often antagonizes labor-management relations fades in these small operations.

Amish enterprises boast remarkably low overheads. They do not have plush retirement plans for employees, and few offer health insurance because the Amish church has its own informal aid plan. Within a church community committed to mutual aid, such benefits are seen as unnecessary and superfluous. Additionally, business owners do not have lavish expense accounts to attend costly conventions, nor do they sport high-priced clothing. Likewise, no carpeted, air-conditioned offices adorned with posh chairs and ornate furniture drain profits from Amish firms. The lack of computers and public utility bills also keeps overhead low. Few businesses hire full-time clerical help. When asked how many of his hundred or so Amish clients have a full-time bookkeeper, a non-Amish accountant said, "Probably none." In most of the smaller firms, owners and spouses manage their own books on a part-time basis. A growing trend among larger firms is to outsource their bookkeeping, payroll, and tax work to the professional non-Amish firms that provide computerized services and, in some cases, produce weekly payrolls.

Flexibility is another mark of Amish-owned firms. Timetables and work calendars follow the ebb and flow of community life itself. The ability to control the terms of their work has been a plus for Amish entrepreneurship. Free to observe religious holidays and keep the Sabbath sacred, the Amish manage their work in harmony with the community's moral order and personal convictions. Flexible work hours allow the community to maintain the rituals that enhance unity and solidarity. Employees, for example, can negotiate extra time off during the fall wedding season. In the same way, business owners and their employees are free to drop their work and lend a hand to rebuild a barn or home when disaster strikes. Owners of farm-based enterprises can slow their shop work during harvest so employees can assist relatives working in the fields. The flexibility afforded by small-scale entrepreneurship strengthens the community and adds a layer of ethnic support and legitimacy to Amish firms.

Amish enterprises also stand apart in their use of technology. Unlike most businesses, which regard "new" and "improved" as synonymous, Amish firms are more skeptical of bigger, faster, and more-automated equipment. The Amish are not opposed to advanced technology, but they use it selectively. They reject tools, equipment, and production methods that unnecessarily disrupt and fragment community life. Additionally, the Amish argue that ready access to electricity from public utility lines encourages materialism and the accumulation of trivial gadgetry. The rejection of high-line power constricts the size of businesses and harnesses technology for specific purposes. Amish entrepreneurs have ingeniously tapped alternative power to replace electricity. Hydraulic and pneumatic power, for example, are used to operate a wide range of tools and machinery. These power sources, along with electricity from generators and batteries, enable the Amish to operate competitively in today's marketplace while maintaining a symbolic separation from the world.

Finally, these enterprises are uniquely tied to the Amish church. Entrepreneurs defer to the guidance of the church on questions of business size, product acceptability, technology, litigation, and the investment of wealth. Independence and creativity—although certainly not smothered—are restricted by the moral boundaries of Amish life. These religious and cultural constraints shape the character of Amish enterprises and distinguish them from their worldly counterparts. By reserving the right to regulate its homespun entrepreneurs, the church is able to channel business activity in ways that strengthen the bonds of community. Thus, the church not only guides the development of flourishing enterprises, but stamps its distinctive imprint on their cultural face as well.

4. Homespun Entrepreneurs

The Amish are proving to be terrific entrepreneurs.
— FORBES MAGAZINE

The First Generation

A surge in small business start-ups in North America led some business leaders to dub the late twentieth century the new age of entrepreneurship.[1] In an increasingly regulated and bureaucratized society, the entrepreneur who can buck the trends becomes a folk hero of sorts. The downsizing of corporate America has encouraged many corporate castoffs to turn to entrepreneurship. In some respects, similar forces motivated both homespun Amish entrepreneurs and their worldly counterparts. Both groups desire the flexibility afforded by entrepreneurship. Non-Amish entrepreneurs seek independence, personal autonomy, and freedom. For the Amish, on the other hand, the appeal of entrepreneurship is not mere individualism but autonomy from the factory and its alien cultural values. Opening small businesses enables the Amish to enjoy the pleasure of profit while preserving the virtues of their religious community.

The vast number of first-generation Amish entrepreneurs is testimony to the demographic changes pressing upon their community as well as to their remarkable entrepreneurial spirit. Although a few owners purchased or received their firms from someone else—most often from a parent or relative—four out of five started their business themselves. Some Amish entrepreneurs work alone on a part-time or full-time basis, but most hire employees.

The Amish have entered the world of entrepreneurship through several different pathways. In the 1980s, a significant portion joined the ranks of entrepreneurship as middle-aged farmers preparing for retirement. By the time they are fifty years of age, Amish parents typically have passed the family homestead on to one of their married offspring. A full quarter of Amish entrepreneurs began their firms at forty-six years of age or older, a slightly higher rate than the one-fifth of all Americans who began a business at the same age.[2] Although parents typically remain on the farmstead in a small "grandfather's house" and assist with chores, the responsibility for day-to-day farming operations falls to the next generation.

Thus, faced with dwindling farmland, many middle-aged farmers establish a business to provide work for themselves as well as for several soon-to-be-married children. The Amish credit this shift to new and harsher financial realities. Although children support their aging parents, the economic burdens of modern farming have forced some retirees to assume more responsibility for their own livelihood, often through a small business.

Amish retirees are involved in a wide range of enterprises. Many retired or semi-retired farmers have taken up woodworking, building virtually anything, from small toys to large gazebos. A few older couples have opened produce stands. Some women have begun to sell quilts in their newly found free time. Many of the enterprises operated by retired individuals remain small. With a modest view of providing dependable income and filling otherwise unproductive hours, older adults are not building large operations. In some cases, however, the business includes one or more of the couple's nonfarming children. With the family farm in hands of another sibling, adult children often join their parents' retirement business and turn it into a full-time enterprise.

Although some entrepreneurs enter business after turning their fields over to their sons, an increasing number of younger persons begin their occupational life in business. Costly farmland in the Lancaster settlement bars many prospective farmers from obtaining fields of their own at a young age. Small businesses have enabled some men to save for a farm without working in a factory or as a day laborer. Most would-be farmers spend the rest of their lives in a shop or store and never return to the farm of their dreams. In other cases, young entrepreneurs earn enough money to buy a farm. One Amish family, for example, opened a market stand that specialized in chicken barbecue. After building up the business, they sold it and bought a farm for themselves and their soon-to-be married children. Another Amish woodworker built fine household furniture until he could afford to buy a farm. Even then, he had to leave Lancaster County for a less populous settlement with cheaper land.

In an ironic twist, some entrepreneurs who were forced into business by the high price of farmland have been able to garner enough profits from business to buy up more farmland. This frequent practice happens two ways. Some business owners sell their successful business to a non-Amish buyer and move to another state where they use the proceeds to buy several farms for family members and other Amish who want to farm. In other cases, successful Amish entrepreneurs invest their profits in high-priced Lancaster Country farmland at home. Indeed, between 1984 and 1996, the Amish bought nearly 180 farms totaling some 15,000 acres. By the mid-1990s, they were buying 20 farms a year, and by the dawn of the twenty-first century, they owned some 1,500 farms, more than 40 percent of the farms in Lancaster County.[3]

In many cases, business start-ups are driven by financial necessity. When falling commodity prices hurt some farmers, they opened ancillary wintertime businesses. For many years dairy farmers—Amish and non-Amish alike—relied on tobacco crops to augment income for their herds. With declining tobacco prices and rising health concerns, some farmers began exploring new sources of cash. Some retrofitted tobacco sheds for machine shops. Others established greenhouses and grew plants during the winter. At the beginning of the twenty-first century, numerous Amish entrepreneurs were operating a business on their farm beside an empty cow barn. Forced out of dairying by low milk prices, they sold their cows, rented out their land to non-Amish "tractor farmers," and devoted their energy to growing a business. They wanted to "stay close to the land," said one businessman, "and raise their families on a farm." One Amishman said, "There are at least fifty empty barns on Amish farms within ten miles of Intercourse." Another one laughed, and said, "The number is much higher than that." In any event, business in the heart of Lancaster County was much more profitable than plowing.

Sudden financial hardships or unexpected medical bills also prompt some families to open a business. Although the church cares for the needy among its ranks, individual households try to meet their own financial obligations as much as possible. Thus, some business ventures are started to provide supplemental income.

In the past, of course, farming was the assumed—virtually legislated—occupation for church members. Other options were unthinkable. With the rise of commercial opportunities, however, many young married couples go directly into nonfarm occupations. The initial investment to begin farming often exceeds a million dollars with the combined costs of land, equipment, and livestock. With low prices for farm products and stiff competition from large mechanized farmers, it is difficult, if not impossible, for a young Amish farmer to pay off such a sizeable initial investment. By contrast, a carpenter or craft maker may be able to begin a small business with an investment of $100,000 or less and grow it gradually. These stark economic realities lure many young people into business.

◆

A greenhouse and salesroom attached to this home reflect the integration of
work and family. Greenhouses provide a direct connection to the soil for some
nonfarm Amish. Amish women often own and operate greenhouses.

Personal abilities and interests have propelled others into business. "I
was born a carpenter, and I'll always be a carpenter. I guess I don't know
any better!" one Amishman laughed, when asked why he had become a
builder instead of a farmer. Without much reflection, the owner of a metal
fabrication shop admitted he had never wanted to farm. An Amish businesswoman said some women simply "have the desire" to enter business.

Many persons are now becoming second-generation owners of firms
that were established in the 1980s or 1990s. Picking up the reins of established firms, second-generation owners typically try to expand their enterprises. An appliance store owner who took over his father's business said
his father would hardly recognize the place now. While first-generation
entrepreneurs struggle to find financing, products, and markets, those who
follow often find their challenge in boosting efficiency, growth, and profitability. As the second generation moves into place, the church faces new
challenges on how to limit aggressive growth.

Some children of entrepreneurs, interestingly, return to farming. Only
one generation removed from the soil and still able to learn the art of agriculture from grandparents and kin, these children revert back to agriculture after a generational detour—if land can be found. One successful shop
owner with five children said, "I'm saving and looking for a farm because
I hope at least one of my children will farm." Another major entrepreneur

was pleased that he was able to buy farms for each of his four daughters. One machine shop operator requires his sons to work on a farm for at least a year before he employs them in his shop so that they learn the lessons of farming and "just in case they want to farm." However, as more and more families spend two or more generations off the farm, the likelihood of returning to the land will surely decline.

The rapid growth of business has stirred many lively discussions in the Amish community about the comparative virtues of farming and business for family and community life. Many voices applaud the importance of farming for preserving the Amish way of life. On the other hand, some nonfarm families herald the values of nonfarm work. One woman, in an essay defending nonfarm work, wrote, "First of all, we don't live on a farm. Secondly, we are a happy family." Echoing her claims, another non-farm mother said, "Something that has often comforted us is that neither Jesus nor his disciples were farmers." A young shop owner probably spoke for many when he said, "I do feel it is best if as a family we keep at least a few fingers in the soil and stay closer to nature, which can teach us a lot about God and his ways."[4]

Entrepreneurs in Profile

Spread across the Lancaster settlement, Amish entrepreneurs—numbering at least 1,600 strong—reflect a diversity of age, background, and gender. About a fourth opened their shops before they turned twenty-six. Some worked in Amish and non-Amish businesses as teenagers and then started their own ventures after marriage. Others, having grown up on a farm but unable to find land, entered business with the hope of returning to the farm some day. And still others have found themselves unwittingly thrust into management by a parent's untimely death.

At age twenty, harness maker Moses Smucker suddenly took over a small family business when his father died in a tragic accident. The young entrepreneur rapidly expanded the enterprise, which had formed in 1970 in a tobacco shed. He turned it into an international business that emphasizes individual artisanship. Harnesses crafted in Smucker's shop pull trolley cars at Disneyland in California. The Clydesdale horses in the Budweiser commercials also wear them. The shop has filled special orders for Kenny Rogers, Michael Jackson, Donald Trump, and the Ringling Brothers Circus.[5]

More than half the entrepreneurs moved into the market place between twenty-six and forty-five years of age, often after an apprenticeship in another business. In a few cases, a second venture into business soothed the pain of an early failure. At age thirty, one businessman sold a struggling

◆

Several unmarried Amishwomen own and operate this bakeshop. Their baked goods are sold to fellow Amish, non-Amish neighbors, and tourists and at public farmers' markets.

engine shop to launch a profitable bulk foods store. After a serious highway accident paralyzed a middle-aged farmer, he and his wife began selling lawn furniture and crafts. Other middle-aged entrepreneurs confess to stumbling into their enterprises with little planning. A forty-year-old farmer inherited a table saw from his father's estate, but he had "never worked with wood" until his thrifty values demanded that he put the new tool to use. Within five years, he was successfully marketing rolltop desks and had turned his farming operation over to one of his sons.

Although nearly all business owners grew up on farms, the bulk of them (67 percent) spend no time farming today. Some assist on farms several weeks a year, helping family members or neighbors during harvesting or planting. Other owners operate a sideline enterprise to supplement their farm income and spend half of their time behind the plow. A few entrepreneurs also work as day laborers for other firms and operate their own businesses in evenings and on weekends. One Amish father who works in maintenance at a nearby motel spends his evenings making mailboxes, birdhouses, and lawn ornaments. A day laborer in a metal shop might buy a portable welder and do repair work for relatives and neighbors in his spare time, hoping eventually to set up his own shop.

Consider the saga of one entrepreneur, the youngest son in a family of eleven children. His father was unable to buy him a farm when he was contemplating marriage. So for three years the young man worked for a large, national non-Amish farm machinery manufacturer. During this time he also worked part-time as a farm hand for five dollars a day. With the combined income, he was able to purchase a small plot of land before he was married. After marriage, he left the factory and worked as a carpenter for half a year and also made wooden feed carts on weekends. Then at age 25, two years after his marriage, he began manufacturing various products on a full-time basis. But in his words, "Many of them didn't work out, and I wasn't doing very well for several years."

Eventually, a salesman gave him an idea for improving a small feeder for cattle barns. He crafted a superior product, which soon found ready markets. A dozen years later his machine shop was manufacturing some twenty different steel products for cattle barns and distributing them in thirty different states. Family members and three other employees work in the shop, which garners annual sales above $100,000 per worker. Moreover, the successful entrepreneur recently purchased land for a second shop to manufacture and distribute wood products on a national basis. The second shop supports the community by providing apprenticeships for would-be entrepreneurs for several years before embarking on their own.

Although the large majority of Amish entrepreneurs are men, one-fifth are women. As shown in table 4.1, women are disproportionately clustered in the smaller firms. Women typically manage firms with fewer than four full-time employees. The rise of female entrepreneurship is a notable shift within this patriarchal culture. The autonomy accorded business owners, coupled with their independent income, formal relationships with outsiders, and the management of employees, will surely alter longstanding gender roles in Amish society. Some entrepreneurs are unmarried women, whose autonomy is less threatening to the church than that of married women. In other cases, married women—including mothers of young children—have embarked on business ventures of their own. Even with the blessing of husband and church, these commercial pursuits will modify gender roles and power relations over time.

Despite some diversity, most entrepreneurs exhibit considerable creativity, energy, and stamina. Tapping their farming heritage, they expect

TABLE 4.1

Gender of Amish Entrepreneurs (in percent),
by Number of Employees

Number of Full-time Employees	Male	Female	Total
0–1	76	24	100
2–3	79	21	100
4 or more	100	0	100

Source: Enterprise Profile (*N* = 118).

their work to define the use of time, not vice versa. The strictures of a forty-hour week do not limit their labor. Many business owners report weekly stints of fifty to sixty hours. The endless flow of energy expended to launch hundreds of new businesses in recent decades is indeed remarkable. While all entrepreneurs exhibit a spirit of optimism, the cultural values of Amish life, rooted on the farm, have fed the entrepreneurial spirit.

Entrepreneurial Education

The making of an entrepreneur requires training and knowledge. In the larger society, business courses, college programs, and self-help seminars offer guidance through the maze of business start-up. Although a limited number of Amish entrepreneurs have taken seminars and short-term classes, most have ignored formal education. Indeed, one of the restraints within their cultural tradition has been a negative attitude toward formal education—especially higher education, which emphasizes science and critical thinking. This cultural restraint has, ironically, turned into a resource in the case of Amish entrepreneurs.

Although the Amish are not opposed to education as such, they are wary of the type delivered by large public schools. Such schools separate children from their communities by busing them away from home and immersing them in a world at odds with Amish values. Both the content and method of public education disturbs Amish sensibilities. They reject higher education because it encourages individualism, competition, critical thinking, and bold faith in scientific progress. The Amish hope to raise children who obey the church, work with their families and neighbors, and espouse communal values of humility and simplicity. Said one father: "I'm not against education. I want my children educated. But there's more to going to school than books." The Amish esteem wisdom and practical experience. Although not ridiculed outright, book learning clearly ranks low. Formal courses, academic transcripts, and credentials carry little weight among a people who cherish useful knowledge. Indeed, high school and college education remains taboo.[6]

Distrust of consolidated schools has provoked persistent conflict between Amish people and the state in the twentieth century.[7] After midcentury, the Amish established their own private schools and received the blessing of the U.S. Supreme Court in 1972.[8] Today virtually all the children in the Lancaster settlement attend some one hundred and sixty one-room schools staffed by Amish teachers who are themselves products of an eighth-grade education. Basic instruction in reading, writing, English, and arithmetic forms the educational core of their curriculum. Amish schools stress cooperation over competition and generally discourage independent thinking on the part of youngsters. Yet the language and math skills obtained in Amish schools, so far at least, have served prospective businesspeople well.

Beyond their classroom knowledge, business owners come to the marketplace with a wealth of practical experience. In the early 1990s, nine of ten entrepreneurs had grown up on a farm, and some 60 percent had operated one before moving into business (table 4.2). The agricultural tradition offers a significant resource for the cultivation of entrepreneurship. Farmers manage sizable inventories of animals, equipment, and land holdings. Engaged in the commodity markets of milk, feed, and seed, they work with wholesale marketers, lending institutions, and sales representatives. Most important, farmers develop a degree of self-reliance and problem-solving skills as they coordinate sizable operations and cope with the vagaries of weather. Although cooperation and communal aid distinguish Amish life, the farmer epitomizes, in many ways, the spirit of independence. As one retired farmer put it, "On a farm you have to be a mechanic, an accountant, and a vet. You've got to do it all."

A few businesspeople cite trade publications as part of their business education. National magazines and specialized newsletters have become regular reading material for some entrepreneurs, but without exception they list on-the-job experience as their most important—and often only—education. When asked about their training, they report "learning by doing" with hands-on experience. Others note learning from relatives, neighbors, or retired business managers. One shop owner learned to mold fiberglass by spending several weeks working with the previous owner. Another shop owner established a second woodworking shop and hired a young couple in what the owner described as a "kind of five-year apprenticeship." After five years, the young couple hopes to set up their own shop elsewhere, and the owner will "start someone else." In many cases, informal networks of advice and wisdom serve dozens of young or beginning

TABLE 4.2

Relationship of Amish Entrepreneurs to Farming

Entrepreneurs	Percentage
Grew up on a farm	93
Previously operated a farm	60
Are not currently farming	67
Operate enterprises on or adjacent to a farm	60

Source: Enterprise Profile (N = 118).

entrepreneurs. This wealth of social and cultural capital within Amish society has stimulated the growth of Amish enterprises.

Amish entrepreneurs believe that hands-on, experiential learning is not only effective but also practical and inexpensive. Working gradually into business parallels the way children learn farming and household chores. Practical skills, learned by trial and error, hold sway in the Amish mind over theoretical knowledge. When asked how he learned to operate a grocery store from scratch, an Amish entrepreneur responded, "How did I learn? By going out and exploring the food world. You have to just do it. ... When you go in and read about how to do it in books, it's not the real thing. You've got to have a work ethic behind it. You've just got to work."

A hands-on method of learning embodies traditional Amish esteem for experience, usefulness, and wisdom. And by learning on the job themselves, Amish managers model the problem-solving approach for their employees. Said one woodworking shop owner, "If I'm going through [the shop] and see something that's inefficient, I point it out. And if someone ever says, 'Hey, no one ever showed me that way,' I can honestly say, 'Hey, no one ever showed me anything either.' I learned it all on my own. I didn't take a class. I figured it out by myself."

More than 90 percent of the business owners received no formal training beyond eighth grade. Fewer than 10 percent have taken courses after leaving the eighth-grade classroom.[9] A very small number have completed high school through correspondence or equivalency exams. Some business owners who are also farmers have taken short courses on the use of chemical pesticides for their farming operations. Several entrepreneurs have enrolled in human relations programs, such as those offered by Dale Carnegie Systems. Students taking such courses cite their need to acquire special skills to deal with non-Amish customers and employees.

Other formal training is geared more directly to technical needs. A number of shop owners have taken hydraulics courses offered by equipment dealers. Amish accountants sometimes take tax courses offered by H & R Block or seminars provided through state extension programs. A craftsman who molds wheelbarrow bodies might take a plastics course offered by a supplier. One Amish inventor enrolled in a one-day government-sponsored seminar titled "How to Obtain a Patent." A craft store-owner attended a business seminar on creating winsome product displays. Dealer-sponsored seminars in fencing, landscaping, or engine repair have drawn Amish participants as well.

Nevertheless, the vast majority of Amish businesspeople have not availed themselves of formal or technical training. While acceding to some seminars and short-term courses for technical knowledge, the Amish refuse to become engulfed in the educational craze of the larger society. Their private eighth-grade education has served them well. The resources of their cultural tradition, embellished by a practical, problem-solving approach, have proven adequate for training business owners. This pragmatic, ethnic education enables Amish entrepreneurs to work within the moral boundaries of their culture as they seek new ways to compete in the marketplace.

Entrepreneurial Ingenuity

Despite their lack of formal education, many entrepreneurs have displayed remarkable ingenuity and creativity. In some cases innovations have sprung, ironically, from the technological restraints of Amish culture. The same moral boundaries that restrict technology also propel creative minds to find new ways of working within community sanctions. Circumventing the taboo on electricity, one inventor created outdoor watering fountains for cattle that remain free of ice in winter without electrical heating. The energy-free drinker uses thermal heat from the ground to prevent freezing. Although other, larger companies have marketed similar devices, the Amish inventor added a float-valve assembly and an insulated baffle float so that sheep and calves could drink with ease. Farmers can easily assemble the product with sturdy clips—thus eliminating the need for wrenches, screwdrivers, and other tools. The inventor is constantly updating his design.

The inventor of the drinker began experimenting with plastics and produced prototypes of the drinker, but he contracted actual production out to other companies. The young entrepreneur also experimented with an energy-free, nipple-style pig drinker as well as stall drinkers for dairy barns. The nonelectric drinker removes the risk of shocking animals and saves utility costs, making it also attractive to non-Amish farmers. Nevertheless, it was the cultural constraints of Amish life that provided the impetus for the new product.

The ready use of plastics reveals another aspect of the cultural bargain the Amish have struck with modernity. Insofar as new technology bolsters

Amish identity and community cohesion, it is a welcome ally. Children often carry colorful plastic lunch pails as they walk to their parochial schools. When used to produce nonelectric drinkers or softer horseshoes, plastics help to reinforce traditional markers of Amish identity. A sizeable Amish firm produces vinyl fencing for lawns, gardens, and swimming pools. If it enhances the welfare of the community, new technology is welcomed. Only when it peels away community cohesion does technology face the frown of the church.

Entrepreneurs are generally free to build or improve farm machinery as long as they honor the longstanding taboo on self-propelled equipment. Several inventors have developed new products for farm use, and many manufacture machinery they have adapted or improved—wagons, manure spreaders, sprayers, plows, and corn planters.[10]

One Amish firm developed an air-powered pump in a plastic tube that is inserted into wells. The pump is powered by air pressure from the air pump on a diesel engine. Many Amish homes use the air pump rather than the old fashioned windmills to pump water from their wells. One young Amish entrepreneur is developing solar applications that provide electricity to Amish homes for small lights and appliances from solar panels on the roof.

The church wholly sanctions inventions that reinforce Amish culture and tradition. One Amish entrepreneur who manufactured horse-drawn and tractor-driven farm machinery created a machine to flip hay upside down in the field in order to speed its drying time. Innovative and progressive by any measure, the hay turner was welcomed not only by the Amish community but also by non-Amish dealers and farmers across the country. Another Amish mechanic created a bale stuffer to force hay bales into large plastic bags for winter storage.

Several farmers and mechanics developed a rather modern horse-drawn riding plow over the course of two decades. The two-way horse-drawn plow has a hydraulic lift that enables the operator to pull the plow out of the ground with the press of a foot pedal. A hydraulic reset uses hydraulic pressure to force the plow back into the ground. Without tractor power, hydraulic pressure is created by the plow's ground-driven wheel and stored in an accumulator. A rather modern implement, it is far superior to the old-fashioned hand-held walking plow.

Although the Amish are apt to scrutinize the benefits and dangers of technology for their own use, they have greater freedom in producing new products for outsiders. Although playing golf is generally viewed as a waste of time, one inventor helped to mechanize a professional golf course. An Amish farmer who operated a welding shop as a sideline began doing repair work for a local golf course. The non-Amish owner of the course was frustrated by the time required to recup his golf greens with a manual digging tool. In dry summer weather on a hard turf, two employees might spend half a day recupping eighteen holes. Many courses had to cut new cups every two hundred rounds, or even daily, during hot weather.

Intrigued by the challenge, the Amish inventor built a gasoline-powered recupping machine. The finished model, weighing a mere fifteen pounds, solved some of the problems of manual recupping. The new recupper bores a clean hole in seconds and discharges the sod plug from the new cup into the old. One person can recup an entire course in a short time with the new implement. Additionally, the new device cuts cleanly, rarely leaving a ragged hole. The inventor and golf course owner, however, have had difficulty marketing the invention. Some golf course owners prefer the manual recupping method, arguing that the new device is too expensive. The Amish inventor noted wryly that traditions also run deep outside the Amish community: "They've been doing it so long the old way, they don't want to change."[11]

Some entrepreneurs have focused on the wholesale craft industry. One Amishman developed a press to stamp out objects—pumpkin faces, Christmas trees, candy canes, Santa Clauses, and stockings—from thin sheets of wood. His unique press enables him to punch out a pumpkin face and its eyes in one operation. Craft stores buy the wooden cutouts in a variety of seasonal shapes. Customers paint the items and use them in holiday displays. Although most Amish themselves would not buy a wooden Santa's face, manufacturing such items is acceptable because it flows in continuity with traditional woodworking.

Other creative products flowing from the offices and shops of Amish entrepreneurs fall within more traditional fields. Two sisters produced and marketed several cookbooks. They advertised in an Amish newspaper, offering a free book to anyone who sent them twenty-five recipes. The women sorted and edited stacks of responses and eventually issued a book with one thousand recipes. One of the sisters and her husband marketed the book. "We've gotten a lot of good compliments on them from our own people, and the tourists seem to like them, too," noted the husband of one of the editors. Since their joint effort, the sisters have also produced cookbooks separately. When asked how his wife and sister-in-law came up with the idea of making a cookbook, the husband of one of the editors explained, "They're just very creative. . . . They just think of these things and want to do something creative."

Creating new products for tourist markets has become commonplace. An Amish metalworker set out to produce pieces for Lancaster County visitors. Playing on the popular image of the horse and buggy, he created metal silhouettes of Amish carriages for sale in tourist shops. The entre-

◆

This recupper was designed by an Amish inventor to recup golf course greens.
It is powered by a gasoline engine.

preneurial spirit was evident in his explanation: "One winter I was sitting in the office and I thought, 'There has to be something else I can make yet.' So I thought, 'I'll do a silhouette of a buggy and cut it out of metal.' So I drew it on paper, transferred it to a sheet of metal, and cut it out with my cutter. I took it to some people who sell to tourists, and I asked if they could sell it." Produced by a nearby fabricating shop, the buggy cutouts return to the inventor's farm, where he paints them black, packages them, and distributes them to his wholesale accounts. Not satisfied with one silhouette, the entrepreneur now offers five different sizes as well as some that serve as letter or napkin holders. Larger ones are attached to metal stakes and sold as lawn ornaments.

One entrepreneur turned a horse collar into merchandise. A craftsman who manufactured harness collars, he placed a timepiece inside the open oval of the collar to create an attractive wall clock. The decorative clocks appealed to the horse enthusiasts who frequented his shop, and within two years he was producing a variety of styles. Transforming a traditional artifact into a decorative piece was not considered a mockery of simplicity.

By using functional clocks, the artisan conferred a measure of practical acceptability on his embellished collars.[12]

Another businessman redesigned a machine to shred newspapers for cattle bedding. In 1989 a non-Amish farmer asked a shop owner to build a newspaper shredder from prepared plans. After reviewing the plans, the Amishman decided that he "could make a better one." He redesigned the machine, sold the improved model to the non-Amish farmer, and built another one for his own use. Because many farmers could not afford the chopper, the Amish inventor began buying and shredding paper and selling bales of it to local dairy farmers for bedding. As the business grew, he continually improved the shredder and increased its capacity. Coincidentally, the local public health agency instituted mandatory recycling and contracted with the Amishman to chop a hundred tons of newspapers a week. As the business grew, the entrepreneur hired three persons to operate the shredder and asked a non-Amish person to handle sales and distribution. A nearby state-subsidized shredding plant cost one-third more to establish than the Amish operation but chops only one-fifth the amount of newspaper.

Beyond the commercial success of his enterprise, the entrepreneur sees his work flowing from Amish concerns for the land. Finding new uses for old newsprint is "a plus to the environment," he notes without reservation. "They say that these landfills are 20 percent newspapers. So if they fill up in five years, pulling the newspapers out will make them last six years— and that's something." He views his work as a service "for the environment and for the farmer" and believes that his services reflect the best values of his ethnic heritage.

Unlikely Professionals

"Professional Amish" sounds like an oxymoron. Without a college education or membership in professional societies, Amish entrepreneurs possess few of the formal marks of professionals. Employed in low-prestige jobs with little name recognition, Amish business owners enjoy little of the popular acclaim of professional status. Yet if the defining mark of professionalism is control over the terms and conditions of one's work, then Amish entrepreneurs, ironically, may be nearer the professional fold than is obvious at first glance.

To a large extent, professionals are able to shape their work by setting their hours and controlling its content and nature. Professionals, of course, work within a subculture of colleagues, accrediting associations, journals, and conventions. The peculiar jargon of a profession creates a kind of dialect that bars the uninitiated. Prescribed clothing in some professions creates insider identity and sets its members apart. Professional groups control the entryway to their professions, and they expel members and revoke credentials. In a word, professions exercise considerable control over the work of their members. Professions also exercise hefty leverage when negotiating with the larger society to enhance their vested interests.

Although the Amish spirit of humility and self-effacement mocks the subtle arrogance of modern professionalism, the Amish do resemble professionals in certain ways. By controlling the terms and conditions of their work, Amish entrepreneurs have created a professional work environment of sorts. They determine where and when they will work. They control their own work calendar and seasonal schedule. As members of an ethnic group, the Amish work within a set of cultural expectations. The Ordnung, like a professional code of ethics, both limits and channels their creativity. The Pennsylvania German dialect, like professional jargon, textures and insulates the workplace. Similar to a professional society, the church exercises control over its members and reserves the right to discipline and expel.

Refusing to be buried in the culture of corporate America, yet forced off the farm, the Amish have negotiated a world of work that champions the joys of entrepreneurship without forfeiting their religious heritage. Combining the frugality of the farm with the opportunities of the marketplace, they have unwittingly acted as professionals in their quest to create meaningful work within the context of their ethnic culture. Using the resources of their community, they have created hundreds of quasi-professional jobs that remain untarnished by the malaise of alienation common in the larger world of industry.

The Amish are not alone in their search for meaningful work. Many of their fellow Americans, disillusioned with factory and office, have established home businesses in vacant rooms, basements, and garages. Alienated by a system of mass production, many would-be entrepreneurs have created alternative, home-based employment, hoping for greater freedom and personal reward. The homeward turn of work is yet another stage in the transition of Western economies as they trek from farm to factory and office and now, with the aid of technology, toward home again.

Lancaster's Amish, meanwhile, have made an end run around the historical trends by moving directly from farm to home-based business. They have tapped some of the rationality of industry along the way but have, nevertheless, bypassed the factory.[13] With this move, the Amish have been able to preserve some of the features of preindustrial, family-centered work. The forces that pushed the Amish toward commerce were far different, however, from those that have pulled office workers homeward in recent years. Many home workers, stressed by impersonal corporate systems, turned to home work in the hope of recovering some measure of satisfaction and pride in their effort. The Amish, on the other hand, facing relentless urbanization, were reluctant to abandon their rural heritage and religious tradition. Sure of their roots and willing to negotiate, they opted to create hundreds of microenterprises where homespun entrepreneurs could work within the context of family and community.

5. Labor and Human Resources

◆

*I could do in a half-hour what some of those English guys did in a day.
They just messed around and goofed off.*

— AMISH SHOP OWNER

The Ethnic Work Force

Although the late twentieth century witnessed a rise in entrepreneurship and self-employment in North America, the majority of today's workforce remains employed by someone else. Among the Amish, growing numbers are also finding themselves on someone else's payroll. More and more Amish are working at a shop or store operated by an Amish relative, friend, or neighbor. Although a few work in non-Amish settings such as feed mills, restaurants, or construction crews, most Lancaster Amish find employment with an Amish-managed firm. The growing ethnic workforce, socialized in the virtues of hard work, has provided an energetic resource for the growth and expansion of Amish enterprise.

The responsibilities of recruiting and supervising employees as well as balancing wages and benefits often challenge novice entrepreneurs. Some are faced with laying off or firing workers. One machine shop owner described personnel management as "a headache," all the while emphasizing that his employees are good workers who never cause problems. Comparing his small-scale operation to a larger neighboring non-Amish business, another owner shook his head, "I don't know how they ever manage with fifty employees. I wouldn't want to do it, that's for sure. That would take all the enjoyment out of it!" Nevertheless, Amish entrepreneurs express universal appreciation for their employees, realizing that their success hinges in large part on their hired help.

Amish businesses do not typically employ large numbers of people. Many, in fact, provide work only for the entrepreneur. Counting only full-

TABLE 5.1

Estimated Jobs Provided by Amish Enterprises in the Lancaster Settlement, 1993–2003

Type of Job	Employees		
	Amish	Non-Amish	Total
1993			
Full-time	1,687	281	1,968
Part-time	1,218	187	1,405
TOTAL JOBS	2,905	468	3,373
2003			
Full-time	2,880	480	3,360
Part-time	2,080	800	2,880
TOTAL JOBS	4,960	1,280	6,240

Source: Enterprise Profile (N = 118).
Note: Estimates based on average of 1.8 full-time and 1.3 part-time jobs per 937 enterprises in 1993 and 1,600 enterprises in 2003.

time help, one-fifth of the firms employ two to four people over age fourteen, including the owner. About another fifth have five or more full-time workers, as shown in table 5.1.[1] On average, each business creates about two full-time and one-and-a-half part-time positions. By 1993, Amish firms had created almost 1,700 full-time jobs and more than 1,200 part-time jobs for Amish persons, in one way or another. Moreover, some 460 non-Amish persons were also employed in Amish enterprises (see table 5.1). In the next decade, the numbers of jobs grew. By 2003, Amish enterprises were providing work for nearly 5,000 Amish and more than 1,200 non-Amish, not to mention the hundreds of non-Amish drivers providing transportation.

Gender roles remain entrenched in traditional patterns, except for the rise of female entrepreneurship, which we explore in chapter 13. As noted earlier, about 20 percent of Amish enterprises have a female proprietor. Very few firms employ women in skilled positions, apart from bookkeeping, and in many smaller businesses the entrepreneur personally handles the "book work." Sometimes spouses do the clerical work for male entrepreneurs. The few businesses that hire full- or part-time office help are as likely to hire Amish as non-Amish, male as female, to fill their clerical slots. The larger businesses typically hire a non-Amish firm to do their payroll and accounting off-site.

Recruiting

Entrepreneurs recruit employees in a number of ways. Often an informal announcement, passed along the Amish grapevine, spreads the news of an opening. Few firms have long-range hiring goals. They simply respond to the flow of orders and customers. Most frequently, new employees of a growing business are members of the immediate family. Sixty-six percent of Amish enterprises employ at least one family member other than the entrepreneur. Twenty percent supply work for two or more kin. Most businesspeople involve their children in one way or another in their work. School-age children often help as needed. Post-school-age children are expected to work on a regular basis in the family business or in one operated by an Amish neighbor or a relative. Members of the immediate family often work without pay. The involvement of children has created some clashes with national child labor laws—a topic we explore in chapter 11.[2]

Extensive social networks within the Amish settlement provide an avenue for recruitment beyond the immediate family. Current employees also help recruit. "We usually ask around to those who are already working here if they know anyone who needs work," reports an Amish contractor. "They usually do. We've had no trouble getting good help." His firm has hired both Amish and non-Amish workers on the recommendation of current employees. Amish persons, however, are the most likely to benefit from the ethnic network.

Other firms seek retired or semi-retired farmers, who may turn their fields over to a son or a son-in-law and move into retirement between the ages of forty-five and fifty-five. Some of the newly retired farmers open small shops of their own or work for a neighboring business. Amish society esteems the wisdom older members bring to the job. Some owners believe that seniors may have a stronger work ethic, even if their physical stamina is not as great. "Some sixty-year-old guys are better workers than some twenty-year-olds," noted a wood products manufacturer who has hired several retired farmers.

Few Amish firms receive walk-in requests for employment from non-Amish people. Often somewhat secluded, many enterprises are not highly visible to outsiders. Few if any Amish firms use public or private recruiting agencies. Likewise, most businesses do not advertise for help in local papers. Even in the Amish press, job openings are rarely listed. In Amish society, employment decisions, like many others, are made in the context of personal conversation and observation.

Amish entrepreneurs do have certain traits in mind when recruiting new employees—primarily dependability and trustworthiness.[3] Amish society, built on the moral assumptions of honesty and integrity, operates largely on interpersonal trust. Without recourse to oaths, law courts, or other civil institutions designed to ensure veracity, the Amish lean on personal trust. Moreover, without extensive supervision, employees exercise considerable independence and responsibility.

◆

A portable hydraulic pump provides power to repair a corn harvester. The fifteen-year-old boy in the center is skilled in hydraulic controls. He is the lead repairman on this job.

Employers also value a willingness to work hard. Although reticent to declare that they work harder than other people, entrepreneurs expect long hours of physical labor. At a young age children begin helping their parents. In one shop, a six-year-old assembles shovels in his father's shop for several hours after school. An eight-year-old girl waits on customers at the reception desk of her father's furniture shop after school and on Saturday morning. Work responsibilities increase when formal schooling ends at age fourteen. In retirement, adults may slow their pace of activity, but virtually none stop working. Employees are expected to take initiative and work diligently. One employer lamented a worker who lacked initiative—"He just wasn't a self-starter."

Other entrepreneurs mentioned religious faith, family background, willingness to learn, and adaptiveness as desirable traits of new workers. When hiring fellow church members or members' children, such information is readily available through personal observation and family informants. Because employees rarely receive formal training, willingness to learn on the job is important. Future employees, in the words of one owner, must be willing to "start at the bottom and work their way up."

Finally, some employers cite the importance of respect and courtesy. "I have no tolerance for abusive language or substance abuse on the job," said one contractor. "I won't stand for it." Another builder asks prospective employees if they smoke, not because it matters what they do privately, "but to make it clear right then and there that we don't have any of that on the job site. That's clear from the start." Amishmen who indulge in a cigar at home often discover that their Amish employer, out of respect to customers, will not permit smoking at work.

Hiring

Few Amish enterprises have elaborate hiring procedures. Owners hiring family members or neighbors may forgo an interview if the person is well known; however, most prospective employees are interviewed. Few enterprises have written job description or even printed employment applications. Hiring hinges on face-to-face impressions rather than written statements.

Those who do hold interviews may do so in unusual ways. Just as printed job applications hold less convincing weight among the Amish, sterile in-office interviews seem ill fitted to their understandings of work. Hence, interviews are often conducted in shops or at work sites. Said one contractor who always meets prospective employees on the job site, "I can tell a lot about a person by the way he approaches me at work—the way he gets out of the car, the way he walks toward me. Is he comfortable at the work site? You can tell a lot just by how they act at the job site, much more than in the office." Others meet potential workers during off-hours or at home, assuming that prospects more often reveal their true character in relaxed and familiar surroundings.

Few entrepreneurs have difficulty finding quality help. The growing Amish population produces dozens of new, willing workers each year. Businesses needing non-Amish workers have also been able to find suitable help. One entrepreneur, however, lamented, "It's very hard to find leadership today." Too many workers—Amish and non-Amish alike—are accustomed to being told what to do, he fears. The independent, problem-solving spirit that first-generation owners brought from their farming background might wane, he warns. On the whole, though, Amish businesses have few labor complaints. Quality workers are in ample supply.

At times, entrepreneurs push aside questions of qualification when hiring new employees. The Amish community has historically provided employment for all its members—mental, emotional, and physical disabilities notwithstanding. The church has never warehoused the disabled, but tries instead to integrate them as much as possible into daily routines. As Amish businesses have grown, they have employed persons with disabilities. One manufacturer, for example, has hired two Amishmen with mental and emotional disabilities. "They were having trouble finding work," he recalls. "We really didn't need them at the time, but we worked them in because they needed work." Employing such individuals is not, of course, without its difficulties. The owner sometimes extends extra privileges to these men and does not expect the same productivity. "I've been more patient with them than with the others," he acknowledged. "Sometimes it's hard on the other employees, but they seem to understand the situation."

A number of Amish firms hire non-Amish employees. Non-Amish people hold about 14 percent of the full-time jobs created by Amish enterprises. Many enterprises employ one non-Amish person in a full- or part-time capacity to provide transportation or special technical services, such as computing. Although a few firms claim to overlook ethnicity, most entrepreneurs clearly prefer hiring fellow ethnics.

Business owners generally agree that, other qualifications being equal, they prefer to hire fellow Amish for several reasons. In the first place, some managers believe that Amish workers are more trustworthy. One store owner said that after having trouble with non-Amish customers shoplifting, she was hesitant to hire outsiders. Reliable workers will let the boss know if they are sick, one contractor noted. Too often, non-Amish employees fail to show up for work and then come in the next day claiming they were sick, he complained.

Other Amish managers worry that the non-Amish will bring a weaker work ethic to the job. One entrepreneur developed a negative impression working for an outside firm as a teenager. Recalling his own memories in the non-Amish shop, he said, "I could do in a half hour what some of those English guys did in a day. They just messed around and goofed off." Although he quickly noted that many non-Amish employees do work diligently, he worries that such diligence is waning with each generation.

Another advantage to hiring Amish workers is the ease it affords in arranging fringe benefits. Amish firms operate with certain assumptions that often clash with those of other American work places. Most Amish businesses do not offer retirement plans, hospitalization insurance, or paid vacations as standard benefits, which non-Amish workers might expect. Employers may feel caught between different expectations if both groups are on the payroll. Said one entrepreneur, "That's one reason I stay with Plain People. . . . Other people want the benefits of other companies. Now,

I don't have anything against that, if that's what they want to do, but that's not the way this business runs."

Some managers also think that Amish employees are more reserved and courteous to customers. Because more than half the firms have a sizable number of Amish customers, having salespeople who know the language and culture of the clientele is a decided advantage. "They get along with each other better, they understand each other better," one businesswoman said, describing the advantages of having Amish clerks serve Amish customers. Owners also report that alcohol and drug abuse is less of a problem among Amish workers than it is in larger corporate world. Moreover, they point out, if a problem of abuse arises with an Amish employee, they can address the problem directly with the employee's family and church. A similar incident with a non-Amish employee would likely involve the police and other government agencies.

Another advantage of hiring fellow church members is reduced paperwork and lower costs. Exemption from Social Security and Workers' Compensation for Amish employees eases clerical and personnel costs. Finally, Amish business owners know that hiring outsiders opens a shop to the threat of lawsuits. Several disgruntled non-Amish employees have repaid their Amish employers by dragging them to court over trivial matters. Hiring Amish employees provides assurance that disagreements will most likely be handled by the church rather than by the legal system.

All Amish entrepreneurs are quick to acclaim their many fine non-Amish neighbors and friends. Most are quite reticent to acknowledge their preference for Amish help. Humility keeps them from charging others with slothfulness. Honesty compels them to point out that a few Amish have poor work habits as well. But most do acknowledge—however cautiously—that hiring nonethnics carries greater risks.

Employee orientation is critical to integrating newly hired workers into a business. Although Amish firms play down the significance of formal education, they do not discount the need to equip workers with essential skills. Some entrepreneurs see advantages in hiring unskilled workers, who are often easier to teach. One general contractor commented characteristically, "I would rather take an eighteen-year-old and break him in the way I want him than to have to retrain someone else. Basically, if I train them, they only know what I teach them." At the same time, business owners often realize that prior knowledge is helpful in approaching a new job. Amish youth, experienced in using tools around the farm, bring a welcome acumen to the job. Similarly, a young floor clerk in an Amish dry goods store would probably bring a knowledge of fabrics from her own sewing experience while growing up.

In passing on technical knowledge and expertise, entrepreneurs employ on-the-job training and apprentice-like approaches. Many employers begin training new workers by having them "start right in." A newcomer hired to operate a lathe, for example, will likely begin operating the machine immediately. The Amish stress learning through doing and emphasize the need for practical training. Employees learn on the job by a combination of trial and error and guided instruction. Either way, the hands-on practice is noticeable and, from the Amish point of view, desirable. Workers trained in a practical, on-site fashion are deemed superior to those who dabble in theoretical knowledge from books or distant classrooms.

Often the owner serves as the training supervisor. Thirty percent of the entrepreneurs reported that new employees learn skills by working alongside or directly with the manager. Because the bulk of Amish businesses employ fewer than five full-time persons, owners typically work closely with new employees—teaching procedures, explaining the use of equipment, and providing technical instruction. Because the boss is rarely hidden away in an office, new workers learn by watching the manager solve problems, relate to customers, and interact with other employees. Learning by imitation meshes well with Amish notions of education. Amish culture esteems experience; learning by doing and by observing others is the preferable mode of transmitting technical skills and wisdom.

Some new workers move into their positions gradually. Newcomers may spend their first days cleaning up the shop, becoming acquainted with the layout, and observing staff and customer interaction. One furniture store owner asks new employees in his establishment to spend several days dusting the stock to acquaint themselves with the inventory. The owner involves the novice in sales discussions, allowing the employee to "make the sale" before he steps in to close the deal. In a short time, the new employee is able to deal with customers from start to finish—as well as price new pieces and offer special discounts.

In orienting new workers, employers stress not only technical skills but also good work habits and timesaving procedures. Owners laud shortcuts that preserve quality. A wood products manufacturer explained the importance of conserving motion—both for efficiency and to keep employees from overworking themselves: "I'm very 'move conscious.' I don't like to see someone picking up a piece of wood over here and cutting it over there and then putting it on a pile over in the other corner. Everything should be close together and efficient . . . If I'm going through [the shop] and see something that's inefficient, I point it out."

One owner, writing about the importance of teaching efficient work habits, noted, "Wasted motion is normally not the employees' fault. The responsibility lies on the owner or supervisor to help his employees to set up, and show him or her, and explain to them."[4] As business owners train

♦

Mobile Amish crews construct residential and commercial buildings.
They often are permitted special access to electrical tools and
earthmoving equipment.

employees and place them in new positions, they seek to equip them not only with technical knowledge but also with "shop sense." Such attitudes reflect a growing rationalization in Amish culture that was less common on the traditional farm.

Few enterprises send their employees to outside classes for specialized training. Because owners rarely have formal training, they see little need to nudge their employees in that direction either. There are, of course, exceptions. One farm machinery manufacturer hired an Amish neighbor with no experience in welding. The owner sent the new recruit to an evening welding class at a nearby vocational school. A landscape contractor occasionally sends his employees to all-day design seminars. Even though the workers do not design landscape plans for customers, the owner thought the seminars would enable the employees to offer helpful suggestions. On the whole, however, Amish firms do not stress formal education. The on-the-job training heralded by Amish entrepreneurs blends nicely with Amish understandings of learning, knowledge, and wisdom.

Wages

Because Amish businesses function within a larger commercial culture, their pay scales are somewhat influenced by prevailing wages. Ethnic employers are partially insulated from outside pressures for several reasons, however. First, Amish employees may be willing to trade lower pay for the chance to work in an ethnic niche with cultural rewards. Second, the modest Amish lifestyle enables employees to maintain a comfortable life with fewer dollars. Moreover, with fewer payroll deductions—Social Security, health insurance, or pension—Amish employees take home a greater share of their hourly pay than do other workers.[5]

Like all businesses, Amish owners acknowledge skill and experience when assigning wages. Unskilled workers typically earn seven to nine dollars an hour and, over several years, can reach the fifteen-dollar range. New employees with woodworking knowledge or welding experience may net beginning wages of twelve dollars per hour. After five years, skilled workers can generally expect at least twelve dollars an hour. More than half of the businesses pay their skilled, veteran workers fifteen dollars an hour or more. Construction workers often command even higher wages. Although one owner gives annual raises to all employees, most enterprises are less methodical. Because owners often hire unskilled workers and train them quickly, many employees enjoy pay hikes as they move from novice to skilled status, often in a matter of five years.

The Amish believe that pay should reflect labor and effort. As a result, owners prefer to hire employees on an hourly basis, which also fits traditional understandings of task-oriented labor. A few prefer piecework pay for much the same reason—to link compensation with productivity. Few businesses offer salaried positions. Even though hourly pay requires overtime wages, Amish employers believe that tying earnings to work motivates employees and encourages diligence. One shop owner noted that employees who are paid on an hourly basis "expect to work and get paid for work."

Their agricultural heritage holds little praise for an eight-hour workday. Farmwork, regulated by the unpredictable interplay of task, season, and weather, often required twelve- or fourteen-hour days in busy seasons. Similarly, Amish shop owners plan their work around particular orders and jobs rather than a forty-hour schedule. Seventy-seven percent of the selected owners report that their workdays average nine or more hours. Larger Amish businesses regularly provide overtime pay. Many routinely expect extra hours, even suggesting that an hourly wage scale assumes some overtime pay. "My employees can count on overtime every week," one businessman reported, "so they take home a nice check" despite a lower wage than what a nearby factory pays for a forty-hour week. For their part, Amish employees expect long days and appreciate the added bonus of over-time pay, which never arrived on the farm.

Traditionally, Amish parents did not pay their children for working until they reached adulthood. Children were expected to help support their families, and they received food, clothing, and lodging as remuneration. Parents were typically generous in assisting children to set up their own households. Today, some parents are beginning to pay their working off-spring, feeling that children need to approach adulthood with some sav-ings. Other entrepreneurs pay their children a lower wage until they reach the age of twenty-one. At that point, the child receives the same wage as other employees with similar training and experience. Still others con-tribute the equivalent of wages to a trust fund for the child, which, after marriage, can be used to buy land or set up a business.

Benefits

Beyond regular wages, Amish firms also provide fringe benefits, although these are often tailored to Amish culture. Retirement plans lose their lure in the context of a culture where families care for their elderly. The need for commercial health insurance is reduced and often negated, due to the financial support of church and family. Although a few shops provide church-based or commercial health insurance for their workers, these are an exception. About half of the businesses provide several paid vacation days a year, but vacations of three or four weeks are not typical. Employ-ees often use their few vacation days to attend weekday weddings in the fall. Free products, employee discounts, and the use of company tools for personal projects are other side benefits (see table 5.2).

In lieu of typical fringe benefits, many employers give handsome bonuses for completed work or new ideas. This direct reward system appeals to Amish values of invention, incentive, and motivation. Firms sometimes offer bonuses to employees who improve products or offer suggestions. Others provide bonuses to workers every time a job is completed without an accident or a customer complaint. "Sometimes their bonuses and wages are equal," said one employer who offers financial incentives for employee-generated improvements and satisfied customers. Employees "work hard and tell me things to do to make the business better. They come and say, 'We got to do this and we got to do that.' That makes the customer happy, and it makes the worker happy. It makes me happy, too!"

Some extra perks in the Amish workplace involve the whole family. The owner of a metal fabricating shop takes his employees and their fam-

TABLE 5.2

Employee Benefits Provided by Amish Enterprises

Benefit	Percentage of Enterprises Providing
Paid vacations	39
Overtime pay	36
Cash bonuses	27
Free products	24
Discounts	24
Health insurance	21
Paid sick days	15
Personal days	3
Retirement plan	0
Other	6

Source: Entrepreneur Profile (*N* = 35).
Note: This profile characterizes larger businesses and may not be typical of smaller ones.

ilies on one-day excursions twice a year to state parks and nature preserves. The owner hires a van and supplies a generous picnic lunch, and the workers receive full pay for the excursion. One contractor who hired non-Amish college students over the summer provided a "family day in the park" at the end of the summer as a farewell for the seasonal help. Because many employees know one another as relatives or members of the same church district, it is comfortable to include families in social affairs. Such family involvement—perhaps considered trivial in the larger society—is a welcomed perk among the Amish.

Amish employees also benefit from their church's commitment to mutual aid. As fellow church members, employers assist their workers as they are able. Employers are often keenly aware of their employees' needs and resources. Sometimes help comes in the form of gifts. At other times, low-interest loans may provide a financial lift for a worker's special need. An Amish farm machinery manufacturer helped a young employee finance a first home for his family. The terms of the employer's loan surpassed those of a commercial bank and represented a significant fringe benefit, likely unavailable from an outside employer.

Amish employers also assist wage earners in starting their own businesses. Experienced entrepreneurs give younger workers technical advice and assistance, and some extend loans and offer help with suppliers and dealers. One businesswoman, a dry goods store owner, helped several of her Amish employees and at least one non-Amish worker to begin stores of their own—either as spin-offs from her shop or as entirely new ventures. By providing the names of sales representatives and other wholesalers, the seasoned owner gave the younger women an added boost as they began operations of their own.

Amish employers also offer their employees freedom from alienation in the workplace. In small-scale operations without assembly line specialization, a friendly, informal ethos ties employees into many phases of the business. Unlike some corporate workers who feel severed from the larger significance of their work as well as from their managers, Amish workers understand their role in the total scope of the shop and know their bosses well. The flat structure of Amish enterprises allows the owners of even sizable firms to play an active role in daily operations, ensuring close ties between entrepreneurs and employees. Bosses work alongside employees, and the frequent interaction fosters communication. Advised a seasoned business leader, "Be open with your employees. You can tap their brains. That's what we do. We get their ideas. We make them talk. That way they feel they're included, they're not slaves. They know when they talk they'll be heard. . . . We ask 'How can we do this better?' They're always giving us ideas to improve. And if someone gives a good enough idea, we give him a $100 bill for it. They like that. They know we care. We want their ideas."

Collaboration between entrepreneurs and employees often leads to delegation of responsibility. As owners work with hourly helpers, train them, and learn to know them well, they feel comfortable granting workers greater autonomy. One Amish contractor had trained an employee in purchasing supplies and turned all buying over to him, leaving the owner free to pursue new job leads. "The employees are more responsible now, and I don't have as many headaches," he said. Another entrepreneur, explaining why his workers express a high degree of job satisfaction said, "I encourage my employees to use their heads." A few larger firms have grown beyond the point where owners can personally work with each employee. Yet these businesses also take steps to solicit workers' views. As its business grew, an Amish fencing company held a monthly "quality circle" so foremen and owners could discuss employee suggestions.

Amish businesses also provide other cultural benefits. For example, most firms allow Amish employees to work in harmony with their community's religious calendar. Employees know that they will not be asked to labor on Sundays, Good Friday, or Ascension Day. Amish businesses also observe church holidays such as Easter Monday, Pentecost Monday, and December 26—a post-Christmas day reserved for family visiting. The right to work within the sacred calendar of Amish culture is a coveted perk that exceeds material rewards. An additional employee benefit is the freedom to work within the moral boundaries of the Ordnung, where they know they will not be asked to sell designer clothes or stock shelves with video tapes.

In all of these ways, Amish businesses offer employees considerable satisfaction. The emphasis placed on skill and quality allows employees to combine production goals with personal artistry. Despite the apparent uniformity of Amish society, individual deftness and creativity prevail in shops that place a premium on artisanship. The opportunity to become an experienced artisan offers job fulfillment and enhances self-worth. Employees know they play a significant role in the business. The unique benefits from working in an ethnic context provide social forms of gratification that supplement regular wages and parallel the benefit packages of corporate America.

Personnel Management

Amish employers discipline their work crews, typically in informal ways. Personal backbiting and carping criticism are discouraged in Amish shops. Employees are expected to treat fellow workers with respect or to find other employment. "A good workplace is a happy workplace," one entrepreneur tells his day laborers. "When one person becomes disgruntled and starts passing that around, there will always be those who side with him. And then there are others who don't agree with him, and then you have a divided shop and there's friction. We don't need that. You need to work in harmony."

Obedience and submission to authority are important Amish cultural values. The Amish view insubordination as sinful behavior that destroys the spirit of cooperation they seek to foster. One manufacturer recalled a situation in which an employee questioned the integrity of the owner. The entrepreneur responded firmly but sought to play down direct confrontation: "I heard some things I didn't like from one of my workers, some comments here and there about the management. I could have called him into the office and talked to him alone, but I didn't. I talked to everyone generally all together one day. . . . That nipped it in the bud. They understood what I meant and they thought about it. We haven't had any problems since then."

Occasionally workers are laid off. Although layoffs are rare among Amish firms, they have occurred. Relatively few Amish businesses have fallen on hard times, so little downsizing has been necessary. When reductions come, employers prefer to rely on attrition instead of direct layoffs. When orders sag and layoffs are necessary, owners rely on church and family values to decide who will go. Younger, unmarried men who live at home or whose employment is less critical to family survival are cut first. Mar-

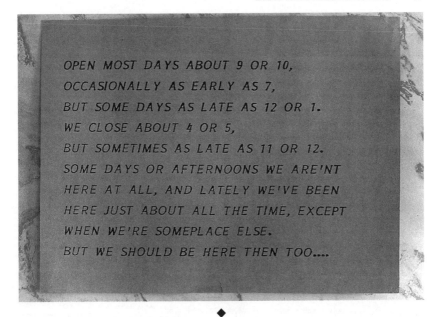

OPEN MOST DAYS ABOUT 9 OR 10,
OCCASIONALLY AS EARLY AS 7,
BUT SOME DAYS AS LATE AS 12 OR 1.
WE CLOSE ABOUT 4 OR 5,
BUT SOMETIMES AS LATE AS 11 OR 12.
SOME DAYS OR AFTERNOONS WE ARE'NT
HERE AT ALL, AND LATELY WE'VE BEEN
HERE JUST ABOUT ALL THE TIME, EXCEPT
WHEN WE'RE SOMEPLACE ELSE.
BUT WE SHOULD BE HERE THEN TOO....

A playful sign announces the hours of a retail bakeshop. Although enterprises located at or near home often have flexible hours, they are not usually this flexible.

ried men and workers who support other family members are retained as long as possible. In contrast to the larger world of work, such family considerations override seniority, which, although important, does not carry ultimate significance. Amish employees understand and accept this system. Indeed, Amish values compel employers to keep family wage earners on the payroll. When asked about his sudden loss of hours at a metal fabrication shop, an Amish teen replied, "[The owner] had married men working there. He had to keep them working. I could go back and work for pop if I had to."

Firing employees is also rare among Amish companies, though a worker may lose a job for reckless, insubordinate, or discourteous behavior. Nevertheless, most Amish employers have never fired a worker. Those who do find it difficult. Remembering her only experience of terminating an employee, one female entrepreneur paused and said simply, "That was the hardest thing." A fencing manufacturer said, "We try to go the second mile with them, and that usually works," expressing his personal policy toward disruptive employees. He believes he has had fewer employment conflicts as a result.

Other Amish owners handle repeated job-site infractions with less sympathy and feel that their approach fosters on-the-job discipline. "We're known to be no-nonsense" about terminating careless employees, one shop owner said simply. "If you're called into the office a second time, you're gone. I give them one warning." A few employers have terminated several workers. One owner of a sizeable firm reported letting one employee go nearly every year. Another manager noted that safety requirements compel him to fire anyone who daydreams, shows off, or operates equipment carelessly. The Amish extend little sympathy to the careless. Negligent employees are let go promptly: "I tell them, after all, they can get other jobs," one shop owner said curtly.

Nonunion Shops

Amish employees do not cooperate with organized labor. The church has taken a consistent stand against participation in labor unions. Members who join a union will forfeit their church membership. The Amish disapprove of labor unions for a number of reasons, but primarily because they view their methods—including strikes and work stoppages—as coercive means that clash with the Amish belief in nonresistance. Amish writers agree that "labor unions came into being because employers abused their authority. Labor unions, by giving a voice and power to employees, served to correct this injustice."[6] Nevertheless, the church feels that "unions are part of the worldly system. They are man's way of correcting wrong, using force against force. Although unions may be useful in their place, they are not in accordance with Jesus' directions to his disciples."[7]

Few Amish have ever taken jobs in unionized industries, but those who have must negotiate acceptable agreements with local officers in order to remain apart from organized labor. Barring such an agreement, Amish employees must find other jobs. From the Amish point of view, the worker must "be willing to suffer wrongfully rather than obtain . . . 'rights' by the use of force." Generally the Amish hold unions in low regard. They typically associate organized labor with overpayment and inefficiency, as well as poor-quality work. Because few Amish have ever held union jobs, their impressions are largely caricatures. Nevertheless, these conceptions reinforce disdain for organized labor.

In some cases, Amish business owners have been forced to forfeit work because of their opposition to unions. Amish contractors who venture beyond Lancaster County to work in metropolitan suburbs are not always welcome because they have nonunionized employees. More than once, a builder has been threatened and had materials stolen or destroyed when he contracted a job in a heavily unionized area. The same principles that stall Amish participation in unions also forbid their reporting such harassment to the police. When faced with opposition, some Amish contractors have silently retreated from the regional market.

The cultural and human resources of skill, ingenuity, fortitude, austerity, and, above all, sheer hard work have empowered and energized Amish enterprises. Without access to these rich resources in the cultural reservoir of their society, Amish shops could not flourish. Nevertheless, the mobilization of this cultural and social capital for entrepreneurial activity is only half of the story, because many restraints afloat in the ethnic reservoir thwart the spirit of entrepreneurship. In the following three chapters, we turn to that side of the story and explore the cultural forces in Amish life that have restrained entrepreneurship.

PART THREE

Cultural Constraints
on Entrepreneurship

6. The Moral Boundaries of Business

Church comes first, then family, then work.
— AMISH CONTRACTOR

The Family Hub of Amish Life

The cultural heritage of Amish life has not only empowered commercial activity, but it has also bridled it. Amish entrepreneurs are constrained in many ways by the moral boundaries of Amish culture that govern, among other things, family life, sacred days, the use of technology, the size of enterprises, the type of products, and acceptable vocations. These cultural restraints that impede entrepreneurial activity often collide with the cultural resources that energize economic growth. Entrepreneurs may work hard to build quality products and expand their markets only to face the frown of the church for getting too big. Without easy access to e-mail and motor vehicles, owners may be hard-pressed to provide prompt service to non-Amish customers, suppliers, and dealers. The clashes between the resources and restraints of Amish culture often produce negotiated outcomes that appear odd to outsiders—telephones in a shed outside the place of business or copy machines powered by homemade electricity from batteries.

Family concerns have exerted many constraints on the development of Amish enterprise. From cradle to grave, Amish life revolves around the family. Most children are born at home, and the preschool years are spent, not in nursery schools, but with the family.[1] Worship services as well as weddings and funerals take place in the context of the home. Recreation is also family-centered—volleyball, softball, table games, and parlor games are played within the circle of extended family. In short, all the major social activities have historically clustered around the family.

Family life is strengthened by the prominence of the extended family.

The typical Amish person has seventy-five or more first cousins, many of whom live nearby. Rejecting retirement homes, Amish seniors live near children and grandchildren, often in an apartment or "grossdaadi house" attached to a main dwelling or in a small home close to a grown child. Families living near each other in a church district are often related. These overlapping social circles integrate faith, work, and family into a common ethnic fabric.

The family channels Amish values, beliefs, and practices across the generations as fathers and mothers pass on the imprint of Amish identity to their children. On farms, Amish children, unlike modern youth, have always worked alongside their parents, learning skills and absorbing attitudes. Despite the shift to microenterprises, farming is still esteemed, in part because it fosters family connections. A shop owner who has never farmed as an adult expressed a common conviction when describing his people: "We're family centered, and the farm is the best place to raise a family." In the words of an Amish grandfather, "Farming is the best family life because father and mother work together to raise the children." The glorification of farming hinges on its ability to hold the family together. "On the farm, we have the opportunity to work together as a family," one Amish publication explains. "The lines of 'your work' and 'my work' become blurred so that it is 'our work.'"[2] Farming remains highly esteemed among the Amish, even though large numbers have abandoned it. "The farm is still enjoyed by our people, even if they're not on it," observed a metal worker.

The legacy of the farm-centered family has shaped the Amish entry into business. Vocational choices are ranked by how well they emulate farm life. Small cottage industries often replicate family arrangements on the farm, and thus the Amish have welcomed home-based firms. "There is always a need for community-oriented shops," one Amish writer states, "but once again, the setting should be such that the father can be at home with the family and there is work for everyone right at home."[3] An Amish minister praised "home shops," but then asked, "What about the many fathers, sons, and daughters who work away from home? Being away from the protection of the Christian home is unfortunate. Working daily under the influence of an unbelieving immoral world is worse yet."[4]

As they leave the farm, Amish persons typically work in one of three settings: at home, nearby, or away. Those who work as day laborers in a neighbor's shop or who have a store or manufacturing establishment within several miles of home fall into the "nearby" category. The least esteemed jobs involve "working away." In describing "away" work, the Amish betray their belief that work should remain near home. "Working away is when you stand at the end of your lane in the morning and wait for someone to come by and pick you up and take you to work—who-knows-where," one Amishman explained. Working away often involves employment with a mobile construction crew or tending a market stand in an urban area. Often young men and women work away until they marry. Once a couple establishes their own household, the husband will try to find work near home. Some men, however, work away for many years, although the cultural constraints to work near home remain strong.

The Constraints of Family Values

The rise of nonfarm work poses challenges to the traditional Amish family as well as to the church. Although Lancaster's Amish have bypassed the factory and professional office, the new patterns of work have brought new challenges. Some at-home enterprises, such as machine shops, involve only the males of the family. Such gender-based work divides households in ways that farmwork rarely did. Although certain agricultural domains were male- or female-dominated, farming was nevertheless broadly cooperative.

Furthermore, some business ventures pull fathers away from home, and children lose a key role model in this patriarchal society. Mothers are left alone to discipline children, manage the home, and meet visitors. Even when work remains at or nearby home, customers disrupt the flow of family life. If the business caters to non-Amish or tourists, outside influences enter the sacred turf of family on a regular and invited basis. In more subtle ways, nonfarm work also disrupts community life because business cycles sometimes clash with the seasonal rhythms of farming. For example, the after-harvest wedding season in November—once ideal for marriages—now coincides with hectic weeks for Amish retailers and wholesalers, falling as it does during the pre-Christmas rush. Small businesses may have saved the Amish from the fate of factory work, but they nevertheless carry some seeds of family disruption.

The Amish do recognize some of the dangers facing their families. They often cite the demise of the traditional family in the larger society as a blight of modern life. An Amish farmer chided his non-Amish neighbors who in his mind had abandoned their children for dual careers. "Their children grow up like weeds," he observed sadly. "Nobody tends them or watches out for them." To the practical Amish mind, neither personal piety nor family devotion can replace an absent father. Warned one Amish businessman, "You have to stay family-oriented. The family with a husband away from home will fall apart. I don't care what your faith is or how strong a Christian you think you are, it won't work. The family has to stay together."

The Amish see clear connections between divided families and broader social ills. They condemn not only divorce but also the occupational and educational mobility that separates parents from children and grandchildren. One contractor recalled meeting a neighbor who was taking a human relations course "to learn how to communicate with his children." The Amishman discovered that his neighbor "was running here and there as a member of this group or that. His problem was spending too much time away from home. No wonder he couldn't communicate with his children!"

Sensing the threats to family life, many businesspeople labor self-consciously to keep their families together. They realize that their new occupational pursuits bring special responsibilities. "If they could, I believe a lot of shop men would farm," said a young Amishwoman. "But since they can't, they're trying to make the best of it for their families." Many entrepreneurs are making the best of it—often with careful planning, sacrifice, and creativity. They are trying to keep enterprises family-oriented and home-centered to maintain as much as possible the lifestyle once fostered by the farm. The arrest of two Amish youth for selling cocaine in the summer of 1998 alerted the Amish community to some of the perils of permitting their youth to work on construction crews away from home.[5]

In many cases, husband and wife work together in a family business in ways that mirror the partnership of farming roles. One young couple works together mounting deer antlers for local hunters. In another case, a retired farm wife paints the wooden toys her husband builds. Even when women are not closely involved in manufacturing, they often help with bookkeeping, mailings, or billing. In so doing, they remain closely connected to the activities of the business. Some women entrepreneurs intentionally include their husbands in their business ventures. One veteran businesswoman declared that every business "should be a man and woman team. It really should. That's important."

Although most entrepreneurs are no longer farming, many follow daily routines that mimic the temporal patterns of a farm day. A manufacturer of barn equipment follows a daily schedule that mirrors his childhood on a dairy farm. A middle-aged father and minister, he rises with his sons well before sunup to tend to stable and shop chores before breakfast. The entire family gathers for an early-morning breakfast and family devotions. At noon and supper, whole-family meals again bring members together to eat and plan their work, which often continues after supper. The kitchen table, not a company lunchroom, remains the center of daily socializing. There is little interest in an eight-hour workday with free time and idle evenings that might welcome mischief.

Business owners also try to balance company size with family interests. Some entrepreneurs turn down work opportunities because of family priorities. Explained one Amish mason, "Church comes first, then family, then work. People say, 'Can't you look at this bid tonight?' If I can't look at a job during business hours, I don't want it. It's that simple." Others keep their work deliberately local. "If we go more than ten minutes by truck to a job, it's too far," said an Amish carpenter. "We want to keep it small and close to home."

The Amish manager of a farmers' market closes his building at four o'clock every Saturday so that stand holders can spend the evening at home. Non-Amish business leaders questioned the practice, noting that Saturday evening hours could easily boost profits. The Amish owner contended that his consideration was not financial but familial. Spending long days away from home is not "good for the stand holders or their families," he reasoned. Amish fathers who do work away from home often preserve their evenings and Saturdays to work with their children in the family garden or around the house. "Saturdays are our time," one father and contractor said. "We have the weekends and evenings. So I tell people, 'Don't bother me with business in the evenings.'" In all of these ways, the longstanding commitment to family bridles the bustling energies of many entrepreneurs.

Funneling Entrepreneurial Energy

The burst of entrepreneurial activity has been both propelled and guided by the values of this unique community. The moral boundaries of Amish culture have funneled entrepreneurial energies toward certain occupations and barred entry into others. By placing limits on education and occupational choice, the church nudges its keenest minds into business, which unwittingly boosts the pursuit of profits.

Several cultural regulators channel Amish creativity toward business. First, the prohibition against high school and higher education blocks youth from the professions and paraprofessional occupations. There are no Amish doctors, pilots, lawyers, scientists, social workers, or high school teachers. Without a high school diploma, they are also locked out of most clerical and white-collar positions in non-Amish firms. Strict adherence to the separation of church and state and the taboo on the use of force prohibits them from entering civil service positions and political or military careers. These moral restraints press Amish job seekers toward manual labor, crafts, retail sales, self-employment, and entrepreneurship.

A young Amishman with an eighth-grade education could hardly hope for a management position in a non-Amish business, but he can start a shop of his own. One young man at the age of sixteen took over the managerial reins of his father's sizable manufacturing plant. Like dozens of other Amish youth in the Lancaster area, he will soon be managing his own firm and building financial security. The cultural lid that blocks the ladder to hundreds of professional jobs encourages self-employment and entrepreneurship for those who are forced off the farm. Barred from professional pursuits by their cultural harness, they have three options: farming, working as a day laborer, or entrepreneurship. Just as many other ethnic minorities have pursued entrepreneurship as a detour around employment barriers, so too the Amish have used the vehicle of self-employment to bypass the larger society's demand for formal education. But unlike other minority groups who often establish ethnic businesses because external discrimination blocks their employment, the constraints that funnel Amish into entrepreneurship are self-imposed cultural restrictions.[6]

The educational taboo channels many of the most creative minds into business. Those Amish who might have been engineers, scientists, and lawyers end up managing small firms. As a result, many of the best minds are engaged in commerce. Although the community has scores of bright farmers, creative minds enjoy the challenge of business. Explained one shop owner, "You have to cultivate your intelligence more if you are in business. You really do, because you don't have anyone to learn from. Your dad can't tell you how to do it. You need to learn the business on your own." The cultural constraints of Amish life have unwittingly, but quite successfully, funneled the best and brightest into business.

Beyond the vertical lid on education, Amish culture sets horizontal restrictions that channel Amish work as well. Religious restrictions make certain jobs unthinkable. Operating a radio station or engaging in television repair is impossible. Auto mechanics, photography, or electrical work are equally discouraged. Likewise, the retail sale of designer clothes, cosmetics, or jewelry is taboo. Although some Amish businesspeople rent vehicles and hire drivers to transport them to and from job sites, a career requiring a vehicle—a traveling sales representative, for example—is off limits. Such a job would carry a double blight if it required extensive travel away from home. And of course there are a host of careers that the Amish believe cultivate pride and self-aggrandizement—theater, the performing arts, and professional athletics. These are naturally out of bounds.

The horizontal boundaries direct business ventures into avenues that harmonize with Amish values. Producing or selling goods that are useful to fellow church members are welcome activities. Providing traditional goods and services for the larger world—harness and tack, furniture, fabric, or food—is well within the moral order. Amish quilts, sold by the thousands to non-Amish and tourists, of course, reflect the heart of Amish life because they are not only a traditional product but are useful as well. An Amish minister suggested that "usefulness" helps to determine what products can be made and sold to outsiders. "It's okay," he said. "to sell items that we don't permit if they are useful to others." But usefulness has its

A young Amish entrepreneur sells Rollerblades from his booth at a public auction.

limits—televisions, radios, and video cameras do not pass the test. Nevertheless, Amish carpenters are permitted to build hundreds of television cabinets and entertainment centers for their non-Amish customers every year.

By tethering work within the boundaries of Amish culture, the church focuses the creative energy of its members on a limited range of jobs. This occupational clustering enhances the quality, artisanship, and public awareness of certain products—especially wood products, furniture, crafts, and quilts—that carry the Amish imprint. Moreover, the ceiling on education encourages self-employment by stripping Amish workers of educational credentials. Unable to work as managers for outsiders, they turn to entrepreneurship within the ethnic community. Although not designed to spawn microenterprises, the moral constraints of Amish culture have channeled enormous creativity into commercial ventures.

Keeping Sacred Time

Cultural understandings of time also impose restrictions. Most enterprises have adapted to the seasonal patterns and traditional tempos of the Amish community. By flowing with the rural cadence of work, they have eased the transition from field to shop. The pursuit of new vocations within their

◆

This state-of-the-art forklift is used to load the cattle feeders manufactured in
this Amish shop. The Lancaster Ordnung prohibits the use of pneumatic tires
on tractors. Because these pneumatic tires are covered with steel wheels, they fit
within the moral boundaries of the church.

community, for example, has not forced the Amish to concede their sacred
holidays or their convictions about Sunday labor for the pursuit of profit.

Sunday is a special day in the weekly rhythm of Amish life—a sacred
day of rest. Church districts gather for worship every other Sunday morning. The "off" Sunday is spent attending services in neighboring districts,
resting at home, or visiting with friends who also have an "off" Sunday.
Drawing on biblical mandates and the Christian tradition, the Amish re-
frain from all but the most necessary work on the Lord's Day. Feeding
animals, milking cows, and preparing simple meals are acceptable Sunday
labor, but fieldwork, business activities, and housekeeping are taboo.

Conducting business on Sunday borders on profanity. In the late 1960s,
when Amish farmers began shipping their milk in large tank trucks, they

refused, under any circumstance, to allow milk to be shipped on the Lord's Day. They would not even be passive accomplices to the desecration of the Sabbath. Because they needed Amish milk, the hauling companies conceded to Amish wishes. They agreed to the inconvenience of scheduling Amish pickups before Saturday midnight or very early Monday morning. The church's taboo on commercial activities on Sunday has remained firm. "God honors the obedience of people who rest on the Sabbath," one grandfather noted, summing up the collective wisdom of the church.

Business involvements have challenged sacred Sabbath boundaries, which differ noticeably from those in the larger society. Many American firms—manufacturers, retailers, and transporters—do a significant portion of business on Sunday. Amish businesses, by contrast, strictly limit Sunday commerce. Amish businesspeople forthrightly oppose Sabbath sales. Many business cards and advertisements clearly state, "Closed Sundays" or "Please, No Sunday Sales." Business signs along country roads announcing "No Sunday Sales" likely signal an Amish business. The deliberate, often unnecessary, announcement of "No Sunday Sales" reminds fellow ethnics that the business defers to the church and informs outsiders of the establishment's Amish identity.

Amishwomen who sell quilts on consignment through non-Amish outlets will not deal with retail shops that are open on Sundays. They worry that customers might purchase one of their items on the Lord's Day and thus implicate them in its desecration. Occasionally, customers are baffled by the Amish stance. Some tourists ignore the "No Sunday Sales" signs and beg to buy quilts from an in-home shop. The Amish turn down the pleas. One storeowner remembers how a non-Amish customer told him with enthusiasm how a business could hike its sales volume with little added cost by opening seven days a week. "He just didn't get it," the Amishman chuckled. By bending their business routines to community norms, Amish entrepreneurs articulate a public boundary that reminds insider and outsider alike of the ethnic identity of their shop.

Beyond retail hours, the Amish also face other points of tension regarding Sunday work. Several Amish manufacturers have surprised large non-Amish distributors by refusing to fill orders or make deliveries on Sundays. Knowing that their contracts are usually coveted by small businesses, major distributors are surprised when Amish firms refuse to budge for a lucrative order. In the end, most are willing to respect Amish wishes, despite their initial surprise.

One entrepreneur received a harness order from an advertising agency shooting a television spot. The agency needed the leather gear immediately. The shop owner agreed to fill the order but refused to deliver it on Sunday as requested. The buyer acquiesced, but flew a representative to Lancaster

County to pick up the harness at Amishman's door at one o'clock Monday morning. Another shop owner had a rush order for wood products that took longer to fill than anticipated. His family worked around the clock for several days to meet the deadline but refused to labor on Sunday. By working late Saturday night and early Monday morning, they were able to complete the order for a Tuesday deadline.

Respecting the Cultural Calendar

Beyond Sunday, the Lancaster Amish continue to observe sacred days long abandoned by the cultural mainstream. Church members faithfully recognize Good Friday, Easter, Ascension Day, and Christmas. They also maintain the old Continental practice of setting aside Easter Monday, Pentecost Monday (Whitmonday), and December 26 ("second Christmas") for family visiting.[7] The Amish also observe a day of fasting in the autumn in conjunction with their Holy Communion service. Although they do not formally observe public holidays such as Washington's Birthday, Memorial Day, the Fourth of July, Labor Day, or Columbus Day, the Amish do recognize New Year's Day and Thanksgiving.

As long as the Amish were self-employed farmers, their cultural calendar remained aloof from the holidays of the larger society. When some Lancaster Amish took industrial jobs in the late 1960s, their traditional calendar was jolted by the civic holiday schedule. The clash of holiday schedules was one of many reasons the Amish became disenchanted working in non-Amish factories. Because Amish-owned enterprises can control the terms and conditions of their work, they are able to flex with traditional patterns and to honor Amish holy days. Being able to control their time and their ethnic calendar has permitted a smoother transition from farm to business. Thus, despite a growing diversity of occupations, the ethnic community still follows a common cultural calendar.

For their part, the Amish have extended flexible holiday privileges to non-Amish employees, allowing them to swap other holidays. One contractor posts this separate-but-equal fringe benefit policy on his office wall:

PAID HOLIDAYS

Amish	Non-Amish
New Year's Day	New Year's Day
Good Friday	Good Friday
Ascension Day	Memorial Day
Pentecost Monday	July Fourth
Fall Fast Day	Labor Day
Thanksgiving	Thanksgiving
Christmas	Christmas

Similarly, an Amish-managed farmers' market also grants an equivalent exchange of holidays of its Amish and non-Amish stand holders. The market does not require merchants to sell on their respective religious or civic red-letter days.

Although most Amish businesses do not offer paid holidays, they are generous in granting days off as needed. This flexibility plays an important role in strengthening the bonds of solidarity and mutual aid in the ethnic community. When disaster strikes, Amish employers can shut down their operation or release some employees to assist in cleanup or rebuilding activities. Amish work frolics and public benefit auctions can also find room in the busy schedules of business. One wood shop owner described his unwritten understanding with his employees: "When we're in a bind, they work with us. When we're not in a bind, we understand their schedule, and they can take off a day or two whenever they have to. And we need that with our people. You wouldn't get that working in a factory." Some of the flexibility afforded by Amish businesses benefits local non-Amish neighbors, as well. Amish businessmen and male employees often serve in volunteer fire companies. When the alarm blares, work stops, and the men rush to the fire station.

The Dangers of Leisure

Sabbath observance and religious holidays are obvious points of friction between Amish culture and contemporary life. More subtle are the challenges business brings to the broader patterns of Amish society. Time for leisure and vacations becomes more available for entrepreneurs, although farm families remain saddled by seasonal cycles and daily milking routines. "Cows tie you down more," one metal shop owner observed frankly. Despite attempts to spread work throughout the day, six days a week, many business people find themselves with more free time than farmers. Day laborers in Amish shops and stores enjoy even greater amounts of discretionary time.

Many elders fear that the generation now growing up off the land might come to expect more free time and—even more dangerous—the right to decide how to spend it. A retired farmer and business owner sees a disturbing side effect of shop work: "Young people have too much free time. They work their eight or nine hours, and then they come home and they're free." That freedom, unaccounted for, could open the door to worldly entertainment and other cultural contaminants. One minister worries that young men working in shops have "too much loose money in their pockets, and that can lead to trouble."

Some entrepreneurs also fear the rise of a "weekend mentality" among

CLOSED SUNDAYS, NEW YEAR,
GOOD FRIDAY, EASTER MONDAY,
ASCENSION DAY, WHIT MONDAY,
OCT. 11, THANKSGIVING,
CHRISTMAS & DECEMBER 26

FISHER'S FURNITURE, INC.

NEW AND USED FURNITURE
USED COAL & WOOD HEATERS
COUNTRY FURNITURE & ANTIQUES

WALNUT • OAK • CHERRY • MAHOGONY

BUS. HRS.
MON. - THURS. 8-5
FRI. 8-8, SAT. 8-12

P.O. BOX 57
1129 GEORGETOWN ROAD
BART, PA 17503

*An advertisement for Fisher's Furniture, Inc., reminds customers that the store
follows the cultural calendar of the Amish community. Many Amish do not
observe Memorial Day, the Fourth of July, or Labor Day.*

businesspeople. Although the Amish have always revered Sunday, the rest
of the week was filled with productive activities. Saturday, like any other
workday, was devoted to farming chores. However, if Amish life coalesces
with the five-day, forty-hour schedule of the commercial world, young people will surely develop new views of work and leisure. Saturday is already
becoming an assumed day off for some Amish teens who have slipped into
the larger society's pattern. One storeowner offers a twenty-dollar bonus
to lure younger employees to work on Saturday. Comparing her youth with
Amish teens now, an older businesswoman remarked, "In our age, we went
away Sunday nights and worked the rest of the week. Now they go away
all the time. They're running around so much, and there are so many activities. It's not right!"

Vacations are a growing possibility for families no longer tied to farming. Many men enjoy hunting for game. Some business owners have invested in hunting cabins. Although farmers also enjoy hunting excursions,

it is more often businesspeople who own and manage these mountain hideaways. Although some cabins are nicely outfitted, many are simple structures that conform to the Ordnung. Many businesspeople work long hours and find little time for excursions, others travel frequently. Hiring drivers and vehicles, or taking the train, Amish travelers traditionally visit other Amish settlements in Florida or the Midwest. Some families now journey to places with no church connections and stay in motels. Trips to Niagara Falls or Prince Edward Island may include a stopover in another Amish settlement, but more often do not. Increasingly, some couples are joining outsiders on bus tours to historic and scenic sites arranged by travel agencies. There are, however, cultural limits to travel—pleasure cruises and gambling casinos are off bounds.

The church officially bans flying in airplanes, so a couple traveling to Europe might, for example, go by ship. Visiting Anabaptist historical sites is, of course, more acceptable than just sightseeing in Europe. Signaling a subtle but significant shift in Amish conceptions of time, more people now use the word "vacation" to describe their extended travels, instead of calling them "trips," as was the longtime practice. "A vacation used to mean a picnic back in the woods," complained one leader. "But now it means touring the country for a week."[8] More and more "trips" and "vacations" are fueled not only by prosperity but also by the more pliable hours of a business schedule. Milking cows twice a day could not be postponed or scheduled around a two-week vacation.

By building their own enterprises, the Amish have been able to tap the prosperity of profit while remaining within the cultural calendar of their community. Constrained by the legacy of the land, many entrepreneurs still strive to keep a daily and seasonal cycle akin to farming. They work without the assumptions of a forty-hour week. They have preserved their ethnic calendar, including Sunday observance and church holidays, in the face of competitive pressure. The flexibility offered by small-businesses enables owners and employees alike to participate in community-based activities, including mutual aid. The moral boundaries of Amish culture have restrained Amish entrepreneurship, but they have also given it a distinctive ethnic imprint—a margin of difference that in many ways serves them well in the public market.

7. Taming the Power of Technology

We try to keep the computer at arm's length.
—AMISH SHOP OWNER

Doubts about Progress

In the minds of most people, technology provides the key to the success of American business. Efficiency and increased productivity—the marks of the successful firm—flow from the appropriation of modern know-how. High-tech electronics, computerization, robotics, and automated manufacturing boost quality and output and lower costs. Indeed, the faith with which Americans approach technology is nothing less than a spirit of progressivism—a belief that improved technique brings progress, advancement, and greater human satisfaction. An unwavering commitment to the spirit of progress drives the effort to appropriate new technology whenever and wherever possible.

The Amish, by contrast, are not progressivists. The weight of their traditional culture constrains their use of technology. They do not assume that novelty and improvement necessarily go hand in hand. Although they selectively use new technology, the Amish worry that its use may erode communal life. A given instrument or mechanical device, while harmless in itself, might trigger broader social consequences. The productive value of a new piece of technology is often weighed against its potential impact on the traditional patterns of work and community. Their cautious use of technology, thus, hinges on an implicit assessment of its long-term impact on community life.

Technology that improves efficiency or reduces physical labor is generally accepted if it does not compromise basic social arrangements. For example, the single-person task of cutting weeds with a sickle is not radically changed when a gasoline-powered whipcord weed cutter replaces the hand sickle. The task remains a solo job in either case. By contrast, tractor farming or automobile ownership would disturb cooperative work and community patterns and lead to greater individuation and fragmentation of community.[1]

Sometimes new technology receives direct approval or rejection from church leaders. In other cases, new machinery slips quietly into use and earns gradual acceptance.[2] In still other cases, the discretion of the local bishop influences the rate of innovation and results in zigzag patterns of change across the community. Thus, some businesses have fax machines and photocopiers, but most do not. Such office equipment is accepted in some church districts, prohibited in others, and "on probation" in still other districts.

Some restrictions stretch firmly across all church districts. Computers were forbidden in Amish-owned businesses in the Lancaster settlement in 1986. Tapping 110-volt electricity from public utility lines is a longstanding taboo, as is the ownership of motor vehicles. Although questions of appropriate farm equipment continue to surface, the use of technology in small businesses increasingly sets the pace for change throughout the community. The pressure of competition from non-Amish businesses has tempted some entrepreneurs to test traditional boundaries. As a result, church leaders continually renegotiate the cultural fences that define technological usage. The pursuit of profit requires new rounds of negotiations with modernity as the Amish struggle to balance the lure of efficiency with the cultural constraints of their tradition.

The growth of microenterprises has stretched some of the traditional lines of propriety in the church's view of technology. The exigencies of the marketplace differ from those of the farm. Businesspeople are increasingly pressed by the necessities of commercial life. Although continuing to eschew many of the amenities of corporate America, Amish businesspeople find it difficult to keep telephones, vehicles, electricity, and computers at arm's length. This chapter explores the Amish struggle over the appropriate use of these four technological tools.

Telephone Reservations

Telephones have a long and colorful history among Lancaster's Old Order Amish. In the early twentieth century, before universal telephone service appeared in rural areas, several Amish farmers had strung lines between their homes to install talking devices.[3] But by 1910 the church had forbidden phone ownership. At first regarded as a benign appliance, church leaders began to view telephones as a threat to community cohesion for several reasons.

First, the telephone line provided a direct tie to the larger world, enabling outsiders to enter private homes by calling or listening to conversations on party lines, thus violating the religious principle of separation from the world. Moreover, phone conversations encouraged gossip—especially on the party lines that were typical of the early phone systems. Third, personal visiting in family and church settings provided a context for face-to-face communication that was sensitive to cultural expectations of dress and decorum. Phone messages lacked the cultural codes of dress and body language so important to a society anchored on oral communication. The telephone, in a word, decontextualized conversation.

Moreover, telephone ownership at the turn of the century involved phone owners in public stocks because most phone companies were organized as stockholders' corporations. Wary of the legal implications associated with participation in chartered organizations, some Amish objected to telephones on ethical grounds. About the same time, a schism within the Amish community split off a flank of the church in 1909. The progressive subgroup welcomed telephones with little reserve, which encouraged the Old Order leaders to tighten the ban on in-home phones, thus making them an important cultural boundary.[4]

Significantly, however, the Amish never prohibited the *use* of the telephone. As with other forms of technology, the Amish often make a sharp distinction between use and ownership. By limiting ownership but not use, the church permits selective access to technology without losing control over its use. Throughout the twentieth century, Amish families used telephones to plan appointments with non-Amish individuals, call veterinarians in an emergency, and make a variety of other contacts. They often used public telephones or the phones of their non-Amish neighbors. After the middle of the twentieth century, many persons increasingly came to rely on "community phones" shared by several Amish families.

With the permission of the church, a few families would band together to install a community phone, often in a shed or shanty at the end of a farm lane or at the edge of Amish property along a public road. Members of participating households walked to the phone, recorded their calls, and received an itemized bill each month from the phone coordinator. With an unlisted number, the phone was primarily used for outgoing calls. Located an inconvenient distance from the home, such phones limited personal calls. While permitting emergency calls, community phones impeded the frivolous chatter that, in the Amish mind, would surely accompany in-home phones. Moreover, the outdoor location and shared use symbolized the principle of separation from the world as well as mutual aid within the community. In both its use and location, the community phone was a ne-gotiated cultural settlement. Striking a bargain with modernity, the Amish permitted community phones but prohibited private, in-home phones.

The rise of small businesses challenged the traditional restrictions. The frequent need to place orders and contact distributors pulled phone shanties closer and closer to many shops. Some phone booths, although outside, were within a few steps of an office. In other cases, telephones were installed inside the place of business itself, often hidden in a back room or in a drawer. The location of phones typically depends on the view of church leaders and the practice of the local church district.

The early businesses that did have access to phones often did not publi-cize their numbers. By 2000, however, many entrepreneurs were publish-ing their phone numbers on business cards or in advertisements. By an-nouncing their numbers publicly, entrepreneurs signaled their willingness to use the phone for business purposes. Although outdoor telephones are useful for placing outgoing calls, receiving incoming calls is more trouble-some. Thus, some owners list the specific hours when they are available to receive calls. Others install devices to amplify the sound of incoming calls so they can be heard at a distance. Some owners hire an answering service provided by a non-Amish neighbor to take calls and relay them once or twice a day. Business owners welcomed voice mail, which quickly became the option of choice. By 2000, much communication occurred through mes-sages left on voice mail.

The acceptable location for privately owned phones varies from con-gregation to congregation. A few bishops permit telephones in shops or desk drawers. Others require telephones to be outside the business estab-lishment in a nearby booth. Still others only permit community phones. To a significant degree, telephones remain as one grandmother put it, "on pro-bation." In outlying areas where agriculture predominates, phone owner-ship is more restrictive. In the heart of the settlement where small busi-nesses abound, the church shows greater tolerance. All church districts, however, prohibit telephones in the home. Speaking of the phone, one busi-nessman reflected, "It's getting to where you can't run a business without one. But it's not in the home. It's here [at the office], so this way we're not talking on it all evening."

The Telephone Bargain

The telephone bargain includes some fine-print exceptions. Entrepreneurs who rent buildings that include phone lines are more likely to use in-office telephones. The church extends greater latitude because the manager does not own the buildings. A few Amish firms have non-Amish partners who

◆

*An Amish businessman traveling in Florida uses his cell phone to check on his
business back home.*

may provide a phone. Occasionally, Amish owners sublease portions of
their buildings to non-Amish employees or sales managers with the understanding that phones will be provided in the subleased space. By allowing
such exceptions, the church permits sizable businesses to operate efficiently,
all the while maintaining a cultural distance from the telephone.

Some entrepreneurs appreciate—or at least rationalize—the church's
resistance to the telephone. They note that a constantly ringing phone
would interrupt their work. Said one shop owner, "If I had a phone in here,
I'd never get any work done." In the words of a manufacturer, "If I had a
phone in here, I'd probably have to hire a full-time secretary to answer it
all day." Instead, he receives business calls in his phone shanty during a
posted answering hour each weekday morning. He believes that loyal, satisfied customers will order a "quality product at the times you're available"
and scoffs at the idea that limited access hinders sales.

Some businesspeople worry that having a telephone too handy will encourage employees to make needless personal calls. In a few cases, in-office
phones at Amish firms have been busy during the lunch hour as employees
jostle to call friends working in other Amish businesses. Keeping the phone

out of the workplace eliminates such problems, one entrepreneur noted with satisfaction.

But few entrepreneurs view the telephone as troublesome. Some are frustrated by the in-office taboo, arguing that church leaders do not understand the competitive world of business. They charge that some bishops act as though all church members are still farming. When some entrepreneurs have asked to install phones in their offices, local church leaders claimed such convenience was unnecessary. A retail storeowner complained that conservative leaders "say that you can run a business this size without a phone. I'd like them to try it. You really can't."

Entrepreneurs cite a number of reasons for needing in-office phones. Wholesalers doing business with Amish firms want easy telephone access. Likewise, Amish businesses that stock retail inventories frequently need to call sales representatives and suppliers. A quick phone call can answer inquiries and enable stores to offer better service. A few entrepreneurs offer arguments of efficiency, noting that when they rely on a community phone, employees are running to and from the phone booth all day. Having an in-office phone saves time and increases profits.

But even leaders who tolerate greater phone usage have not handed entrepreneurs a blank check. One businessman was permitted a multiline phone hookup inside his office because it was some distance from his home. However, the business had to dedicate one of its lines to an outside community phone for neighbors. A phone connection could not be completely private. Sharing the telephone with the larger community was an assumed and unbending requirement. Some businesses have a non-Amish neighbor or a nearby business that owns a phone and provides an extension line to the Amish business.

Although many firms have regular access to telephone service, they often restrict their availability in two ways: by using an answering service or being available only for a short time in the early morning or evening. The Nickel Mine Paint Store, for example, advises customers: "Call between 6:30 and 7:00 A.M." An ad for the Peach Lane Harness Shop says, "Reach me Mon. Wed. or Thurs. evening between 6:30–7 EST." A more typical pattern urges callers to "leave a message" or carries a prefix of "Ans. Service" with the phone number.[5] In the Lancaster area, locals often remind each other that when calling an Amish shop, "You have to let the phone ring a long time until someone answers or the answering service kicks in." Considerable telephone communication occurs by leaving messages, thereby avoiding direct conversation and adding to the ethnic enigma that helps to sell Amish products.

These unusual practices show how Amish firms that use telephones do so on their own terms and in ways that are inconvenient for customers and that defy the logic of contemporary marketing. Such practices illustrate how the Ordnung of the church restrains telephone use. But such restraints, ironically, become an economic resource by heightening the public identity of Amish shops and thereby adding to product distinction and the ethnic mystique surrounding Amish goods. The telephone barriers, announced in public ads, make it clear that an Amish shop is not just another place of business, but a special place that sells special products in special ways.

Cell phones have brought challenges and controversies.[6] Small, mobile, and easily hidden, this postmodern technology challenges the old cultural rules. Amish contractors find cell phones valuable to coordinate construction jobs as they travel from site to site. "But sometimes they forget to leave them in the truck," complained one bishop. Although cell phones are publicly discouraged, a growing number of businesspeople use them. "They are nice," said one entrepreneur, "because you can hide them and turn them off if company comes. The bishops will never be able to get rid of them." On the one hand, cell phones do not violate the old taboo against private phones in homes, but in fact, they provide instant access—anytime, anywhere.

The terms of the telephone bargain are still evolving, complicated now by cell phones. Although the phone has moved closer to offices and in some cases into the office, it remains barred from the home—the vital center of Amish life. In-home businesses continue to use telephone shanties outside the home. By maintaining the in-home taboo yet granting flexibility for commercial use, the Amish have enabled businesses to prosper within the boundaries of ethnic identity.

Motor Vehicle Use

The use of motor vehicles brought another round of negotiations between the restraints of Amish culture and the pressures of commercial life. Using public bus and train service was always permitted. The Amish believe that private ownership of cars will fragment their community by scattering family members to distant jobs, schools, and places of entertainment. The automatic mobility provided by motor vehicles offers easy access to the worlds of perdition, vice, and sloth. The prime symbol of American individualism, independence, mobility, and status, the automobile threatens many traditional Amish values. Personal ownership of vehicles, holding a driver's license, and driving vehicles remain forbidden activities. For a people who wish to remain separate from the world and nurture a family-centered life, easy access to motor vehicles is a menace.

TABLE 7.1

Technology Used by Amish Enterprises

Technology	Percentage of Enterprises
Battery-operated calculators	91
Telephones	91
Diesel engines	66
Air power	60
Vehicle service	57
110-volt electricity	51
12-volt electricity	49
Inverters	43
Hydraulic power	40
Electric typewriters	37
Electric cash registers	29
Fax machines	17
Portable phones	6
Computers	6

Source: Entrepreneur Profile (*N* = 35).
Note: This profile characterizes large businesses and may not be typical of small ones. Use of technology does not necessarily imply ownership. In the case of 110-volt electricity, the source may be a generator, an inverter, or a public utility line at a construction site.

Vehicle ownership, prohibited throughout the twentieth century, stirred little controversy among the Amish. Although the Amish have always shunned the *ownership* of vehicles, they have always permitted their *use*.[7] Hiring a driver and van to deliver a load of goods or to visit a distant relative is acceptable. The inconvenience of waiting and paying for a ride limits personal mobility and unnecessary use. The use of "taxi" service, prodded by Amish business involvement, grew rapidly in the Lancaster area after 1980. Indeed, hundreds of non-Amish persons provide taxi service to the Amish community on a regular basis.

The move into business challenged some of the traditional understandings governing motor vehicles. Amish manufacturers of wholesale materials need to make frequent deliveries. Custom cabinetmakers must visit the homes of prospective clients to take measurements and later to install finished cabinets. Even retailers, feeling the heat of competition, are often compelled to deliver products such as storage barns. And mobile Amish contractors must travel every day to outlying job sites. Traveling work crews need ready access to inexpensive but dependable transportation. Contractors often need at least two vehicles on the road—one for employees and another to shuttle the owner between various jobs. Produce stand holders in urban areas also need vehicles to ship their meat or vegetables to market as well as to transport their employees. As shown in table 7.1, about 57 percent of the owners use some type of vehicle service on a regular basis.

Businesses that depend on regular delivery service often negotiate contracts with non-Amish persons for vehicle service. In some cases, an Amish business may provide full-time work for one or more drivers. Other firms contract for part of a hauler's weekly time. In a few situations, an incorporated business includes a nonethnic partner who owns a vehicle and leases it to the business. In other cases, a non-Amish employee of a firm provides vehicle service as needed.

Mobile work crews, however, pose a larger problem, because employees and tools must be transported to construction sites on a daily basis. This need has brought a variety of arrangements. Some Amish contractors hire a non-Amish employee who provides his truck for business use, with reimbursement for mileage. However, if a worker quits, transportation may suddenly stop. Non-Amish employees who serve as drivers occasionally complain that their bosses may ask them to go out of their way for personal shopping errands.

Similar problems plague Amish employers who buy vehicles in the name of a non-Amish employee. If the worker becomes disgruntled, the vehicle may disappear, leaving the employer with little recourse. Another, more stable arrangement involves the use of vehicles owned by family members who have not yet joined the church. Some young males join the church in their mid-twenties. The son of an Amish roofer, for example, might own a van and transport his father and other crewmembers from job to job. Such arrangements evaporate, of course, when the child joins the church, which most do in the Lancaster settlement. As a result of these complications, some contractors have begun leasing vehicles. A conservative Mennonite, whose church permits ownership of motor vehicles, has a firm that leases vehicles to some Amish businesses. Leasing allows a few entrepreneurs a small cushion of distance from actual ownership.[8]

No matter how a business gains access to motor transportation, every entrepreneur must hire drivers. Company drivers, often non-Amish employees, transport the crew to job sites and work alongside Amish employees. In other cases, they make regular treks to work sites twice a day. Close relationships often develop between entrepreneurs and their non-Amish drivers. Indeed, for some, their driver is their closest non-Amish contact. The entrepreneur may acquire an ear for the style of music the driver plays. In other cases, the driver's political opinions may shape the views of an Amish contractor. As a gateway to the larger society, the news, information, and opinions offered, even casually, by non-Amish drivers may tint an entrepreneur's view of the world.

Acknowledging the necessity of transportation for many businesses, Amish leaders have permitted various vehicle arrangements to evolve, including, in some cases, company leasing and ownership of vehicles. Re-

Non-Amish drivers hauling an Amish construction crew fill their gas tanks
early in the morning before heading for a construction site.

gardless of the details of these cultural compromises, they remind members of the church's authority over vehicle ownership. All of these negotiated cultural arrangements, which seem so silly to outsiders, symbolize the
Amish fear of unbridled mobility and their reticence to allow motor vehicles to jeopardize the virtues of a stable community.

Amish Electricity

As they mushroomed in the 1970s, manufacturing and carpentry shops
faced yet another technological taboo: the church's opposition to electricity. Easy access to electricity carried the danger of wholesale materialism,
convenience, and exposure to mass media. Around 1919, the church forbade the use of 110-volt electricity for electric lights and other equipment;
however, batteries had always been acceptable. Thus, during the first half
of the twentieth century, a cultural distinction between 12-volt electricity
from batteries and 110-volt electricity from public utility lines gradually
gelled. By not tapping public utility lines, the Amish were able to keep at
bay not only televisions and computers but also the avalanche of other
appliances that hit twentieth-century households. The rejection of electricity from public power lines eventually became a symbolic mark of
Amish identity in the modern world.[9]

In the 1960s, because of new sanitary regulations, Amish farmers began chilling their milk in large bulk tanks. Diesel engines powered the refrigeration units. However, the agitators that stirred the milk in the tank required 110-volt electricity. Reluctantly, some church leaders permitted portable generators to create 110-volt current for bulk tanks; but others required that 12-volt motors, powered by batteries, spin the agitators. Nevertheless, self-generated electrical power was strictly limited. Portable generators were permitted to charge batteries and to operate portable welders, but home-generated electricity was otherwise prohibited. Yet increasingly, manufacturers needed power for large equipment.

By the late 1960s, stationary diesel engines had become popular sources of power to operate a variety of machines in Amish shops. Entrepreneurs often operated large drill presses, lathes, and saws by belts spun by the power shaft of a diesel engine. Some tools, both small and large, were difficult to run from a line shaft. The cultural taboo on 110-volt electricity blocked the use of many power tools that were essential for efficient shop production. In response, inventive Amish mechanics turned to hydraulic (oil) and pneumatic (air) power. This pivotal change gave a major boost to Amish enterprise.

Mechanics began stripping electric motors off shop equipment and replacing them with oil- or air-driven motors. Diesel engines could run hydraulic and pneumatic pumps, which in turn could power a variety of tools with pressurized oil or air (fig. 7.1). Amish mechanics might take an electric table saw, for example, strip off its electric motor, and replace it with an air motor. In other instances, the electric motor was replaced with a hydraulic motor. Today, pressurized oil or air powers dozens of shop tools— metal presses, sanders, drills, and saws. This so-called "Amish electricity" has enabled shops to use sophisticated equipment without tapping electricity from public utility lines. The cultural compromise has also preserved a symbolic sign of ethnic identity. The ingenious use of "Amish electricity" not only preserved the line of cultural separation but also boosted productive efficiency and bolstered the collective confidence of Amish society.

Some shop equipment is not easily adapted, however. Machinery with electronic controls cannot be operated with oil or air. For example, an Amish grocery store that uses a large machine to flatten cardboard boxes faced several obstacles. The device is normally powered by an electric motor, which includes electronic sensors and control switches. When converting the machine for use in a nonelectrified store, Amish mechanics had to make two replacements. First, the electric motor gave way to a hydraulic one. Second, the electronic controls were hooked to an inverter, which converted current from a 12-volt battery into 110-volt electricity. Thus, with a hydraulic motor and the help of an inverter, the large equipment could be operated without high-line electricity.

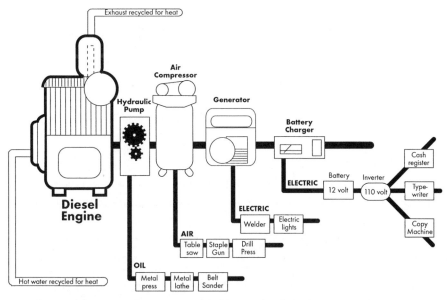

Figure 7.1 Power Sources Provided by a Diesel Engine

The use of inverters to make homemade 110-volt electricity from 12-volt batteries has grown rapidly in recent years. About the size of a car battery, an inverter can power a wide range of small electrical tools—copy machines, typewriters, fax machines, electronic scales, and cash registers. Inverters enjoy widespread use among Amish businesses in the Lancaster settlement. Electric typewriters with a memory and small screen are also used, as are a variety of battery-powered calculators (see table 7.1).

Shop owners have adapted hydraulic and pneumatic power for a wide variety of uses. The so-called Amish electricity allows businesses to operate competitively within the moral strictures of the church. In this way firms can use state-of-the-art equipment while still keeping wide-scale change and modernization at bay. Many entrepreneurs argue that hydraulic power saves money as well. Although more costly to install, air and hydraulic alternatives are virtually maintenance free and are cheaper to operate than electrical systems. Many households also use hydraulic power to pump water, run washing machines, and operate other equipment.

In recent years, many shops are using more homemade electricity. Electric lights are often permitted in paint rooms and for other tasks where gaslights would be dangerous or where special lighting is needed. Electrical lights for these purposes are run off a generator powered by a diesel. Battery-inverter combinations offer another source of homemade electricity. An alternator on a diesel recharges batteries that feed inverters that can provide 110-volt power for a coffeepot, a copy machine, large overhead doors, or for other specialized purposes. The more progressive shops use a combination of air, hydraulic, and electrical power produced by their diesel. Heat from the diesel is also used sometimes to warm water and/or air to heat the building as well. Nevertheless, traditional propane gas lamps provide the bulk of the lighting along with skylights that funnel sunlight in through the roof.

Consider how technology is tapped and tamed in a typical welding shop in a newly constructed 40 x 120 foot building. Each morning the 35-year-old entrepreneur starts the 300-horsepower diesel that powers equipment and heats the shop. Hydraulic power operates about a dozen different machines, including a large one that bends and cuts giant sheets of steel. Air power turns ceiling fans and exhaust fans. A generator, running off the diesel, provides 220-volt current for the state-of-the-art electric welders and 110-volt current for electric lights in the paint room. Skylights in the roof and portable propane gaslights illuminate the remainder of the shop. Batteries and an inverter provide a continuous supply of 110-volt current for a copy machine and a large garage door, which can be operated at night when the diesel is off.

◆

Virtually all Amish businesses depend on diesel engines rather than electricity for power. The engines operate air and hydraulic pumps, which run much of the equipment in Amish enterprises.

◆

A variety of machines in this welding shop are powered by air and hydraulic.
Pressurized air and oil travel through hoses that go from the diesel power plant
to the machinery.

A coffee break room on the second floor provides amenities for the five employees. A radiator filled with circulating hot water from the diesel heats the room. A battery pack and inverter provide 24-hour 110-volt electricity for a coffee maker, microwave oven, water cooler, and copy machine. The wall clock is battery-powered. A refrigerator runs on propane. In lieu of air conditioning, an air-powered ceiling fan stirs a breeze on sultry summer days. A daily newspaper, a battery-powered Black Jack and Poker hand game, and a portable phone lie on the table. The phone operates from a stationary phone installed in a phone shanty outside the shop. This mix of technology from multiple sources of power illustrates both the complexity and ingenuity of the adaptations that have emerged as Amish entrepreneurs struggle to compete in the marketplace within the moral order of their community.

These negotiated cultural arrangements enable the community to modernize without losing its sectarian soul. But the cultural deals did even more; they generated new enterprises. Numerous shops have sprung up to serve ethnic needs. They convert electrical equipment to hydraulic or air and repair the equipment as well. As their reputations have grown, the hydraulic firms have also attracted non-Amish customers, who bring large trucks and bulldozers for repair. Amish businesses that sell and service alternative equipment provide employment for community members—but more important, they make it possible for other ethnic businesses to tap the power they need to remain competitive in the larger marketplace.

Keeping Computers at Arm's Length

The massive growth of computer applications in business and the widespread use of the Internet have created new challenges for Amish entrepreneurs. In the mid-1980s, the church banned the ownership of computers, fearing that they would lead to the acceptance of television. Computer monitors and television screens were simply too much alike. Nevertheless, as with many other forms of technology, the Amish make a distinction between use and ownership. In the words of one businessman, "It's okay to work on a computer if someone else owns it." Thus, while it is rare to find individual members who own computers, many businesses do have access to computer services in one way or another.[10]

The taboo on computer ownership creates challenges in three areas: production, accounting, and marketing. How can Amish entrepreneurs compete against high-tech firms that have easy and full access to technology? The vast majority of Amish businesses have not integrated computers into their production process. The only way you can do that, explained one shop owner, is "to sell the business to an outsider and still work there, have an English partner who owns the computer, or outsource some things." He concluded, "We try to keep the computer at arm's length."

Some shop owners lament that they cannot use computerized controls to automate production. A few shops "out service" some production jobs to Old Order Mennonite or other non-Amish shops that have computerized controls for automated production. A growing number of businesses are using pneumatic controls to automate their production process. Ingenious Amish mechanics have developed sophisticated control panels that use air switches to operate repetitive and sequential processes. Sheets of vinyl can be sized, cut, and fabricated into fence parts in a fully automated process without computerization. A drilling machine programmed by air controls can bore multiple holes in metal or wood and repeat the action hundreds of times. Amish "engineers" are creating a whole new generation of automated manufacturing equipment programmed by air rather than electronic controls.

In terms of inventory and accounting, many of the smaller operations keep their records by hand. A number of self-trained Amish accountants provide services and advice to business owners. The larger Amish firms typically outsource their accounting, payroll, invoicing, and tax work to non-Amish firms that provide computerized services. In some cases, the outside firm will send a courier twice a day to pick up and drop off recent transactions. Smaller firms may have weekly or monthly visits by third-party providers. In all of these cases, Amish owners are tapping off-site computerized services for accounting, payroll, and other clerical functions.

A search of the Internet will show hundreds of Web sites hawking Amish products. Indeed, Internet marketing has boosted Amish sales in recent years. How do entrepreneurs find access to the World Wide Web despite the church taboo on computers and Internet use? Amish Web sites are also at arm's length from Amish ownership and control. Non-Amish distributors typically own the Web sites that sell Amish products. In other cases, outside firms provide Web service to Amish shops. Most of the larger Amish firms have distributors and dealers across the country who create a Web site for various Amish products. In any event, the Web sites are not directly owned by Amish and cannot be accessed from computers in Amish offices unless a non-Amish partner owns shares in the business.

One successful Amish crafts maker buys services from a non-Amish neighbor who lives within a block of the business. The neighbor provides phone, computer, accounting, and Web site services that are within reach, yet outside the legal ownership of the Amish firm. These and various other arrangements have enabled Amish firms to gain access to computer services and Internet marketing without transgressing the moral boundaries of their community. However, one Amish shop owner is dismayed that some Amish businesses form partnerships with an outsider "just so they can use a computer." In his words, "That's just down right hypocrisy."

Using the Fruits of Technology

Although the Amish have placed restraints on certain forms of technology, they have warmly welcomed technological advances that fit within the traditional patterns of their culture. Many Amish businesses use synthetic materials and integrate them into traditional products. When carriage makers had difficulty finding properly cured wood for buggy bodies, they searched for alternative materials. Fiberglass solved the quandary. Carriage makers could substitute synthetic fiberglass for wood and still allow buggies to retain their traditional look and design. The wooden shafts that connect the carriage to the harness were also replaced by fiberglass. In the process, new Amish enterprises sprouted as fiberglass shops began producing carriage shells. Thus, fiberglass makers, negotiating still another cultural deal, have taken a new technology and used it to serve their community by preserving the symbolic features of the traditional Amish carriage with high-quality synthetic materials.

Others have used synthetic materials to produce wheelbarrow basins, farm carts, utility buckets, and many other items. With raw fiberglass and the appropriate molds, a small shop could produce a variety of products. Because fiberglass products can be molded in small shops, they make an ideal cottage industry for an Amish family, given adequate ventilation and safety precautions.

Other business owners have also used new technologies to produce new products. An Amish contractor sold fencing products and installed picket fences throughout southeastern Pennsylvania and Maryland. Picket fences typically have a picket cap placed on the top of each fence post or stave. Because of faulty manufacturing, picket caps sometimes became discolored. Responding to customer concerns, the Amish contractor built a picket crimper, which presses a spade-shaped picket on top of each stave. Eliminating the possibility of discoloration, the machine also saved on-site labor costs because work crews no longer had to attach individual picket caps. The entrepreneur soon obtained a patent on his picket-crimping gadget. Mixing creativity and new technologies, he and many others have created new competitive products.

The fence business also sells polyethylene lumber, a product of recycling efforts. Since 1990, the enterprise has distributed Resource Lumber, made from consumer waste products such as plastic milk or water jugs.[11] The recycled plastic comes in a variety of nonfading colors, in the size and shape of traditional lumber. But it does not crack, split, or rot. The Amish firm cuts the plastic and makes a variety of products, such as mailboxes, birdhouses, and fence posts. Much of the plastic lumber is used to build porches, decks, and patios on new and existing homes. Another Amishman uses recycled lumber to build large fire trucks and trains as playground equipment. The bright colors and lack of splinters make the oversized toys ideal for playgrounds. Using promotional materials provided by the manufacturer, the Amish agent emphasizes the convenience of his product and the fact that recycled lumber saves valuable natural resources.

The use of these new products does not trouble Amish sensibilities because the materials use traditional woodworking methods. Indeed, the Amish entrepreneur had worked as a carpenter for eleven years before moving into the fencing business. Using plastic lumber did not change the nature of his work or threaten Amish lifestyles. And for those Amish who are buying polyethylene decks and porches, the new technology does not pose a problem because the synthetic materials do not alter the architecture or function of Amish homes. Indeed, the fact that the plastic porches were built by an Amish enterprise gives the new material an ethnic endorsement.

The flexibility of church leaders in permitting Amish shops in Lancaster County to use air and hydraulic power, forklifts, generators, inverters, and off-site computer services has clearly contributed to their success. Likewise, the freedom of contractors to use cell phones and electrical tools at construction sites enhances their productivity. Restrictive Ordnungs that forbid the use of these technologies in some other Amish settlements retard the growth of shops and business productivity.

Churchly accommodations to the technical needs of entrepreneurs do not receive universal praise within the Amish community, however. In fact, they frequently ignite controversy between farmers and shop owners. A young shop worker claims that farmers and shop owners "bicker just like republicans and democrats" over the guidelines of the Ordnung. Entrenched in centuries of tradition, the rules governing the use of technology on the farm are rather firm. By most accounts, church leaders have granted more freedom to shops to tap and adapt modern technology. The rapid rise of businesses, the lack of knowledge by church leaders about new technology, and a dearth of business tradition have all contributed to the flexibility granted to shop owners and contractors.

Many farmers feel the Ordnung hinders them and favors business. In a letter to Amish bishops, farmers pled, "Please, let's be fair. You don't forbid any of their [shop owners] equipment or where they can use it. We see the shops with their automatic, push-button, handy equipment—whatever they need to do the job. They run their tow motors back and forth, and some even have remote controlled gadgets to open and close their overhead doors without getting off the tow motor seats." The letter continued, "Please let's be fair. Shop and other businesses are favored over farmers. We do not want the shops to change anything, just be fair with us."[12]

Although many shop owners would concede that the church has tolerated new shop technology, they think the Ordnung favors contractors. Moving from site-to-site, often out of sight of church leaders, contractors enjoy the greatest use of technology, including electrical tools that are banned back home. In the blunt words of one shop owner: We have three Ordnungs, "one for contractors dated 2002, one for shop owners dated 1980, and one for farmers dated 1930." Contractors and construction workers, in the mind of one shop owner, are freer because "they are out of sight, out of mind. They drive to Philadelphia to a job, and nobody sees much what they do. They have cell phones, electrical tools, skid loaders on rubber tires, and sometimes they lease vehicles."

Clearly, the rise and growth of business has moved the cultural fences that regulate the use of technology, but the changes are not always seen as even or fair within the community. In bargaining with technological progress, the church seeks to permit new technologies as long as they do not disrupt traditional lifestyles or disturb the quality of community life. Although technological restraints in some ways hamper productivity, they also, like other moral boundaries, etch an ethnic trademark on the face of Amish industry. Thus the cultural constraints, which often bridle the power of technology, also contribute to the vitality of Amish enterprise by reinforcing its distinctive ethnic character.

8. Small-Scale Limitations

The hardest thing about a small business is staying small.

— AMISH CONTRACTOR

The Problem of Size

An unflagging commitment to growth and expansion is a common ingredient in the conventional recipe for business success. The Amish story offers a challenge to this cherished ideal. Indeed, the bosom of Amish culture is filled with many values that restrain commercial growth. One of the salient features of Amish enterprises is their small scale.[1] Even firms with significant sales have few employees and rather modest facilities. Only about 10 percent of Amish businesses have seven or more employees, and some of those may work part-time. The small size of Amish shops is not accidental. The church has worked self-consciously to keep enterprises small. Said one Amish contractor; "The hardest thing about a small business is staying small."

The favorable business climate in Lancaster County encourages growth. Indeed, the expansion of many businesses is unplanned. Explained one Amish owner, "Things just take off. It's hard to keep a progressive business on an even keel. When customers call and there's more business out there, it's hard to say no. Some people can do it. They can control the business, but it's hard. Some let it get out of control." Although outsiders might consider such easy growth a boon, the Amish eye it cautiously. They see dangers lurking behind the lure of expansion. Working without a set of specific guidelines, the church has, nevertheless, been successful in keeping enterprises small.

The Amish fear large businesses for a number of reasons.[2] First, they worry that bigger establishments will weaken the involvement of the family. One of the reasons they established small shops was to keep work integrated with family life. A large business easily encroaches on family life, as entrepreneurs become engulfed in manufacturing, sales, or bookkeeping. Although the community values hard work, it frowns on jobs that completely dominate everything else. "A lot of Amish are workaholics," said an Amishman who manufactures storage barns. "They pretty easily get too caught up in their work. The church doesn't want a business to get too awfully big, or pretty soon you're living for your job. You get too caught up in it. That's not right."

Second, the Amish fear that large operations will lead their owners away from the church. "I think people are afraid that if you get too big, you'll go against the church rules," admitted one businesswoman. Bigger businesses demand more advanced technology, education, and scientific know-how and greater interaction with outside support professionals, such as lawyers, engineers, and accountants. "When a business gets too big, it's harder to follow church rules," a wood products manufacturer admitted. "That's one of the dangers of not putting the brakes on your business." Uneasiness with commercial insurance and government entanglements adds to the anxiety over size. By staying small, the church hopes to avoid many of the complications that trouble larger firms.

Third, the church frets that large operations will cultivate conceit. Much of the success of farming rests in the hands of God, who sends the sun and rain. Successful business operations, independent of the weather, point to the owners' personal skills of management and planning. Unlike farming, a successful business is more likely to cultivate pride in personal achievement. Such self-adulation mocks the quiet virtues of Gelassenheit—modesty and humility. Large businesses, in other words, contradict the core values of Amish culture by focusing attention on personal accomplishments.

Finally, the Amish worry that the emergence of large businesses will disrupt the delicate balance of social equality. When most members were engaged in farming, the church enjoyed homogeneity of social status and financial means. As more people follow entrepreneurial pursuits, there is greater opportunity for wealth to settle in the hands of a few. Growing income in entrepreneurial pockets may encourage the formation of a wealthy managerial class. Such stratification runs counter to the egalitarian understandings that have shaped Amish society. Moreover, large business operators might not bend as easily to the collective will of the church. Wealthy individuals could, in the words of one church member, "begin to make their own rules."

Establishing Limits

Responding to the incipient dangers of growth, church leaders try to limit the size of enterprises. However, drawing exact lines is a delicate and ambiguous matter. The church has never legislated specific limits, and when asked, members are unsure of the precise boundaries of growth. They do know, however, when businesses have crossed the lines of propriety. And there are many stories of business owners who, unwilling to yield to the communal limits on size, have left the church.[3] Sometimes the adult children of the owners of overgrown businesses leave the church. One Amish writer concerned about the growth and consequences of big shops called the trend "tragic."[4]

"When you get too big, it shows up," said one owner simply. Another entrepreneur, struggling to explain the limits on growth, noted, "When people get too big, one thing leads to another, and then it's out of control." An Amishwoman described the moment when a successful owner realized that "he had too much money coming in for his comfort." He knew that his firm had gotten "too big for an Amishman." A machine shop owner pointed to a similarly imprecise, yet significant, moral boundary: "The church doesn't have an exact limit [on business size]. They'll let you go, but they'll want to know *why* you want to get so big. . . . And the only answer to that, when it comes right down to it, the only answer is *money*. . . . You know what the Bible says about the rich man. It's not impossible for the rich man to get to heaven, but it's pretty hard. It's pretty hard."

Entrepreneurs agree that there is no church-wide cap on sales or on the size of facilities. Nor has the church issued pronouncements on the maximum number of employees that a business may have. One shop owner suggested that a firm should stop growing "when you have to hire outside help," or when you "start crowding the church's standards by getting bigger equipment."[5] One storeowner suggested ten workers might be an unofficial limit, but others say that there is no employment ceiling. The structure of the Amish church creates some of the vagueness. Each church district, under the leadership of its bishop, holds final authority over matters of ethical practice. Thus, acceptable standards vary from one district to another. What one bishop considers "too big" may be acceptable to another.

Yet certain cultural regulators have evolved that effectively stifle expansion. First and most obvious is the church's regulation of technology, including motor vehicles. A retail storeowner pointed to technological restraints when describing the lid on his business: "The church doesn't have a problem with size *except* when the size necessitates a phone [on the

◆

*A tractor-trailer delivers raw lumber to a storage barn builder in an Amish
industrial park.*

desk]." Other practical parameters emerge from the choice to forgo certain
fruits of modernity. The lack of electricity from public utility lines, for
example, is a barrier to unlimited growth. Although, as we have seen, entrepreneurs utilize pneumatic and hydraulic power to operate a wide array
of equipment, this so-called Amish electricity cannot power electronic
equipment. Even with the use of inverters, which convert electricity from
batteries to standard voltage, the output is somewhat reduced.

The church's rejection of computers also curbs the size of some shops.
"If it gets so big that you can't handle it yourself and you need a lot of fancy
equipment to manage your books, that would be too big," ventured one
entrepreneur. When asked if a computer would increase production in his
metal fabrication shop, the owner chortled, "Oh yes! That would save me
so much time, especially in billing. I could just type in their customer number and how many of what they got, and it would all print out in a bill.
That would be a big savings." But he also feared that more office efficiency
would only encourage him to take on more work.

Another regulator of size, albeit indirect, is the cultural lid on formal
education. Although businesspeople have performed remarkably well in
the modern marketplace with only an eight-grade private education, such
training may retard growth. Said one businesswoman and quilt shop owner,
"I think [one] reason some Amish say they don't want to get too big is sim-

ply because they don't have the education for it. They wouldn't say that, but that's probably part of it. I enjoy book work, but I still feel dumb about all these taxes and government forms." Although many entrepreneurs are quite fluent in commercial jargon, others are unfamiliar with the vocabulary and feel somewhat lost in the maze of modern business. No matter how developed their products or markets, some feel intimidated by non-Amish competitors in the larger business world. Amish schools and child-rearing practices produce hard-working, thoughtful adults, but they do not prepare assertive, competitive marketers.

A third factor retarding growth is the Amish aversion to government regulation. Wanting to distance themselves as much as possible from entanglements with the state, some entrepreneurs try to huddle below thresholds of size. Having few employees exempts owners from certain requirements that they see as "needless paperwork." The problems businesses encounter with municipal government and zoning often concern size as well. In some areas of Lancaster County, public ordinances keep businesses small. Local officials in some townships regulate the size and number of buildings, the square footage of lots, and the number of nonfamily employees a business may have. In some cases, Amish firms are more limited by zoning officers than by the rules of their own church. By keeping their work near home, away from commercial zones and industrial parks, the Amish have subjected themselves to zoning laws that keep their operations small.

But the most important limit to growth is not measured by physical or financial size. The most significant moral boundary is the owner's attitude. In the Amish context, a haughty disposition reveals a sinful and rebellious spirit. Gelassenheit, willingness to yield to the community, is a cardinal Amish virtue. To be humble—to submit to the will of the church—is to lose oneself for the sake of the community and follow the ways of Jesus and the martyrs, who literally gave up all. Arrogant expressions of pride are seen as detrimental to the church and to one's relationship with God and others. Gratitude for what God has given, not boastful declarations of personal accomplishments, form the bedrock of Amish life. Humility, gentleness, and meekness are the marrow of a yielded life.

Big business becomes dangerous because it so easily leads to pride, self-confidence, and a spirit of independence. When an owner begins to exhibit an attitude of arrogance, the church knows that the business has become too large. An enterprise can grow until its owner "gets too big a head," one Amish grandfather explained. An owner might enjoy some private pride with a small business, but the Amish fear that larger operations will surely lead to big and bloated egos.

If an entrepreneur maintains a discreet spirit of humility and a willingness to operate within the limits of the Ordnung, the church will typically smile on success. Larger establishments that camouflage the size of their operations and marketing efforts will more likely win the blessing of the church than those seeking attention. A silo contractor who builds hundreds of silos but operates from a modest home base may avoid undue criticism. An entrepreneur with several retail stores that are dowdy in appearance may avoid church sanctions by maintaining this unpretentious posture, even though collectively the stores are a large operation. Some sizable businesses enjoy the blessing of the church because of the owner's humble demeanor. "He's got a big business," one Amishman said, describing a large entrepreneur who remains in the community's good graces. "It's a lot bigger than most people realize. But see, he can go to church and sit beside you and sing the same songs, and after church he can have dinner with you and talk just like anyone else. You'd never know his business is in the seven-digit range. He acts just like the farmer or small shop man sitting next to him." By exhibiting a spirit of Gelassenheit, this businessman is able to retain his place of honor in the community.

Not all big operators are so successful. Some have allowed their business, in the words of one Amishman, "to go to their head." A sizable manufacturing firm became embroiled in controversy when its owner was unable to balance personal humility with financial success. The entrepreneur began flagrantly deviating from church standards. "He started making up his own rules," a neighboring farmer remembered. "He set it up and then he went to the bishop and said, 'I did it and I'm going to keep on doing it.' That didn't go over too well." Eventually the church forced the owner to sell the business to non-Amish investors. In the view of some observers, the owner's attitude, rather than the size of his business, was his downfall. A more diffident person "could have run it and kept it Amish," some church members averred. Even so, the Amish are quick to note that larger businesses are more liable to produce arrogance and pride. The church tries to rein in excessive growth before its lures become too tempting.

Most entrepreneurs support the church's attempts to limit size. News of Fortune 500 companies downsizing, mountains of regulatory paperwork, and labor disputes in the larger world of industry confirm in the Amish mind that smaller is better. Said one Amish mason: "Our ministers preach this all the time in their sermons and at their conferences: 'Keep it small. Keep it small.' They really try to drive that home. And some people wonder why. Well, when you get to be where I am, at my age, with a business like this, you see why. They're right. You've got to keep it under control or it'll get out of hand. Where does it end? You just get bigger and bigger. Our preachers are right." Another manufacturing shop owner agreed.

"I'm not limited by the church. I've limited myself. . . . I wouldn't want to get any bigger. That would make it more of a headache than it's worth." Such voices reveal the humble spirit of Gelassenheit, which voluntarily forgoes growth for the sake of unity and equality in community life.

Strategies for Downsizing

The Amish have engineered a number of strategies to trim their firms in order to preserve family-centered, manageable businesses. Self-imposed limitations are the most basic way to ensure that firms remain small. Entrepreneurs are encouraged to make a conscious effort to keep their businesses slim, despite opportunities to expand at every turn. "You start out small, just making a few things," one entrepreneur explained. "Then you're employing your son and it's fine. Then out of nowhere you get this big order from somewhere for $50,000, and you think, hey, we can't let this get away. That wouldn't be good for business. So you hire some neighbors, and after awhile hire them full-time, and then where does it end?"

Many owners choose to limit their growth. Said one businesswoman, "I don't want to get any bigger, but I could have. We had the chance last year to get another shop, a good opportunity, but we turned it down. We just said, 'Why do we want to get bigger? We have enough. We have as much as we can handle. Why get bigger—we'll just have more headaches.'" Another owner described his difficulty scaling back "when you get enough." He had "to say no sometimes," even when refusing work meant jeopardizing important contracts. The informal guidelines of Amish culture enable these entrepreneurs to keep their businesses in check. Few would have the personal fortitude to limit growth, but within the context of church and family, they are able to make such choices.

Another method of downsizing involves dividing successful firms. When a business grows too large, the owner may offer a segment of it to an employee or a family member. Others create divisions or new independent businesses. Founded in the mid-seventies, a farm implement manufacturing firm outgrew its first home within eight years. With several employees, it had exhausted its zoning permit and was too large for one person to manage. Conventional wisdom called for adding a second layer of management, creating separate production lines within the company, and finding a new location for expansion. Instead, the firm split in half. The owner, who lived at the original location, retained the Amish clientele and continued to produce horse-drawn-wagon gears and steel wheels. One of his brothers relocated part of the enterprise and produced wagons and cattle feeders for non-Amish customers. Both businesses retained the small-

scale ethos of the original operation. The brothers could operate their separate shops with a small number of employees without becoming full-time
managers.

A very successful machinery manufacturer with about ten employees
discussed his personal dilemma with growth. "I could really grow the
business if I wanted to—the market's out there—but what's the purpose?
Why?" Instead, his present plan is to divide the business into four different divisions and transfer the ownership of them to some of his children.

In another case, an Amish-owned dry goods store became a mother store
to eight other retail outlets—three more dry goods stores, a shoe store, two
housewares shops, and two grocery stores. As the parent store grew beyond
the owner's comfort, she sold off divisions or product lines to employees.
Employees and assistant managers bought various portions of the business,
carving it apart to keep it from becoming too large.[6] This strategy not only
multiplied the number of operations and allowed wider ownership within
the church, but it also prevented the development of a large department
store with layers of management, which would surely have separated the
owner from employees. Each of the new owners retains a hands-on management position within his or her own store. And interestingly, dividing
the parent business did not damage the viability of any of the firms. In fact,
most of the spin-offs spawned new growth.

Some entrepreneurs have negotiated a different solution to the problem
of size. A few owners have formed mixed partnerships with non-Amish
individuals. Others have incorporated their businesses—with or without
non-Amish shareholders. Such a move does not necessarily downsize a
business, but it does distance the Amish owner from a firm that may be
evolving toward greater worldliness. Relatively few Amish have used this
tactic to remove themselves in a symbolic way from their businesses; only
about 5 percent of Amish firms are mixed partnerships or corporations. As
some enterprises expand to the point that they need computerization, a
hybrid partnership may allow such a convenience. A non-Amish partner
might sublease office space from the partnership or corporation and then
install computers, public utility electricity, and telephone service. Mixed
partnerships have allowed some Amish-related businesses indirectly to
own vehicles and engage in practices otherwise prohibited for individual
members.

Businesses that become mixed partnerships do not necessarily disregard
all church rules, however. Most continue to limit their size and are selective in their use of technology. "We only take it as far as we have to," said
one Amish shop owner who formed a partnership with a non-Amish
neighbor. His partnership installed in-office telephones but retained gas
lighting. The non-Amish partner contributed a computer and photocopier

to the business but keeps these at his home. Moreover, some partnerships involve conservative Mennonites who are permitted more technological freedom than the Amish but who nevertheless espouse basic Amish values. The church has never prohibited mixed partnerships, but they are strongly discouraged by church leaders.

Hybrid partnerships and corporations receive mixed reviews in the Amish community. Some members view owners of these businesses as both successful and faithful to the church. They have created large enterprises without overstepping the bounds of propriety and have, at least symbolically, distanced themselves from their companies. Other Amish are less charitable. A businesswoman and craft storeowner is dismayed by a large Amish-founded business that formed a mixed partnership: "He had to go into partnership with an English man to be able to do what he does. That's too big if you ask me." Still, hybrid partnerships and corporations are a generally acceptable means of resolving difficult circumstances and enabling businesses to grow or gain access to technological convenience. At the same time, partnerships and articles of incorporation force founders to relinquish some measure of control, because the Amish partner, in deference to cultural taboos, never holds direct ownership of electrified buildings, vehicles, or computers. Nevertheless, these arrangements are a major cultural concession to the forces of commerce.

A new strategy for coping with success emerged in the late 1990s when several owners sold their overgrown businesses to outsiders. More than a dozen large Amish businesses have been sold off.[7] Some owners took their profits, bought several farms out of state, and tried to return to farming themselves. Others invested the funds from the sale in new business ventures. One creative entrepreneur founded and sold two successful firms and now is growing a third.

Another way of balancing growth with the size constraints of Amish culture involves subcontracts within the Amish community. Instead of building a larger plant, a successful entrepreneur will contract with an Amish family to produce a particular item at their homestead. The larger entrepreneur may purchase the necessary equipment, provide training, raw materials, and quality control. However, the work is performed in a small shop or barn at the home of the subcontractor. This arrangement has many benefits. The size of a successful operation *appears* smaller, and labor costs and personnel problems are reduced. The small subcontractor can keep work close to home, involve family members, and control the hours and rate of the work. This growing practice also provides a way for young entrepreneurs to get a start in business.

Not all growth situations are resolved so easily, however. Some businesses have grown too rapidly, employed questionable technology, and

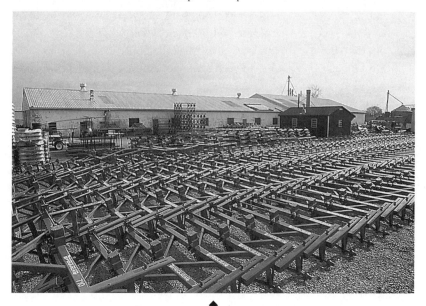

◆

*This large machinery shop outgrew Amish limits and was sold to
non-Amish buyers.*

alienated church members. Owners who refuse to bend to the collective
will of the church and operate an offending enterprise demonstrate an
arrogance that will ultimately trigger excommunication from the church.
Over the years a number of Amish owners have left the church and taken
their growing businesses with them.

The Amish commitment to small-scale operations diverges from mainstream society. To submit all of one's life—including personal business
decisions—to the authority of the church is alien to Western notions that
prize individual autonomy, economic independence, and expansion at any
cost. The sacrosanct right to freedom of choice in all decision making suc-
cumbs to the welfare of the larger community in this ethnic culture. Amish
entrepreneurs stand apart from their worldly counterparts in their willingness to surrender their business endeavors to the authority of the church.
And although the church rarely exercises that right of sovereignty, it will
do so when necessary to protect the ethnic community from the arrogance,
autonomy, inequality, and expansion of power that typically follow in the
wake of unfettered growth.

Lingering Questions

Even with the attempts to cap business size, entrepreneurship poses subtle challenges to Amish peoplehood. Church members tend to hold owners of larger businesses in high esteem. Even those who discreetly bend the rules of the church are admired for their hard work, creativity, and know-how. The respect accorded to successful entrepreneurs may also encourage others to test the limits of acceptable behavior. Larger businesses touch the Amish community in another way as well. Many church members employ other members. Although such links reinforce community solidarity, they also may disturb the long-time egalitarianism of Amish culture. Might employees be more influenced by their bosses than by their bishops? If a business owner encounters difficulty with the church, employees—caught in the middle—may side with the owner.

Some entrepreneurs provide employment for a sizable number of people in their church district. Will the church be able to scale down such a business if it means the loss of jobs for fellow church members? Already some large operators regard attempts to limit business as less than serious. In the words of one wood products manufacturer: "Normally the ones [in the church] who think you're too big and talk about you being too big will eventually come and ask you for a job, or they will want to subcontract things from you to do at home, or come and ask you for a loan. That's how it works." He anticipates that the church will find it increasingly difficult to restrain growing firms.

Challenges can come even under the guise of traditional practices, such as mutual aid. Many entrepreneurs are generous with their earnings. Businesspeople have bailed out families burdened with hospital bills, provided low-interest or no-interest loans to young farmers investing in land, aided young families starting new businesses, and supported members struggling to recover from a fire or flood. One father told of a typical occurrence. Several days after a neighbor lost his barn and farm equipment in a fire, a truck pulled up to the still-standing house and delivered a new manure spreader. The truck driver announced that it was an anonymous gift from a fellow church member. Although no one knew for sure, most people believed that a businessman had donated the spreader. The church is grateful for its generous entrepreneurs. Mindful that wealth does not always lead to generosity, ministers stress charitable, big-hearted giving.

But privately, some worry that members may use their gifts to earn community respect. At worst, large-scale operators could someday build a private base of support and command enough clout to snub church counsel and do as they please. If enough other members feel beholden to the generosity of an entrepreneur, the community's delicate balance of power may totter. Even now, a few members think that wealthy businesspeople sometimes stand above the church. One small shop owner worries that the generosity of a large operator has earned him the privilege of tampering with the Ordnung. "My neighbor is always there to help the next guy. When someone has a hospital bill or has a fire, he's right there to help. So a lot of people don't think they can say anything critical about his business."

Well-heeled businesspeople also feel the moral responsibility of wealth. They sense the shifting economic balance. One businesswoman confessed struggling with her financial success, although others have tried to calm her anxiety: "There are some who tell me that it's not bad that I'm big. You need bigger businesses for when the catastrophes come," she reasons. When major disasters strike, "the little guy can't do much. You need some big businesses to help out. When you have a little, you can give a little. When you have a lot, you are expected to give a lot." Yet others remain concerned. The historical strength of mutual aid among the Amish rested on an equal sharing of burdens. The lack of large donors united the community. Will the emergence of wealthy entrepreneurs spoil the church's egalitarian commitment to mutual aid? That possibility makes efforts to keep businesses small even more critical.

Modest Investments

As businesses generate profit, owners face new questions about investments. Several patterns have emerged in recent years. Most entrepreneurs seek to make accelerated payments and clear any loans as quickly as possible. Beyond debt repayment, earnings often find their way back into the businesses. Most owners agree that plowing profits into the enterprise is their most important business strategy. A dormant savings account is considered money wasted. Keeping new earnings at work in their operation is an almost universal goal. As a business nears the brink of acceptable size, reinvestment may stall or stop. As the moral boundaries of growth cap expansion, owners must explore new investment options. And at that point, the church offers guidance.

The church encourages members to make mutual aid their first priority. Successful business owners are expected to extend low-interest loans to fellow members. Most make funds equally available to prospective farmers and beginning entrepreneurs. Some owners channel profits to Helping Hand, an informal Amish network that makes low interest loans to church members to buy property or start a business. Many business people claim they are happy to help other church members. Said one machinery manufacturer; "I've had enough help in my years getting started that I like helping other people with what they're doing." About one-fifth of the business owners have assisted a relative in beginning a new business, and one-quarter have made loans to relatives buying farmland.[8] Some buy land themselves, hoping to offer farms to their children later in life, should their children choose to farm. Ironically, as one entrepreneur pointed out, "Many times only the business owners have the funds to buy expensive farmland when it comes on the market."

Some entrepreneurs have also engaged in other types of investments. A few have purchased mountain land in northern or western Pennsylvania for hunting camps, which often include mountain cabins. Some business-people buy rental properties—single-family homes or houses remodeled into apartments. Many rent to non-Amish tenants. Occasionally, a business owner will purchase commercial property to lease to other businesses. Some have bought interests in other Amish firms. Still others invest in mutual funds on the stock market. Several financial brokers have a sizeable number of Amish clients who make monthly investments in mutual funds.

This new wave of investment, beyond the traditional parameters of mutual aid, worries some church leaders. They fear that such investments, generally not possible for farmers or day laborers, might further encourage economic stratification in the church. With already flush business owners earning additional money through farm or apartment rentals, the possibility of accumulating wealth becomes a growing threat. Some leaders feel that a prosperous class of entrepreneurs may forgo the wisdom of the church in the pursuit of profit. Confirming the worst fears of some conservatives, word circulated that a few owners, citing poor returns on farm loans, had declined to loan money to young farmers but instead had bought cabins and rental apartments for themselves. Amish leaders, who condemned the incidents, insisted that they were aberrations.

Not all Amish view the emerging entrepreneurial class as a threat to community life. At least some feel that business owners are sharing their earnings fairly. Far fewer private loans would be available to help young couples enter farming or commercial pursuits without the generosity of Amish entrepreneurs. Others note that an occasional mountain cabin or apartment house is a rather modest use of wealth. And of course, there are no private jets or lavish mansions among the Amish elite. No beach houses along the Outer Banks or ski trips to the Rockies absorb excess Amish income. Prescribed clothing patterns, limits on transportation, and the informal scrutiny of a close community constrain wealthy members from spending too much on themselves. Although vacation trips have become more frequent, they still pale in comparison to the dollars spent by corporate America on recreation and leisure. By limiting the size of businesses,

◆

The crafts and vegetables in this roadside stand are sold to non-Amish neighbors and tourists. The crafts are made in various Amish shops.

the church has been largely successful in spreading the new wealth rather widely across the community.

The Positive Side of Restraint

The rise of microenterprises was a negotiated compromise between the countervailing weight of cultural resources and cultural restraints in Amish life. The resources embedded in the Amish heritage provided the social capital to underwrite the formation of hundreds of productive shops. But what about the cultural constraints, the curbs on entrepreneurship—the moral restrictions, technological taboos, and limitations on size—that ostensibly block the path of progress? These cultural strictures hamper the entrepreneurial spirit, but they also inadvertently serve many positive functions in the Amish community. Although unintended, many of the consequences that flow from these cultural restraints help to undergird the long-term welfare of Amish life.

The cultural fences encompassing Amish firms grant them a distinctive identity that enhances their marketing efforts. The Amish margin of difference is attractive to consumers searching for handcrafted products with an ethnic mystique. Moreover, the moral boundaries that stifle entrepreneurial enthusiasm heighten the community's own sense of identity and self-confidence. The vigorous productivity of nonelectrified shops and the state-of-the-art hydraulic systems built by Amish mechanics are cause for ethnic pride, albeit camouflaged.

The cultural boundaries that have restrained Amish shops have also spawned a coterie of new enterprises specializing in ethnic products for the special needs of the Amish community—products that fit the ethnic code of propriety. The dozens of enterprises specializing in pneumatic power, hydraulic systems, gas appliances, gas lighting, clothing, carriages, and all sorts of horse-drawn machinery have all developed because of the restrictions of the Ordnung. Thus, the limits on technology have in turn birthed many firms that cater to the special needs of Amish society.

The church's restrictions on technology have also bolstered creativity. The ban on 110-volt electricity and the use of horse-drawn equipment has generated imaginative technological detours. Because the larger world has discarded so many products still in use by the Amish, shop owners have mustered great creativity to design alternate equipment. Replacing electric motors with hydraulic systems or manufacturing gas lanterns, for example, continually underscores the church's identity while also producing work for its members. The rise of ethnic-specific technologies has thus bred it own class of business ventures.

By limiting the size of their enterprises, the Amish have scattered entrepreneurial opportunities widely across the settlement. Without the restrictions on size, a handful of large operations might dominate the landscape, instead of hundreds of small shops. The large number of shops in each church district reinforces traditional patterns of horse-and-buggy transportation and strengthens the social bonds of local congregations. By widely distributing entrepreneurship, the Amish have successfully kept their work tied to family life. This in turn encourages large families and contributes to the numerical growth of the community. Home-based industries can more readily involve children. Thus, children remain an economic asset, encouraging large families, which in turn, produce more potential members for church membership. And as noted before, the widespread ownership of shops scatters wealth more widely throughout the settlement.

By spreading entrepreneurship across many small-scale shops, the benefits and satisfactions of entrepreneurship are shared with many owners. But even among those who labor by the hour, the alienation that often accompanies factory work diminishes in the context of a small shop. Employees feel directly tied to their work because they understand how their role meshes with the whole and see how their artisanship benefits or hinders overall productivity. Thus, the small-scale operations increase the satisfaction of everyone and contribute to the long-term stability of the community.

In all of these ways, the cultural restraints that appear to thwart entrepreneurial dreams, in reality, contribute in significant ways to the long-term stability of the Amish community. Moral boundaries, technological taboos, and limitations of size often indirectly strengthen the viability of Amish life. Microenterprises were produced by the dynamic tension between the resources and restraints inside Amish culture; but they also have a public face that looks to the outside world—a world that once persecuted them and from which they still try to keep a discreet distance.

PART FOUR

The Public Face of
Amish Enterprise

9. Promotion and Professional Networks

Advertising really pays.
— AMISH BUSINESSMAN

Facing the Public

Amish entrepreneurs do not work in an ethnic cloister. Business involvements push them beyond rural enclaves and challenge the longstanding Amish principle of separation from the world. Although most employees are church members and many sales are conducted within ethnic circles, all enterprises are linked to the outside world in some way. Indeed, as Marc A. Olshan has argued, the foray into business signals the "opening" of Amish society. Moreover, Olshan notes that the "Come In-We're Open" signs hanging on the doors of retail shops are "a graphic denial" of the Amish claim to separation from the world. Such signs both welcome and endorse interaction with outsiders.[1]

As business owners enter the public marketplace, they meet an assortment of clientele and sometimes join business associations and trade groups. Such affiliations provide them with information and identity and also legitimate their role in the commercial realm. Outside ties shape a firm's relations with the surrounding culture and open avenues of commercial interaction.

More broadly, advertising is a deliberate attempt to go public and penetrate the larger world. The public face of a business is presented through its name, business cards, brochures, advertising trinkets, and print advertising. Many Amish businesses take promotion, advertisement, and public relations seriously. Others depend primarily on word-of-mouth promotion. Traditional Amish values of modesty, humility, and simplicity often clash with the aggressive techniques of promotional efforts. Balancing historic religious taboos and the latest sales gimmicks, entrepreneurs have had to negotiate their way between the quiet, unassuming ways of Gelassenheit and the splashy, assertive manners of advertising.

As they venture into the public square, the Amish face challenges common to all entrepreneurs. Although their responses have been guided by the cultural norms of their religious faith, they have exhibited enterprising creativity. Typically declining to participate in professional associations and business syndicates, they have created their own ethnic trade groups that incorporate Amish values into their design and function. The use of advertising has produced some unique expressions as entrepreneurs have tried to harness their promotional efforts inside the moral boundaries of the church. The search for new clients has sometimes stretched the norms of the church, but most entrepreneurs have tried to keep one foot planted in the tradition of humility while leaning farther and farther into the public arena.

The Struggle with Advertising

As Amish firms venture into the realm of public image making, they enter a complex, costly, and confusing world—one that often clashes with their traditional values of simplicity and humility. Advertising presents many practical and moral challenges. When the first generation of businesses began in the 1970s and 1980s, many owners gave little attention to promoting their products. As businesses have matured, much more money and effort is devoted to advertising. Like other businesspeople, Amish entrepreneurs turn to advertising agents for help in developing brochures and placing ads.

Some owners advertise sparingly, arguing that word-of-mouth praise and satisfied customers are the best and cheapest means of promotion. In fact, some sizeable enterprises, boasting annual sales of a million dollars, use only a simple roadside sign. In so doing, they reveal an Amish skepticism toward glitzy promotion and worldly fanfare. Others disagree with such a cautious approach. Said one Amish businessman, "I've found that advertising pays. Some Amish would say that it's money thrown away, but I've found that it really pays." Convinced of the importance of advertising, an Amish businessman who runs a sizable farmers' market requires each of his stand holders, Amish and non-Amish alike, to offer an advertised special each week. All the evidence suggests that advertising has grown as businesses have matured and moved into their second generation.

Beyond mere finances, advertising challenges other Amish values. The prized virtues of humility, diffidence, and integrity often clash with the hype of public billboards and high-pressure pitches. The world of promotion, laced as it often is with veiled half-truths, pompous claims of product superiority, and the degradation of competitors, conflicts with Amish commitments to cooperation, simplicity, and reserve. The very idea of self-promotion runs counter to the Amish impulse for modesty and self-effacement. To trumpet one's name or announce one's accomplishments mocks the virtue of humility. Although the Amish have not rejected advertising, neither have they fully embraced Madison Avenue methods. In expressing caution and reserve, they have negotiated carefully between their historic values and the necessity of commercial promotion.

Amish values govern even the most basic form of advertising—the business name. Business owners rarely include their own full names in the business title. More often, geographic locations identify Amish firms: Bird-in-Hand Window Sales, Buena Vista Upholstery, Centerville Variety Store, Gap Hill Wagons and Gates, Georgetown Hydraulics, Pequea Planters, Rocky Ridge Construction, Scenic Road Manufacturing, and Sunny Slope Woodworks, to name a few.

In recent years, more surnames are being used. For example, Stoltzfus Woodworking, Fisher's Quality Furniture, and Beiler's Pneumatics. Some businesses do include an owner's initials—J. and B. Crafts, D. S. Machine, and B. B.'s Grocery Outlet. The use of initials underscores a degree of anonymity and personal reserve often missing in the larger world. By keeping first names from the spotlight, owners defer to the group and deflect individual attention. And because there are few Amish surnames in the settlement, the use of a surname does not compromise privacy. With one in four Amish families named Stoltzfus, a business called Stoltzfus Woodworking hardly identifies a particular individual. By using obscure place names, Amish firms reveal their local orientation. Although conventional advertising wisdom suggests that grand geographic references— "East Coast" or "National"—increase status and market, Amish business names betray a commitment to the parochial worlds of family and local community.

Roadside signs announcing a modest business are typically small, often hand-lettered, and never electrified. As businesses grow, they often replace hand-painted signs with professionally lettered ones. In some municipalities, zoning ordinances keep signs small, but even without restrictions, Amish signs are rarely large or flashy.

Most firms are reluctant to promote their Amish identity on their product labels or brochures. Fearing that using the Amish label to garner profits will prostitute the soul, one minister said, "I'm really opposed to sticking the Amish name on all of our products. If it's a high quality product, it will sell itself." Non-Amish distributors and retailers eagerly stamp the Amish label on everything they handle. Unscrupulous merchandisers sometimes paste the Amish name on products, even computer software, that are not Amish made.[2]

The moral boundaries of Amish culture severely restrict some types of advertising. The Amish rarely use radio and television promotions. Viewed as worldly gadgets that channel violence and immorality into the family, televisions and radios are not found in Amish homes. In fact, owning such devices is cause for excommunication. Thus, it is not surprising that the church frowns on members marketing on the airways. Moreover, such advertising would be worthless for the firms that cater primarily to Amish customers.

Despite the church's prohibition, a few Amish entrepreneurs who target non-Amish customers have experimented with advertising on the airways. One owner reasoned that church leaders "who don't like it, don't listen to it or watch it anyway." Does such advertising increase sales? In almost every case, experimentation with broadcast advertising has flopped—not because of church rulings, but because of high costs. An advertising agent with many Amish clients said Amish advertising uses print mediums, does not "over promise" its products, and targets local markets. She was never asked by an Amish client to "exaggerate" or make "false claims" about a

◆

This roadside sign on the edge of a field advertises three Amish businesses.

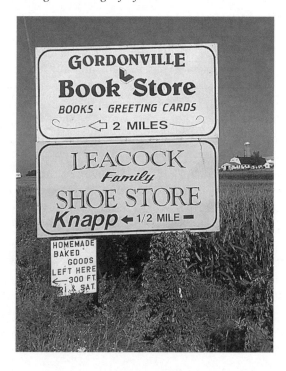

Non-Amish distributors of Amish products have created dozens of Web sites that market Lancaster Amish products worldwide.

product. Moreover, she finds that her Amish clients are "a little more patient than the English clients," in seeing quick results.[3]

Print Advertising

Amish business owners use a variety of print advertising. Business cards are now widely used. They signal the growing acceptance of individuation and public recognition that has accompanied the rise of microenterprises. Even new and relatively tiny enterprises have cards bearing their name, location, and hours. Most list an on-site phone number, an answering service number, or the hours they may be reached at a community phone. The most traditional ones invite prospective customers to "Drop us a card and we will call you."

Entrepreneurs post their business cards on bulletin boards in stores, restaurants, or community phone booths. Accumulated cards also serve as an address and telephone directory of sorts. Some Amish children collect business cards, much as children in the larger society amass sports trading cards. This activity socializes Amish youngsters into a community where business is an assumed and approved vocational option.

Many businesses hire ad agencies to create attractive brochures. One brochure designer noted that although non-Amish businesses conspicuously announce their name and address on the cover, Amish firms highlight the product itself. Sometimes the enterprise name will only be listed on the inside or back of the brochure. Striking a deal with promotional necessity, the Amish have chosen to advertise their products while trying to keep a low personal profile.

Brochures also pose a challenge to the traditional taboo on photography. Although the Amish oppose the vanity expressed in human portraits, they generally permit photos of objects. Occasionally, youth will appear in advertising photos because unbaptized children are not bound by church regulations. In one case, an entrepreneur's children were in school when the photographer arrived to shoot a brochure. Undaunted, the manufacturer went to a neighboring Amish family and borrowed their preschool children for the shot. The bulk of promotional photos, however, appear without people. A few businesses have developed full-color catalogs filled with photographs of their products.

Retail advertising in newspapers is rather common. Due to their low cost and guaranteed circulation, print ads offer a cost-effective means of publicity. However, few Amish businesses advertise in the two Lancaster County daily newspapers. Instead, Amish entrepreneurs tend to use specialty papers and directories to promote their businesses. Those that target an Amish clientele advertise in ethnic newspapers that circulate in Amish Communities. *The Budget* and *Die Botschaft* (The Message) both issue weekly editions filled with short news columns from correspondents across the country.[4] *Die Botschaft* only prints correspondence from Old Order writers and will not print ads that violate the Old Order moral code. Ads promoting television, videotapes, and self-esteem books, for example, are off-limits. Advertising in ethnic newspapers heightens a firm's ties to the church and the ethnic community.

Amish businesses with farm-related products frequently buy space in *Lancaster Farming,* an agricultural newspaper that circulates from New York to the Carolinas. The paper is widely read among the Amish, although they represent only a small fraction of its readers. Some Amish businesses with listed phone numbers appear in the yellow pages of the Lancaster telephone book.[5] An Old Order newspaper, *Plain Communities Business Exchange,* appeared for the first time in November 1993. Devoted exclusively to Old Order business concerns, it soon became a popular medium for advertising. Published in the Lancaster area, it enjoys national circulation.

One measure of the growing Amish commitment to advertising is found in the *Lancaster County Business Directory.* The 300-page directory is filled

TABLE 9.1

Number and Type of Selected Businesses Advertising in the Lancaster County Business Directory

Type of Business	Number
General woodworking	100
Household furniture	77
Lawn furniture and ornaments	65
Welding and machine shops	55
Storage barns/sheds	52
Builders and masons	44
Playground equipment/playhouses	24

Source: Lancaster County Business Directory, 2003.
Note: These are the largest categories of businesses listed in the *Directory.* A few businesses may not be Amish owned.

with over 1,000 attractive ads, the bulk of which feature Amish or Amish-related firms (see table 9.1). The directory began in 1988 with 80 ads on 46 pages. Within ten years, it jumped to 700 ads displayed on 200 pages with a distribution of 50,000 copies. Sales agents for the directory take photos of Amish products and write attractive display copy. Many ads appear in full color glossy print. The index of the directory lists some 400 types of business and product lines.[6]

A growing annual trade market that brings Amish producers and wholesale dealers together also signals the growing Amish commitment to promotion. Begun in 1994 in a large auction barn, the trade market is a bonanza for outside buyers, who can see and compare hundreds of products in a few hours instead of searching for shops on obscure back country roads. Amish producers rent a booth for two days where they can display their wares—furniture, storage barns, playground toys, leather products and crafts—to wholesale buyers from many states. Although it is organized like a trade show, the organizers were careful to call it a "trade market" to avoid offending longstanding Amish traditions against ostentatious and showy display—farm shows, fairs, and other worldly exhibitions.[7] Beginning with about three dozen Amish booths and two hundred wholesale buyers, the trade market soon grew to more than three hundred producers and a thousand wholesale buyers from many states. Organizers also added a complimentary feature: a reverse market for firms selling lumber, hydraulics tools, and other equipment to Amish shops. The mostly non-Amish suppliers rented space to display their products to hundreds of Amish shop owners in an annual two-day event.

The growth of Amish businesses has spurred competition within the Amish community. As shops proliferate and become more specialized,

◆

Amish shop owners inspect products at a trade market organized by Amish
businessmen. Some of the markets display Amish-made products for wholesale
dealers. Other markets exhibit special manufacturing equipment for Amish
shop owners.

they frequently compete directly with each other for both Amish and non-Amish customers. The dynamics of internal competition have also propelled the growing interest in marketing and advertising.

Promotion and Public Relations

Promotional trinkets are another common way of publicizing Amish businesses. Calendars, mugs, pens, thermometers, rain gauges, letter openers, and rulers—all emblazoned with a business name—are frequent handouts. Although many entrepreneurs view such items as a token of thanks for patronage, the items also promote visibility. The most common giveaway items are calendars. One business gives calendars with large colored pictures of different styles of Amish buggies across the United States. Medium-size wall calendars are especially popular, because their lovely pictures make nice decorative pieces in Amish homes. Although encouraged not to adorn their homes with paintings or photographs, picture calendars are permitted because of their functional purpose. But even then there are limits. Amish businesses generally do not distribute calendars that include close-up pictures of people.

A few business owners have begun distributing T-shirts and baseball caps imprinted with their business name. Such advertising marks a departure from Amish tradition because the Amish do not wear T-shirts and bill caps. "There was a time they would never think of buying bill caps," says one advertising agent who has handled Amish accounts for years. "Our sales reps don't push them [T-shirts and bill caps] because they know most Amish wouldn't want them," the agent continues. "But we sell them at the Amish request." The lures of advertising in this case have led some owners to use promotional items that are otherwise forbidden for church members. Here, the moral parameters have created another negotiated agreement of sorts, for the Amish distribute, but do not wear, these novel advertising specialties.

Beyond product advertising, many businesses also engage in broader efforts to enhance public relations. Many Amish businessmen and farmers serve as members of local volunteer fire companies. Their participation is acknowledged and appreciated by neighbors and other non-Amish businesses, who rely on the quick response of local firemen in rural areas. Many volunteer fire companies hold benefit auctions or dinners to raise funds for their operating expenses. Amish businesses not only donate products, money, and time for such endeavors, but they also purchase space for fund-raising ads in promotional fliers.

During the Christmas season, the owner of a produce market in an urban area set up tables to collect donated food and children's gifts. He gave the gifts to local churches and family shelters. "I want to be a part of the area," the Amish owner explained. "I want to help the area. I don't like the image that we're going down there to get their money and scoot back to Lancaster." His market also regularly provides free space for local charity groups to conduct fund-raising campaigns. Being "part of the area" is a constant struggle for Amish businesspeople, who in many ways straddle two worlds. Rooted in the ethnic community, entrepreneurs venture daily into the public marketplace, which tests personal convictions and group loyalty. Interacting with non-Amish businesses becomes routine, yet remains problematic.

Promotion is a delicate issue for a people who espouse self-effacement and humility. Bowing to the necessity of advertising, Amish firms have nevertheless negotiated modest means of presenting themselves on the public stage. Non-Amish distributors who develop and operate the Web sites, as noted before, typically handle Internet advertising. Shying away from individualistic promotion and eschewing electronic media, Amish businesses have adopted promotional techniques congruent with their ethnic values. As they have entered the marketplace, they have allowed their cultural heritage to shape their public posture.

Professional Ties

Amish entrepreneurs, new to the business world and anchored in their three-hundred-year history of cultural separatism, are ambivalent about participating in business organizations, chambers of commerce, and regional trade groups. Preaching separation from the world for centuries, the Amish church has been wary of "worldly" connections. Using biblical imagery of the yoke of oxen, such entanglements are often called "an unequal yoke." The Amish fear that being "yoked" with outsiders in a common harness will unwittingly snare them into practices and activities they oppose—such as lawsuits and flashy self-promotion. These associations, the Amish worry, might eventually drag them into the whirlpool of assimilation.

At the same time, however, many business groups appear quite benign even to the tender Amish conscience. Trade groups that simply promote products or hold educational seminars do not necessarily threaten Amish values. Although participation in such groups is not, strictly speaking, off-limits to Amish entrepreneurs, the church certainly does not encourage such outside ties. A few entrepreneurs have joined the ranks of Lancaster's commercial associations, but most Amish businesspeople keep a respectful distance.

A number of business groups in Lancaster County welcome Amish membership, but participation is weak. The Building Industry Association of Lancaster County, one of the larger local trade groups, holds regular meetings, seminars, and a well-attended trade show. The few Amish builders who have joined the association operate more progressive firms involved in specialty work—custom fencing, copper roofing and spouting, or whirlpool installation. Neither their products nor their involvement reflect traditional Amish carpentry.

Several Amish contractors participate in the group's annual trade show, but they attend members' meetings and other seminars only sporadically. The handful of Amish contractors who participate in the builders' group does so to meet new customers at public trade exhibits rather than to enjoy the camaraderie of professional peers. The fraternal aspects are neither important nor attractive to Amish entrepreneurs, who derive their social identity from family and church.

As early as 1896, a Chamber of Commerce and Industry had formed in

Lancaster.[8] With more than 3,000 members today, the Lancaster Chamber of Commerce is the area's largest business advocacy group.[9] The few Amish entrepreneurs who have cautiously joined the chamber are typically engaged in manufacturing and join primarily to make customer contacts. Chamber members receive a directory of members and a mailing list, which Amish affiliates may use to contact new clients. With several notable exceptions, Amish entrepreneurs rarely attend chamber meetings and seminars, nor do they participate in the group's political lobbying or advocacy efforts. For its part, however, the chamber has paid attention to issues of concern to Amish enterprises—especially zoning and commercial ordinances in local municipalities. The chamber has also worked to allow farm-related businesses to operate in agricultural districts, which, of course, benefits the Amish.

Unlike local trade groups, the National Federation of Independent Businesses (NFIB) is a private small-business network operating across North America. The NFIB is active in Lancaster County, and federation officials estimate that some two hundred Amish individuals, about half of whom are farmers, hold membership in the NFIB.[10] The surprising participation of the Amish likely stems from the fact that the NFIB employs a traveling representative to solicit memberships. Federation officials are able to win some Amish entrepreneurs by speaking to their traditional fears of government encroachment and the creeping tentacles of the "welfare state." Other Amish join to learn from the traveling representative, who serves somewhat as a business consultant. A modest membership fee and use of the word "independent" in the group's title attract Amish who feel that affiliation will not compromise their autonomy.

The NFIB primarily engages in political lobbying. Because the Amish have historically shunned the world of politics, their involvement in a political interest group is a surprising move that has nudged some of them toward greater political awareness. Several times a year the federation conducts issue referenda among its members. Although Amish members do respond to the organization's polling on particular issues, they often do not vote in public elections. They are more likely to express their views to a private lobby group than to vote at the public ballot box. Such activity, they feel, would implicate them in activities of government and blur the separation of church and state.[11]

Encouraged by NFIB mailings and group representatives, however, some Amish members have gone to the polls. One Amish contractor carefully studies the group's voting guide before voting each November. A mason contractor had hoped to travel to Washington, D.C., for a national NFIB meeting but was unable to make the trip because of other obligations. An NFIB representative noted that a number of Amish members have become more politically active as they have read federation materials over the years. On the other hand, most Amish businesspeople have avoided membership in such groups. To the practical Amish mind, membership in a distant lobbying group that produces dubious results hardly warrants an annual fee. Others are cautious about affiliating with any politically oriented group. So although some Amish entrepreneurs have joined the federation, most remain skeptical.

Tourism

In 1957 as the number of annual visitors to Lancaster County approached one million, the Lancaster Chamber of Commerce established a tourism committee to coordinate and promote tourism. Ten years later the organization moved to a new suburban location, and later it became an independent, self-supporting agency.[12] Now called the Pennsylvania Dutch Convention and Visitors Bureau, it serves both local businesses and upwards of seven million yearly visitors to Lancaster County.[13]

Most first-time and many repeat tourists visit the bureau to locate lodging, restaurants, attractions, and shopping opportunities. Several hundred enterprises hold membership in the bureau, which displays and distributes free literature and promotes tourism.[14] The bureau's annual "Free Map and Visitor's Guide" lists member establishments and locates them on a large map, which visitors find useful. The bureau does not highlight Amish-owned businesses but features all member firms on an equal basis.

Lancaster's Amish have a love/hate affair with tourism. Although some church members resent the touristic intrusion and the invasion of their privacy, others gladly cooperate in tourist enterprises. In fact, 10 percent of Amish businesses report that sales to tourists account for more than half of their retail volume. A few Amish firms rely entirely on tourist dollars. Dozens of Amish establishments are closely linked to tourism, and many others lean on it for marginal income. Church members often work in restaurants, stores, and motels owned by non-Amish who cater to visitors.[15]

Despite their practical involvement in tourist-related businesses, few Amish entrepreneurs are affiliated with, or hold membership in, the Visitors Bureau. Women entrepreneurs are more heavily involved in bureau membership, because the firms they operate tend to be aligned with tourism. Single women head up some of the member enterprises and married female entrepreneurs manage others. Amish members of the bureau have not tried to capitalize on their Amish identity. Only one shop announces that it is "Amish owned & operated." Enterprises owned by non-Amish, however, often deliberately try to promote the Amish name.

The Amish affiliates of the bureau do participate in some of the organ-

◆

An Amish manufacturer of vinyl fences displays samples outside its plant for tourists and other onlookers.

ization's regular activities—the annual meeting and member seminars. Bureau-sponsored workshops on improving business skills, increasing sales, and designing brochures draw Amish participation as well. One Amish member called the bureau staff for advice on how to prepare an advertisement. A bureau executive voiced appreciation for the group's Amish members and noted that the bureau has "every reason to believe that" Amish entrepreneurs participate "with the blessing of the church."[16] In fact, an Amish minister is one of the members. Beyond formal membership, several other Amish enterprises have lent symbolic support to the bureau by accepting public contracts with the agency. When the bureau expanded its headquarters in 1980, a number of Amish contractors received subcontracts for portions of the job. As a result, Amish carpenters constructed much of the visitors center.

Like those firms that participate in the builders' association or the Lancaster Chamber of Commerce, Amish members of the Visitors Bureau often lead more progressive enterprises that are comfortable with outside connections. Nevertheless, Amish businesses across the spectrum are notably cautious about joining outside trade associations. Participation in ethnic trade groups, however, is quite another matter.

Amish Trade Guilds

Skirting professional outside business groups does not mean the Amish disdain ethnic trade group involvement. Indeed, their historic patterns encourage banding together for common purposes. Church-based mutual aid groups receive strong support from members.[17] Many Amish farmers and businesspeople are also active members of local volunteer fire companies. The recent foray into business, however, has given rise to a number of new Amish trade guilds that serve as an alternative to worldly trade associations.

These ethnic occupational fraternities are loosely coupled and carry little of the prestige and clout of public trade associations. Unlike their secular counterparts, the ethnic guilds have no formal membership, annual dues, or public lobby efforts. In the family-style atmosphere of Amish culture, participants often call the gatherings "reunions" or "meetings," not conventions. The reunions combine fellowship and trade talk, and provide access to many ethnic resources. In an Amish nod to wisdom, the technical input comes from older, seasoned entrepreneurs, not professional experts or itinerant speakers. Questions from novice entrepreneurs may set the direction of discussion, but the response of business veterans shapes the content of the program.

Amish harness makers are one of several guilds that hold a well-attended yearly gathering. Scheduled for the third Friday of each July, the meeting rotates from settlement to settlement across North America. Generally the larger communities host the meetings, since the gatherings require room and board for hundreds of participants. Unlike some worldly conventions, which pitch their programs as a getaway from home, Amish trade reunions typically welcome spouses and children.

A standing committee of six harness makers convenes the reunion each year. The six represent various states and settlements, but their selection is informal and self-perpetuating. Committee members serve as long as they are able and then find their own replacement. Although the reunion is primarily Amish, a conservative Mennonite currently chairs the standing committee, because of his easy access to a telephone. In addition to some Old Order Mennonites, sales representatives from various leather companies and harness suppliers also attend.

Those attending the reunion usually arrive on Thursday—while the standing committee is planning the next day's program. Thursday also includes an auction of used harness-making equipment and materials. The sale is a highlight for many. It permits experienced leather workers to dispose of older equipment, while allowing newcomers access to inexpensive tools. Meanwhile, wives, children, and other family members visit and play nearby, adding to a reunion atmosphere that fosters the integration of work and family.

Counting family members, as many as five hundred people may attend the all-day Friday program. The activities begin when the local host welcomes all attendees and explains procedures. Then harness makers from the local area speak in turn, describing their latest products and specialty lines. They share unusual orders, novel products, and innovative equipment. Representatives of leather companies often present a show-and-tell of their latest products. The program includes a general question-and-answer period. The host, acting as moderator, takes questions from the floor. Shop owners pose specific technical queries as well as general questions or broad requests for advice. Everyone is free to offer suggestions. The gathering often closes with door prizes, which serve as advertising. Shop owners and sales representatives donate samples of new products or tools. Someone holds up each item, describes it, and announces the donor. Using a random drawing of registered attendees, prizes are dispensed.

Like the harness makers, Old Order tax preparers have formed a similar support group. A number of Amish and Old Order Mennonites prepare taxes during the winter for supplemental income. Despite their lack of formal education, the tax accountants are highly knowledgeable in tax laws and skilled in preparing complicated returns. Although no Amish have become certified public accountants, many prepare personal, farm, and small-business returns for scores of Amish and Mennonite clients. Some perform accounting functions on a regular basis for Old Order firms.

Largely self-taught, Amish accountants advise each other in interpreting the ever-changing tax laws. Each fall many accountants attend tax courses offered by commercial companies and public seminars sponsored by state universities. In mid-December, they gather for a day to pool their knowledge, share seminar handouts, and discuss thorny changes in federal regulations. Novices receive extensive assistance from seasoned preparers. Everyone is free to pose questions, clarify tax codes, or offer helpful suggestions.

By 1990, about two dozen Amish tax preparers were attending the trade reunion. Increasingly, some of the conservative Mennonites began to employ personal computers in their bookkeeping. As a result, the gathering now includes discussions about computerization. This turn of events has led to a new twist in the format of the meetings. Participants continue to attend the one-day gathering in December, but those who work without computers meet again—on the following day—for a discussion of manual calculations. Although the entire group has formed a fraternal bond, the second gathering is an even closer group, sharing not only technical knowledge but also friendship and a commitment to prepare taxes without electronic assistance.[18]

Amish carriage makers, metal workers, woodworkers, and schoolteachers also hold regular trade reunions to discuss work-related problems and share techniques and products. In addition, Amish entrepreneurs who manufacture farm equipment often attend the national Horse Progress Days each summer, which typically are hosted in an Amish community. Both Amish and non-Amish inventors demonstrate their newest models of horse-drawn equipment.[19]

The guilds provide fraternal support even seasoned entrepreneurs crave, because smaller settlements do not have large cadres of specialized businesses. Despite a dozen shops in a given church district, few are involved in the same craft. A harness maker told of a neighboring farmer who jokingly complained that farmers never get to travel across the country for a farmers' reunion. The shop owner reminded his neighbor that every Sunday after church, the farmers discuss crops, cattle, and the weather all afternoon, while the businessmen sit and listen. "I only get together with other harness makers once a year," the young man retorted, but "you farmers talk together every week."

The rise of business gatherings has paralleled the growth of small enterprises. Trade reunions are popular for several reasons. The gatherings provide excuses for memorable trips and family relaxation in a culture where vacations are frowned upon as pleasure-seeking frivolities. Reunions also provide informal networking within the business community. The gatherings pool the cultural and social capital of Amish communities across the country. New business contacts, product information, and technical advice readily flow throughout these informal gatherings. Newcomers in business find the trade reunions helpful places to solicit advice and encouragement in the context of the church.

Craft guilds and trade reunions provide entrepreneurs access to the technical resources of the ethnic community and keep their identity rooted in the church. These ethnic guilds spur both competition and cooperation by providing a context for learning about competitive products as well as for strengthening social networks. Ethnic trade groups reinforce an Old Order identity and energize their participants with good feelings about their vocation and their people.

Promoting their products and developing professional ties, entrepreneurs occasionally step across the cultural lines of Amish propriety. However, they face even greater challenges to traditional norms as they cope with litigation and liability in the public arena.

10. Coping with Litigation and Liability

These Amish businesses aren't going to just roll over anymore.
— A LAWYER

Going to Law

Entering the public marketplace has strained the church's traditional teaching on litigation and insurance. The historic Amish commitment to nonresistance—not using force of any sort to resist evil—received a fresh review as business owners found themselves considering insurance coverage and visiting courtroom chambers. Moreover, the Amish culture rests on oral communication and verbal agreements based on trust, not written legal documents. Commitments to these principles long upheld by the church began to sag under the weight of profits, investments, and sizable inventories. In response to these challenges, the church has bridled some questionable business practices, placed hurdles in the way of others, and negotiated cultural detours around other thorny issues.

As more and more people plunge into business, Amish opposition to litigation has faced new challenges.[1] The Amish have regularly used lawyers to draw up wills, conduct transactions, and establish legal partnerships. Yet they have always been wary of using the law to protect their personal or business rights. "Going to law," as the Amish put it, is contrary to the submissive spirit of nonresistance that undergirds their culture. Members are not to defend themselves with lawyers or courtroom tactics; rather, they are called to follow the meek example of Jesus and bear injustice without complaint. Indeed, filing a lawsuit is cause for excommunication. Although the Amish have reluctantly appeared in court to defend their principles or to test government regulations, they oppose plaintiff litigation and will not initiate lawsuits.[2]

Involvement in the marketplace has pushed the church to the brink of using legal force. Cutthroat politics in the world of commerce raises the specter of lawsuits—both those filed against the Amish by disgruntled customers or competitors and those filed by the Amish themselves when they have no other way to settle financial disputes with outsiders. While Amish society functions under an umbrella of trust and integrity, the larger culture often operates under the veiled threat of legal force. The authority of the state—police, magistrates, and judges—stems from its legal ability to enforce decisions and rulings, even with violence if necessary. Such coercive force collides with Gelassenheit, the core value of Amish culture. The Amish commitment to nonresistance and dependence on divine solutions makes them uncomfortable with a legal system based on force.

If word spreads in the community that a business is filing a suit, the owner can expect a visit from ordained leaders. One entrepreneur who was called to testify in a bankruptcy hearing explained, "The ministers came and checked over my books and records to make sure that I wasn't filing a suit. They were satisfied that everything was in order." Had the ministers found evidence of litigation, the owner would have been asked to confess his transgression or face excommunication.

As Amish enterprises grow in size and number, they often become entangled with legal issues. Rather than bringing legal charges against offenders within their community, the Amish have tried to resolve problems within the authority structure of the church, which serves as a court of sorts. They are reluctant to bring charges against outsiders who have wronged them. Shoplifting has hurt some Amish retail businesses, yet the church bars storeowners from prosecuting thieves. In their eyes, turning a robber or shoplifter over to civil authorities violates the spirit of nonresistant love. Some merchants post vaguely threatening signs to deter shoplifters. Others are uncertain how to respond. Said one storeowner: "About all we can do is let them know that we're watching. There have been a few times we've actually caught them, you know, with the stuff, and we've talked with them. But what can you do? It's terrible the way society is these days."

Despite their aversion to the legal system, the Amish are sometimes inadvertently pulled into its web. When two Amish teens employed by a fellow church member died in a work-related accident, their deaths were mourned but accepted as "part of God's will." The state, on the other hand, routinely investigates all nonagricultural on-the-job deaths—"God's will" notwithstanding. When Labor Department investigators discovered that no charges had been filed against the employer, they proceeded to enter a case in the name of the boys' families as required by law. This sudden turn of events shook the Amish community because it now appeared that two Amish families were suing another church member.

The church pressed the families to drop the suit, but they were unable to do so because Workers' Compensation required it. The businesses, though Amish-controlled, were incorporated and thus not exempt from the legal jurisdiction of Workers' Compensation. In an effort to satisfy both the church and the state, the Amish asked an attorney to settle the case out of court. The lawyer arranged a modest out-of-court settlement agreeable to all parties. Had the accident not involved the Amish, it would likely have resulted in a multimillion-dollar courtroom confrontation. The Amish acceptance of death and their refusal to sue resulted in a very different settlement. Nevertheless, the whole situation underscores the ways in which the Amish can become unwittingly entangled in legal events beyond their immediate control.

Collecting Debts

A more troubling issue for Amish entrepreneurs concerns the degree of force they will use in collecting bad debts. During the 1980s a number of businesses developed what one observer called "a major problem" with uncollected bills. Knowing that the Amish do not sue, some non-Amish began systematically bilking Amish businesses. The Amish coped with this dilemma in four ways: they used collection agencies, filed formal complaints, used confessed judgment notes, and engaged third-party litigation.

Amish wholesalers were especially susceptible to unpaid bills because they often delivered large orders and offered new accounts a customary line of credit. Unfamiliar with business law and unwilling to sue, those who were bilked had little recourse for recovering their losses. Although many had legal counsel on other aspects of their businesses, they hesitated to report their collection difficulties, knowing that lawsuits were off-limits in their moral order. Additionally, because many of the defaulting customers lived outside Pennsylvania, the owners assumed that any legal action would be costly, complicated, and time-consuming.

One gazebo builder, frustrated after months of trying to collect debts from a wholesaler in Virginia, hired a truck and, under the cover of darkness, picked up the unpaid gazebos from a display lot and brought them back to Pennsylvania. For other owners, the bad debts piled up faster than their businesses could absorb them. Although unwilling to "go to law," they decided that something must be done. Some turned to bill collection agencies that had offered to settle bad accounts. These private agencies provided a quieter, less public way of settling differences. Because they avoided legal entanglements, private collection efforts received the church's guarded approval.

Some bill collectors, however, exploited the Amish as much as did the debtors themselves. Taking advantage of Amish trust and naiveté, collection agencies promised quick action to recover debts. With a mere verbal agreement, some agencies began proceedings against delinquent customers. The collection agents then insisted that Amish owners sign a contract because the agency had already taken action against the debtor. Bowing to the pressure tactics, some owners signed collection contracts. But the contracts, in some cases, were as expensive as the unpaid accounts and left the Amish feeling confused and angry.

Frustrated with debt collectors, a few entrepreneurs asked local district magistrates for help in collecting bills. Although local justices are part of the state judicial system, the Amish did not view them as a court and were willing to talk with them. Realizing that some collection agencies were preying on the Amish community, sympathetic magistrates urged the Amish to bring overdue bills to their offices. The justice then drafted a formal complaint and sent a registered letter to the debtor, hoping that the implied threat might produce some action. Some business owners also had their lawyers draft and mail similar complaints. This strategy also proved unworkable because debtors stalled, contested complaints, and demanded hearings. Some Amish were reluctant to attend hearings because they were too much like a court trial, so they often dropped their cases. Others who did attend hearings often saw their complaints dismissed in the face of sophisticated arguments from lawyers representing delinquent parties. To avoid the appearance of a lawsuit, the Amish often did not take lawyers to the hearings and were outmaneuvered when they spoke on their own behalf.

As businesses grew, the problem of debt recovery persisted, underscoring the inability of registered complaints to produce fair settlements. Some lawyers working for the Amish proposed a solution by suggesting that customers sign a "confessed judgment note" as part of any sales contract. If payment was not forthcoming as stipulated by the contract, the note was automatically registered in court against the defaulting business and a lien was placed against the customer's property. The effect at that time was almost identical to a trial verdict. The judgment note seemed like a good resolution. The Amish could remain somewhat aloof from the judicial system yet be reasonably sure that their bills would be paid. They did not have to file an actual lawsuit or appear in court, but the result was nearly the same; moreover, the weight of the court was behind them.

But even this novel arrangement was not always satisfactory. In the first place, the Amish were hesitant to have customers sign such an agreement, which seemed to imply mistrust and ill will. The note offended honest buyers, while less veracious individuals, knowing its meaning, were able to argue their way around it. They asked business owners to document the legal foundation of the note. When owners were unable to do so, buyers

♦

A non-Amish dealer picks up a wholesale purchase of gazebos at an Amish shop. Commercial interaction with the outside world has raised a variety of new legal issues for the Amish community, including collecting debts from out-of-state buyers.

refused to sign, saying owners had no right to ask anyone to sign a document they could not explain. Meanwhile, the Pennsylvania confessed judgment law changed, making signed judgments open for review, appeal, and the possibility of public hearings. Again, the Amish wanted no part of such hearings, which would occur in the county courthouse.

By the late 1980s, the situation had reached a critical point. Bill collection, formal complaints, and confessed judgment notes had all failed. By this time, some non-Amish partners proposed filing suits in their own names against debtors. Neither the business nor the Amish partners would be named as plaintiffs. Sometimes grudgingly, other times with encouragement, the Amish agreed. The cases were called and quickly settled in favor of the suing partner, much to the surprise of some debtors, who thought they were insulated from their nonresistant creditors.

Other Amish enterprises without non-Amish partners decided to follow suit. Temporarily signing over their rights of action to a non-Amish friend or to their own lawyers, a few business owners filed suits against bad debtors without having Amish names associated with the case. Although this is somewhat problematic because assigned rights are only temporary and are directly derived from the owner, some church leaders have reluctantly allowed this form of indirect legal action.

After a number of successful non-Amish-partner and third-party law-suits in the late 1980s and early 1990s, debt collection problems subsided. Although the suits were relatively few, they sent a powerful message to those engaged in systematic exploitation. One lawyer noted, "People began to realize that these businesses aren't going to just roll over any more."

The Amish have negotiated a delicate cultural compromise with the legal system of adversarial justice. They will not file a lawsuit or allow their names to be associated with a court case. Neither will they appear in court. If their public testimony or presence is required at a hearing or as part of a trial, they will typically have the proceedings dropped. At the same time, they have granted the legal system the legitimacy that comes from necessity. Caught without recourse to debt collection, they have turned to lawyers and to the judiciary. Without making regular use of the law, they have used the threat of law as well as third-party lawsuits to protect their interests and to break the cycle of bad debts.

Amish Arbitration

Although the Amish have agreed to cooperate with the judicial system in certain cases involving outsiders, they remain adamant in rejecting the law to settle disputes among themselves. Instead of resorting to litigation, they seek mediation within the church. The result is similar to the modern use of binding arbitration. However, in the Amish version, binding acceptance is based on moral, rather than legal, authority. The forces of tradition and submission to religious authority, not the coercive force of law, bring dis-agreements to resolution.

When members find themselves in a business dispute they cannot re-solve, church leaders typically intervene. The bishop or bishops involved consider the case and decide whether they are able to judge it themselves. Giving a nod of approval to growing specialization, church leaders may invite other Amish businessmen known for their wisdom and knowledge to serve as mediators.

The mediators meet with each side privately, hearing both sides of the story individually. Later, all parties are brought together, and the arbiters take testimony from those involved in the dispute. Non-Amish persons may be called to offer their perspectives as well. Testimony is given with-out sworn oaths, relying instead on affirmations of the truth. Lawyers are noticeably absent. When the mediating committee renders its judgment, all sides know that it will be the final word. There is no provision for appeal. If amends are to be made or an apology offered, the parties obedi-ently acquiesce. Moral and communal authority enforces the decision.

In some instances, non-Amish persons who have had a conflict with an

Amish business have also settled their differences within the context of the church. Going to church leaders, non-Amish businesspeople have been able to settle their problems without the cost and trouble of the courts. Although church elders will not award a million-dollar settlement, they will use their authority to reconcile disputing parties, achieving sometimes what even the law cannot do by force.

Fire and Storm Insurance

Commercial insurance poses another significant challenge to historic church teaching. Traditionally frowned upon, commercial insurance policies have become more common among individuals engaged in business. The Amish have long avoided commercial insurance, and in the past they have typically created ethnic alternatives to "worldly" commercial plans, symbolized by their barn-raising frolics. Conceding the need for financial planning, they nevertheless still maintain some distance from secular coverage. Yet the new situations that entrepreneurs now face—especially those involving product liability—have brought them back to the bargaining table. As before, the Amish have negotiated new, creative mutual aid programs.

The Amish have historically shunned commercial insurance for a number of reasons.[3] Christians, they believe, should turn to family and church members in times of need, not to government or commercial interests. Reliance on a commercial company compromises their religious principle of separation from the world. Moreover, coverage reflects an individualistic spirit because it shields people from communal responsibility and obligation. Insurance is also built on a fear of the future and, in the case of life insurance, of death. Moreover, insurers often engage in lawsuits, implicating their policyholders as well. Most important, insurance signals a lack of faith in divine protection and care and symbolizes individualistic attempts to control the future.

The Amish seek to face the anxieties of tomorrow by quietly waiting and trusting in divine providence. Wrote one Amish leader who discouraged insurance, "The New Testament teaches that we should not seek to make our future secure by means of earthly possessions." Instead, to the traditional Amish mind, needy members should rely on alms from the church, collected by the deacons. Commercial insurance departs from both the theory and practice of church-based mutual aid. "There is a great difference," the leader noted, because "the world's system of insurance is designed for the protection of one's earthly possessions. . . . In the Scriptural pattern, the situation is reversed. The brethren gladly share of their means to help those who are in need. There are no selfish motives involved."[4] For similar reasons, the Amish have consistently avoided what they call "government insurance" programs—Social Security, Medicare, and Medicaid.

Yet Amish aid has not always been as spontaneous as their commitment to goodwill offerings would imply. The more progressive leaders and church districts have supported organized programs of mutual aid within the church.[5] The more conservative sectors prefer spontaneous mutual aid as needed. At times, the church has developed intentional sharing plans. One of the earliest efforts to organize mutual aid was the Amish Aid Society. Created about 1875, the church-linked group collects a "fire tax" of one dollar per thousand dollars of property value from member families.[6] In the event of a fire or natural disaster, the plan supplies new building materials for a barn raising or house rebuilding. By paying in cash, the plan's managing committee saves thousands of dollars a year. As Amish Aid depletes its coffers, they are replenished with periodic collections. The program has no paid staff, agents, or profits. Although participation is strictly voluntary, most families in the settlement are members of the plan.

Amish Aid enjoys wide support among church members and leaders, and many businesses have made ready use of its protection. Almost all enterprises are members of the plan. Virtually the only ones who buy commercial fire insurance are those who own rental properties and have non-Amish tenants. If the occupants of rental buildings are not church members, the property does not qualify for the Amish plan. Amish Aid had operated successfully for nearly a century when another group of laymen decided to copy its success. This time, changes in the surrounding culture, not the vicissitudes of storm and fire, forced their hand.

Liability Coverage

As the United States became more litigious during the 1950s and 1960s, Amish families were increasingly caught in precarious situations. An accident on the road or an injury on an Amish property could trigger a crippling lawsuit. Although the Amish had always sought to make fair restitution when responsible for wrong, they were unaccustomed to the idea of punitive damages. Such payments—often far beyond the real costs of an accident—became typical in courtroom awards. These new and sometimes frightening realities gave birth to a new form of ethnic aid.

After the mid-twentieth century, some families began buying liability insurance for their horse and carriage because of legal complications surrounding highway travel with horse-drawn vehicles. By 1963, one observer estimated that some eight to nine hundred commercial liability policies were in Amish hands. Some church members, uncomfortable with this form of commercial insurance, organized Amish Liability Aid in 1965 as an alternative. Like the earlier fire and storm program, Liability Aid assessed members in order to build a sufficient reserve fund. The fund covers the costs of non-Amish who are involved in an accident or injury involving Amish property. As funds dwindle, the directors take up new collections. Many Amish did not consider Liability Aid an insurance program as such because it was "protection for the other fellow" rather than for themselves. Within a short period of time, some eight hundred families joined the ethnic plan, although others still sought commercial coverage. Newly established business enterprises often join Amish Liability Aid for liability coverage.

Some businesses faced further liability needs when their companies became involved in vehicle use and ownership because motor vehicles are required to carry insurance. During the 1970s some Amish businesses used cars or trucks owned by non-Amish employees. These employees, of course, were responsible for their own liability coverage. Some business owners moved away from using employee-owned vehicles because of liability problems. Employees—and thus vehicles—could quit at any time, leaving the business in a jolt. Some of the larger firms evolved into joint partnerships where a non-Amish partner provided a vehicle with liability insurance.

Entrepreneurs who are not in mixed partnerships and who do not wish to have employees own company trucks seek other options. As noted before, a few bishops allow church members to own vehicles in the fictitious name of their business. Another increasingly common strategy is leasing. In either case, the entrepreneur is responsible to hold commercial insurance, although not legally owning the vehicle. Most leasing contracts, however, also include collision insurance in the terms of the lease. Although enterprises using motor vehicles are required to have commercial liability coverage, such plans are not as offensive to the church because they are viewed as protection for other drivers rather than for the Amish themselves.[7] Nevertheless, the growth of business has increased the need for liability coverage.

Medical Insurance

Health care has also created insurance problems. Rising health costs in the 1960s prompted some Amish families to buy hospitalization coverage. The Amish do not accept Medicare or Medicaid payments but rely instead on alms money from the church to cover major doctor bills. In 1969, a group of laymen began an informal hospitalization plan similar to the fire-and-property program. Known as Amish Church Aid, the medical plan sought to coordinate giving and sharing across the settlement. Families—regardless of the number of children—contribute $150 per month (single adults, half that amount). After paying a thousand-dollar deductible, families are reimbursed through the Church Aid fund. Like the other plans, provisions are made for extra collections if central funds dry up. Supporters laud the program as "the perfect opportunity to help other people in a way that lets you remain anonymous."

However, not all church members have joined the plan, and some leaders do not permit their congregations to participate because the fund, in their view, is too much like commercial insurance. By the early 1990s about half of Amish households were enrolled in the plan. Many of them lived in the more progressive northern half of Lancaster's Amish community. Households outside the plan cover sizable medical costs by relying on alms money and the generosity of friends and extended family. A few families who did not participate in Church Aid continued to carry commercial health insurance.

About one-fifth of Amish businesses, especially large firms, offer medical benefits to their employees. Several of these offer Church Aid to their Amish employees. If the worker lives in a participating district, some employers make the employee's monthly payments on his or her behalf. In such cases, the owner also provides comparable commercial insurance for non-Amish employees. Some entrepreneurs discovered that their church plans were at times more expensive than standard medical insurance. In some cases, owners dropped out of Church Aid and took up commercial health insurance for themselves and their employees—Amish and non-Amish alike. They continued to contribute to the church's alms fund but sought personal protection in outside plans. Others, citing loyalty to the church, have remained committed to Church Aid, despite its sometimes higher cost, because they are wary of the legal and moral entanglements of commercial insurance.

The church has been unable to bring all Amish businesses into the church-related health plan because it is divided on the matter. If more districts would participate and costs would drop, more entrepreneurs might rejoin Church Aid. Most entrepreneurs offer no coverage and rely on alms funds to supply their own and their employees' needs. Others wholeheartedly support the Church Aid plan, while still others participate in commercial programs. Rather than leading or pushing the church, business owners have mirrored their community's mixed response to medical coverage.[8]

Product Liability

Product liability is perhaps the most important insurance issue facing Amish business owners today. With the rise in consumer litigation, businesses of all types have sought financial protection through product liability plans. Among the Amish, dairy farmers were the first to take out liability coverage for protection against contaminated milk.[9] Growing numbers of manufacturers and contractors also began taking out commercial liability coverage. To counter these trends, the church responded with a plan of its own.

In the early 1990s, business owners established a church-based product liability program. Three factors spurred this development. First, many businesspeople were uncomfortable holding commercial liability policies. Newspapers frequently carried stories of insurance companies initiating lawsuits around the country. The Amish wished to distance themselves from such litigious organizations and hoped to find ways of settling product disputes out of court and in harmony with their cultural values. Second, many Amish manufacturers were losing commercial coverage because their products were considered too risky. "They'd just walk in one day and say 'We don't need you any more,' and [you] couldn't get coverage anywhere else," a stove manufacturer lamented. Finally, Amish construction crews needed product liability insurance in order to win subcontracts. Without liability coverage, Amish builders, roofers, and plumbers were forced to forfeit important work.

The ethnic alternative, Amish Product Liability Aid, was the brainchild of several Amish entrepreneurs. Demonstrating financial creativity and sensitivity to church teaching, the entrepreneurs hoped to create a product liability program similar to the church's other mutual aid programs for fire, health, and accident. The early planners were driven by a desire to strengthen the church. Said one of the organizers, "I thought that as a church family, as a community, we have to do something to help each other out."

After four years of discussion, a group of business leaders approached a half dozen or more senior bishops with the idea. They explained their ethical quandary and proposed a church-based plan to cover product liability. The entrepreneurs wanted the approval of church elders before bringing their plans to the wider fellowship. The bishops presented the idea at one of the semi-annual gatherings of ordained leaders. Church leaders argued that rather than "relying more and more on worldly insurance, which could prove harmful to the Old Order Amish way of life," Product Liability Aid "would show better honor and trust to our Lord, who does not

◆

Air-powered hand tools are sold by this Amish retail store to Amish and non-Amish customers. The manufacture and distribution of products on public markets has introduced product liability concerns for Amish entrepreneurs.

forsake those who trust and rely upon Him according to His will."[10] Following approval by church leaders in 1992, the plan went back to the businesspeople, who launched it within a year.

A board of five laymen oversees the plan, and an advisory board of six ministers and deacons provides ethical counsel. A contact person in each church district provides a direct link to local church districts. The product liability program runs with remarkably little organizational red tape. Unlike the other mutual aid plans, no sign-up is needed; all church members are automatically covered. Equating coverage with church affiliation distances the plan from traditional insurance. When claims arise, the directors meet with the parties and attempt to work out a mutually suitable settlement. After determining the costs, they ask local representatives to collect the needed funds. Collected funds are used to reimburse claims by outsiders, not the Amish who caused the damage.[11]

One of the early cases involved a farmer's tank of spoiled milk, which ruined a large truckload of milk. A church collection reimbursed neighboring non-Amish farmers for their innocent loss without ruining the offending farmer. In another instance, an Amish carpenter had completed a new house. While another contractor was backfilling earth around the building, a wall buckled. The homeowner sued the Amishman for real and punitive damages. The Product Liability Aid board offered to settle out of court and to cover the real damages. The plaintiff accepted. The board divided up the costs and collected freewill donations from church members to cover the loss.

For the fiscal year 2002, over $110,000 was paid because dairy farmers had shipped high-bacteria milk that contaminated good milk from other farmers on bulk tank trucks. Claims for faulty construction work totaled $6,100, and those for spoiled produce $2,700. These product liability costs are remarkably low in the midst of a multimillion dollar ethnic economy.[12]

The church-wide liability program encourages greater product care and safety. Product offenses are no longer private matters between a businessperson and a distant insurance company. Offenses become general church knowledge, creating community pressure to ensure the quality and safety of Amish products.

Some Amish worry that the plan relies too heavily on the good will of others to settle claims out of court. They fear that vengeful individuals could snub the program and ruin any number of firms. Other difficulties surface for partnerships that mix Amish and non-Amish owners. The non-Amish owners are not eligible for coverage under the church plan and need to secure their own policies. However, insurance companies cannot write a policy for only one member of a partnership. In such cases, the Amish partner or partners must obtain commercial coverage.

The story of Product Liability Aid illustrates the complexity of issues faced by Amish enterprises in the world of entrepreneurship. It also reflects the expanding size and scope of Amish business. If shops were merely selling to their own ethnic community, product liability would not be an issue. But, in the words of a gazebo builder, protection is needed, "with all these Amish products being distributed all over the United States and Canada, and some going to Europe." This is especially true, he said, "because there are lots of people out there who will sue at the drop of a hat."[13] Amish entrepreneurs no longer operate as naive newcomers in the world of commerce. Yet the emergence of the liability plan demonstrates a commitment to operate their businesses within the constraints of their cultural tradition. They hope to settle disputes personally, outside the courtroom, and without the entanglements of litigation. Most importantly, Product Liability Aid represents a continuing commitment of entrepreneurs to the church and to mutual aid in a changing economic context.

The Lure of Life Insurance

More problematic for the Amish is the increasing lure of life insurance. Although they have been willing to negotiate acceptable alternatives to other types of financial coverage, the Amish have refused to debate the merits of life insurance. Historically, they have prohibited life insurance, believing that such coverage exploits a matter that rests solely in God's hands. The Amish view such insurance as the merchandising of human life. Moreover, life insurance not only belies trust in God; it also encourages each family to secure its own financial future apart from the church. Yet despite the historical taboo, a scattering of Amish farmers began taking out coverage during the 1960s. The rising cost of land forced some to obtain insurance in order to qualify for farmland mortgages. Most called their policies "savings plans" rather than life insurance and kept their involvement in such plans rather secret.

The growing involvement in business has brought about more life insurance plans. Some Amish entrepreneurs are attracted to life insurance for two reasons. In the first place, unlike farmers, many do not hold large assets in land. They view life insurance as an investment akin to real estate. Second, lawyers and accountants frequently encourage business owners to buy policies. The professionals are not trying to test Amish conviction but merely contending that life insurance is a simple necessity for business people, especially those who carry considerable debt.

Although involving only a small portion of the community, life insurance poses a significant challenge to the church. Given the church's long-standing opposition, it is highly doubtful that leaders could ever fashion an acceptable church-based alternative as they have for property, health, and product liability. The church's firm stand leaves little room for negotiation. Those wanting life insurance need to buy it through commercial carriers, albeit secretly. Church leaders have been able to curb many aspects of the emerging entrepreneurial culture, but life insurance remains elusive. The private nature of such plans keeps them out of public scrutiny and thus makes regulation difficult. If the church grants tacit approval to life insurance, it will mark a quiet concession to business owners.

The threads of Amish life tie faith and work together. There is little separation of religion and everyday life in Amish society, no compartmentalization of the sacred to a few hours on Sunday morning. Religious values imbue all aspects of Amish life. And while business activity remains beneath the sacred canopy of the church, it has produced some creative arrangements in litigation and insurance. These hybrid arrangements reflect the crisscrossing constraints of Amish culture and the legal realities of the marketplace. An even more difficult challenge emerged, however, as Amish entrepreneurs faced the growing tentacles of the welfare state—a story to which we now turn.

11. Negotiating with Caesar

◆

Where does my right stop for your rights?
— AMISH CONTRACTOR

The Amish and the State

Amish involvements in business have stirred new conflicts with the government, conflicts that reflect the cultural tension between Old Order ways and modern society. The impersonal, bureaucratic policies of the modern state sometimes clash with the informal nature of Amish life. An adversarial system of legal justice flies in the face of humility and nonresistance. Except for their early persecution in Europe, the Amish have experienced more conflict with the state in the twentieth century than in any other time of their history.[1]

As conscientious objectors, the Amish have refused to participate in military affairs. Their efforts to educate their own children erupted into a spate of conflicts with the government in the mid-twentieth century. Likewise, the rise of the modern welfare state placed the Amish at odds with government. Social Security and other welfare programs, immunization requirements, workplace regulations, and zoning ordinances all spring from the popular desire to control civic life and to care for the common good. Drawing on modern notions of civic duty, many of these government programs threaten Amish understandings of communal and familial responsibility.

Unlike many modern citizens, the Amish present themselves to the seats of power as humble subjects. Citizens feel a compelling loyalty to the state and expect government to work for them. Subjects, on the other hand, live under the rule of a civil authority from which they receive privileges and freedom. The yielding spirit of Gelassenheit compels the Amish to forfeit claims of rights and produces "humble petitions" and "appeals to our men in authority."[2] Amish attitudes and actions arise from biblical teachings to respect and honor civil officials and from their Anabaptist heritage as social outcasts in Europe. Although non-Amish citizens develop a sense of civic obligation and public duty, Amish devotion tilts toward church, family, and ethnic community.

The Amish may send appeals to government leaders and will meet with key officials, but they rarely try to force the state's hand through marches, protests, or other forms of political action. However, when state requirements conflict with religious conscience, the Amish can become rather stubborn. Indeed, they will accept fines and imprisonment and will even migrate to other locations before surrendering core religious convictions. Their conflicts with the state are usually resolved, not within the traditional avenues of power politics, but through various types of informal negotiation.[3]

A History of Compromise

The forces of modernity have compelled the Amish to modify their ways of dealing with government. Without a centralized organization at the regional or national level, the Amish have sometimes found it difficult to cope with government mandates. Thus, in 1966, some church leaders organized a group known as the National Amish Steering Committee as a means of speaking to officials in Washington about the military draft.[4] Authorizing a single group to speak in a unified voice was a new and unusual step for a church that lacked an organizational structure beyond the local settlement. Members of the Steering Committee are laymen, which ensures that their powers and opinions will not spill over into church doctrine. Although the Steering Committee originally addressed conscription issues, it more recently has spoken to a variety of church and state frictions—Social Security, Workers' Compensation, unemployment insurance, and child labor regulations, to name a few related to business.

Amish firms generally do not work for government agencies, but there are a few exceptions. Under a public contract, a fiberglass manufacturer produces lids for township septic tanks. Another Amish entrepreneur shreds newspapers for a county-sponsored recycling program. Generally, however, entrepreneurs remain aloof from government agencies. Some Amish firms are frightened by the reams of red tape that municipal contracts often entail. One Amish mason lamented government regulations that "keep the small guy out of competition and cost taxpayers a lot of money." Although he once built public restrooms at a township park, the extra expense and complications were so frustrating that he is hesitant to take on similar projects. "You have to have a full-time employee just to handle the paperwork for a job like that," he grumbled.

Frictions between the Amish and the state are often more than mere legal haggles; they are cultural struggles as well. The assimilating forces of the larger society find their regulatory power in government. Consequently, the cultural stakes are high when the Amish tussle with the state. If the church surrenders too much too often to the political order, it endangers the future of Amish society. Thus, when the Amish bargain with government agencies, they negotiate carefully and cautiously.

Negotiating with Washington

Historically, the Amish have fared well in their negotiations with the federal government. Washington, for instance, has permitted alternatives to military conscription, and in 1972 the U.S. Supreme Court granted legitimacy to Amish private education. When Amish and federal officials sit at the bargaining table, the church has generally received favorable settlements that acknowledge the government's authority but also preserve religious freedom.

Social Security triggered a major conflict between the Amish and Washington that festered for years before being resolved.[5] Although the Amish pay all typical taxes—income, sales, property, school, and inheritance—they are conscientiously opposed to Social Security and have struggled to free themselves from its tentacles. They view it as a commercial insurance that would supplant the church's commitment to mutual aid. Established in 1935 as Old Age and Survivors Insurance, Social Security sought to ensure adequate care for aged and orphaned Americans by transferring responsibility to the national government. When Social Security was voluntary for the self-employed, the Amish opted not to use it. In Amish eyes, the care of the elderly, widowed, and orphaned was clearly the responsibility of the church, not the state. In 1955, however, Congress expanded the program to include the self-employed, and conflict erupted when the Amish refused to participate.[6] In 1965, after a decade of controversy, Congress resolved the stalemate by exempting self-employed Amish persons from Social Security and the newly created Medicare system.

With the rise of Amish enterprise, Social Security problems surfaced once again. Amish employees in shops and stores owned by fellow church members were not exempt. Ethnic employers were required to pay Social Security for both their Amish and non-Amish employees. In the 1970s and 1980s, with increasing numbers of businesses sprouting, the situation became acute. In response, some entrepreneurs established multimember partnerships so that employees could be part owners and thus claim self-employed status and exemption. Multimember partnerships proved problematic, however, both from a legal and a practical standpoint.[7]

In 1988, after years of backstage negotiations, Congress exempted the Amish from Social Security if both employer and employee are Amish.[8] Clearly not a blanket exemption, Amish employers must pay Social Security taxes for their non-Amish employees. Furthermore, Amish who work for non-Amish firms must likewise contribute. The exemption encourages the Amish to remain within ethnic networks of employment, which, of course, bolsters the in-group economy.

Since the 1988 congressional exemption, conflicts with the Internal Revenue Service (IRS) have subsided. Nevertheless, as with other businesses, there are occasional audits and problems with compliance. In one case, the IRS charged an Amish grocery store owner with failing to make payroll deductions for non-Amish employees, only to be rebuffed later by the firm's accountant, who proved the IRS wrong. Still, the Amish are not exempt from federal tax laws. The IRS did close one business in the late 1980s, when an audit revealed a confusion of business and personal records. The family was, in effect, "living out of the cash register" explained another Amish person. Somewhat confused but undaunted by the ordeal, the entrepreneur created a new record-keeping system and opened a new woodworking business, which has operated smoothly.

Many of the federal tax policies governing retirement savings are geared to Social Security laws. Because of their exemption from Social Security, the Amish are only able to make annual maximum contributions of $12,000 to Individual Retirement Accounts. U.S. Representative Joseph R. Pitts of eastern Pennsylvania proposed tax law changes in 2001 that would allow Amish people to deduct contributions to three other retirement plans: Keogh accounts, simple employee pensions, and simple IRAs, all of which allow larger contributions than regular IRAs.[9] The growing business income made all of these private retirement accounts more attractive to the Amish community.

Safety standards have produced another area of conflict between Amish businesses and the federal government. The Occupational Safety and Health Administration (OSHA) required, among other things, that construction workers and employees in some manufacturing firms wear regulation hard hats. Hundreds of Amish workers received furloughs when they refused to comply with the law and wore traditional Amish hats to work. A symbol of ethnic identity and affiliation, the church has always insisted that men wear the prescribed Amish hat when they appear in public.

A member of the National Amish Steering Committee made several trips to Washington and met with Labor Department officials to work out alternative arrangements. Negotiation between the federal government and the National Amish Steering Committee resolved the impasse in 1972, when the government exempted Amish workers from the hard-hat requirement on religious grounds. However, Amish workers must wear the prescribed Amish hat in order to obtain the waiver. Ironically, this compromise puts the government in the unusual position of enforcing the church's own standards of dress. In practice, of course, the church, not the state, ensures that members don their symbolic hats during work.[10]

Other OSHA rulings establish workplace safety standards. Most Amish businesses are small enough to be exempt from many of the regulations. Larger firms, however, must comply, although many owners consider the rules unnecessary and confusing. The Amish feel that their own safety record speaks for itself. In the words of a knowledgeable Amishwoman, "The businesses and shops actually have a good record. They have a very good safety record." Moreover, the Amish have historically worked in agriculture—one of the more dangerous occupations—and they see little need for a raft of new rules regulating shops, which to many, appear to be safer. Nevertheless, the large shops face OSHA inspections related to a variety of safety and environmental issues.

Child Labor Issues

National child labor laws have also triggered tension between the Amish and the state. Amish children attend school until they turn fourteen, the age at which children may legally begin to work.[11] In reality, however, regulations keep children from performing many tasks with power tools until they are eighteen. These restrictions have caused much concern on the part of Amish leaders and parents. Said one father; "Fourteen to eighteen is a tender age. If we wait too long to teach children, too much of what's learned is learned. We want to have the children working with us when they're learning." One non-Amish woman charged that "some Amish know the child labor laws but pretend they don't until they get caught."[12]

The words *child labor* conjure up negative images of children working twelve-hour days in dangerous conditions in sweatshops, coal mines, and brothels. For the Amish, child labor means apprenticeship, family solidarity, and learning the basic values that form the foundation of their way of life. Rooted in farming, the Amish believe that children and parents should work together. Not only does child labor make an important contribution to the family's well-being; it also serves as an important channel for passing on skills and values. Leaving youngsters idle invites mischief, even rebellion, and opens the door to the "the devil's workshop," as the well-known adage warns. Many Amish persons tie the woes of the modern world to its disdain for work. The Amish believe that labor brings dignity. "No one in this county is abusing their children by teaching them to work," asserted one father. "There probably are people in this county who abuse children, but it's not with work. In today's world, the way I see it, we don't need laws which keep children *from* work."

Although Amish parents feel a God-given responsibility to provide labor for their offspring, few employ school-age children on a full-time basis. Many school-age children work before and after school by cleaning up around the shop, helping to pick produce for roadside stands, or waiting on customers at an in-home store; but they do not put in regular workdays. The work of younger children is interspersed with play, care of pets, or running errands for the extended family. After eighth grade, children often begin working full-time in the family business or for a neighbor or nearby family member. The Amish system of apprenticeship involves youth in business at an early age and especially after they complete eighth grade. Instead of attending trade school, vocational-technical school, or high school, Amish youth serve apprenticeships in shops where they learn a variety of trades.

Concerned about the impact of enforcement on family, apprenticeship, and business, an Amish lobby effort swung into action in the 1990s under the coordination of the National Steering Committee. Amish representatives met with more than forty members of Congress to plead their case. Congressman Joseph R. Pitts, representative from Lancaster County, tried without success to persuade officials in the Department of Labor to respect Amish concerns by using light-handed enforcement. Eventually, he scheduled a hearing with a subcommittee of the House of Representatives and introduced a bill that addressed Amish needs.[13] The legislation specified that fourteen-year-old youth in religious groups that forbid formal schooling beyond eighth grade could work in manufacturing plants if they were supervised by relatives or other members of the religious sect. The U.S. House of Representatives approved the legislation in March 1999, but the bill stalled in the Senate even after it received a hearing in 2001.

In his testimony at the subcommittee hearing, the chairman of the Amish Steering Committee said that after eighth grade, Amish youth "learn by doing . . . we cannot tolerate idleness during these adolescent years, therefore we see a dire need that our youth learn a trade . . . we believe that forced idleness at this age is detrimental to our long-standing Amish way of raising our children and teaching them to become good productive citizens. Keeping young hands busy, keeps them out of mischief."[14] To Amish thinking, keeping children busy in meaningful work is central to their entire way of life.

The child labor laws were designed to protect youth in the larger soci-

◆

Amish youth learn vocational skills by working in apprenticeships in Amish shops. Their employment and use of equipment has created child-labor conflicts with some regulatory agencies.

ety from danger and exploitation in large manufacturing plants, not from the needs of small family businesses providing an apprenticeship for their own children. One Amish businessman, complaining about Department of Labor officials said, "They're trying to tell me I can't have my own children working for me. My kids have been coming up here [to the shop] since they were two years old. This is part of our house. This is where we keep an eye on them."[15]

Even the *Wall Street Journal* joined the debate with an editorial by an Amish-raised woman who argued that America's "child-spoiling culture—TV instead of work and encouraging youngsters to challenge parental discipline—contributes to the boredom and dissatisfaction that cause America's problems with juvenile violence." She noted that some of her most gratifying childhood memories involved work, and she urged the government "to stop causing stress for those who choose to raise their children close to the instincts of nature."[16] In any event, Amish apprenticeships faced stiff challenges from the regulatory apparatus designed to protect childhood in the modern state.

Bargaining with the Commonwealth

Workers' Compensation, designed by the Commonwealth of Pennsylvania to compensate employees who are injured on the job, became another point of friction as more and more Amish moved into nonfarm occupations. The Amish declined to participate, voicing objections similar to those with Social Security. Practicing their belief in mutual aid, the Amish care for their injured members because they believe that tapping public funds violates the separation of church and state. Paying their own medical bills and rejecting plaintiff litigation, the Amish have less need for on-the-job liability insurance.

When the Commonwealth of Pennsylvania began enforcing a stricter Workers' Compensation law in 1975, the Amish objected. The chairman of the National Amish Steering Committee, who lived in Lancaster County, met with the state attorney general as well as with legislators to seek an amiable solution. According to one Amishman, "The governor put a moratorium on enforcement and asked the legislature to draft a new bill. It took three years to get it through, but the House of Representatives passed it unanimously in 1978."

The new bill exempted the Amish and other religious sects that have "established tenets and/or teachings which oppose" receiving public or commercial insurance benefits for death, disability, old age, or medical services—including Social Security.[17] Amish employees must sign a notarized affidavit declaring that they will waive all benefits and rights from Workers' Compensation. Paralleling their exemption from Social Security at the federal level, the exemption from Workers' Compensation was a significant concession by the state to the Amish. For their part, the Amish agreed to stay off the public dole.

Another point of friction with the state flashed in 1993 when the *New York Times* published a story implicating some Amish farmers for violating health standards in dog kennels where they raised puppies for pet shops.[18] Opponents of puppy breeders charged that "puppy mills" were sending thousands of sick, undernourished dogs into an already overpopulated market. Animal rights observers accused several Amish kennels with inhumane treatment of animals. State Senator Stewart Greenleaf, complaining that Pennsylvania had "turned into the puppy mill capital of the world," introduced legislation to regulate unsupervised operations.[19]

By the turn of the twenty-first century, Lancaster County had about 230 licensed dog kennels for breeding purposes, many of which were Amish owned.[20] Amish owners typically had twenty-five to fifty breeding dogs in licensed kennels that were inspected by the state Department of Agriculture. The issue flared up again in 2000 when several Amish people in three different townships requested zoning approval to build more kennels.

Public zoning hearings, generous newspaper publicity, and active opposition by the Lancaster Humane Society stirred lively debate.[21] The issue pitted three Amish farmers, "who treated dogs like any other animals," against Humane Society officials who wanted better care. An Amishman charged that "the animal rights people are more concerned about dogs than their own children." One township received more than 120 emails and 55 faxes from "crazy people on a crusade," in the words of a zoning officer. Most of the protests came from outside Pennsylvania.

Some of the planned kennels were approved, but those that failed township codes were rejected. To many Amish, dogs—like cows or chickens— were simply another source of income. As long as they met licensing and inspection standards, they saw no problem producing puppies just like they did pigs and peeps. For animals' rights advocates, however, the so-called puppy mills mistreated dogs and produced an unneeded surplus. One woman leaving a public hearing was so incensed that she doubted "that the Amish will go to heaven" if they continue raising dogs. Another person called the Amish farmers "killers." One member of the audience said, "You people disgust me and make me sick. I'm going outside and throwing up."[22] A few weeks later, irked by all the commotion, an Amishman wrote the editor of a local newspaper. "I'm surprised these folks come from so far away to mind our business. Seems to me someone needs something to do. Why not start some dog kennels?"[23]

The Amish practice of shunning has stirred another controversy with the state of Pennsylvania. In accordance with church teaching, Amish persons may not accept payment for products from excommunicated members. This complex issue pits the religious rights of the Amish to practice shunning against consumer rights in the marketplace. Amish entrepreneurs may give goods or services to banned persons, and they may accept third-party payments, but they may not receive direct reimbursement by excommunicated members. At the same time, antidiscrimination laws hold that public businesses must serve all customers and cannot discriminate on the basis, among other issues, of religion. Several past court cases upheld the legal validity of shunning as a method of church discipline and censure. However, such cases always focused on private, interpersonal relationships, not public sales transactions.[24] The Amish entry into business complicates the church's historical practice and illustrates how church and state can become entangled in odd ways.

In 1990, former Amishman Aaron Glick, who was expelled from the Amish church in 1945, filed a formal complaint with the Pennsylvania Human Relations Commission. He charged two Amish business owners with unlawful discrimination because they would not accept direct payment from him. One Amishman, Bennie King, operated an auction service and refused to accept a check from Glick. As a result of the charges, King closed his business. Chris Stoltzfoos, the other Amish owner, operated a hardware store and would not accept payment in checks from Glick, who forty-five years later, remained under the ban of the church.

The complaint against Stoltzfoos simmered in the offices of the Pennsylvania Human Relations Commission for three years. Eventually, the commission sided with ex-Amishman Glick in "believing that discrimination had occurred."[25] In 1994, the state ordered the Amish storeowner to "cease and desist" from treating ex-Amish differently from his other customers.[26] Amish leaders urged Stoltzfoos to accept the ruling, indicating that the church was retreating from its three-hundred-year tradition of restricting commerce with shunned persons, at least in public settings. Amish habits were conceding to economic forces and state-enforced rules of the public marketplace.

This significant issue addresses one of the most sensitive areas of religious liberty—the freedom to act on one's convictions. By moving into the public realm of business, the Amish have become more vulnerable to complaints from disgruntled neighbors, former members, and commercial competitors. No longer secluded on the farm, traditional Amish face new challenges in the world of commerce. As the plaintiff in the recent case complained, "The Amish years ago were farmers. They did not mix with outside interests. Over the last twenty years, many have set up businesses. . . . If they want to practice it [shunning] in their home, fine. I don't think they should practice it in business."[27] With one foot in the public arena, Amish religious practices will likely face ever-growing legal and public scrutiny.

Zoning Conflicts

The most intense conflicts with the state in recent years have surfaced at the local level. Amish businesses and municipal officials have clashed repeatedly over zoning issues related to land use.[28] Zoning is the primary technique municipal officials employ to regulate land use and manage growth.[29]

Pennsylvania zoning laws are particularly complicated because they vary from one municipality to another. In Lancaster County alone, more than sixty local bodies—townships and boroughs—determine zoning regulations. The resulting jumble of mandates confuses Amish and non-Amish alike. Said one government official, "Unfortunately, most zoning and planning in this county is done by Xerox. Municipalities copy ordinances from other areas that may not be suited to local needs to all." One municipality, using standard ordinances, found it difficult to allow Amish families to stable a horse on a two-acre plot.

During the 1970s and the early 1980s, some Amish entrepreneurs found themselves at odds with zoning officials. Because commercial and manufacturing establishments are normally not permitted in rural and agricultural zones, starting a cottage industry or farm shop was often illegal. Some civic officials directed the Amish to rent or buy property in industrial areas for their new businesses. A few municipalities offered lenient zoning regulations, which encouraged small businesses, farm shops, and cottage industries. Other local governments ended up with ordinances that stood somewhere in the middle—quite restrictive, but not completely prohibitive. The various shades of permission often confused business owners. Amish people could not always rely on the advice of friends because the Amish settlement spanned dozens of municipalities, each with different regulations and enforcement officers. Remarked one Amish shop owner wryly, "I know of some [Amish] people who said 'I'll never challenge anything the government says.' And then they move to a place where the township is unreasonable, and they soon have a conflict. A lot of Amish don't realize how bad it is here [in my township]."

Yet local officials are not capricious in setting restrictions. They fear that if Amish families scatter small shops along country roads, industrial parks might spring up in the middle of cow pastures. "Uncontrolled industrial waste disposal—that's what scares me the most," said one civil engineer. "We're sitting on limestone soil here. If you dump solvent or oil on the ground here, it goes right into the drinking water." Some officials argue that consistency requires the prohibition of all commercial businesses, stores, and shops in residential and agricultural zones, irrespective of their size or environmental impact. Older enterprises, however, are often grandfathered into acceptance when a zoning code is adopted.

As a result of some zoning laws, dozens of would-be entrepreneurs were denied permission to open new cottage industries or fined for operating household firms illegally. Some Amish began to operate shops clandestinely, offering no visible indication of their enterprise. As the number of Amish businesses grew, conflicts mounted. As shown in table 11.1, a third of the owners in the Entrepreneur Profile reported difficulties with zoning. Many of the problems were clustered in a handful of municipalities.

Mounting Concerns

Although the Amish are not the only people with zoning difficulties, they have been entangled in conflicts for a number of reasons. In the first place,

TABLE 11.1

*Amish Enterprises Reporting Difficulties with
Government Regulations*

Type of Regulation	Percentage of Enterprises
Air pollution	0
Noise pollution	0
Safety	0
Water pollution	3
Hazardous waste	9
Zoning	32
Other	9

Source: Entrepreneur Profile (*N* = 35).

in the words of one Amishman, "We are used to being our own boss. We don't understand someone coming in and telling us what we can and can't do on our land if we aren't bothering anyone else." The multiplicity of zoning codes confuses and irritates rural minds reared on the freedom of the farm. Amish entrepreneurs see little reason for having one set of business ordinances in one township while the next one—equally rural—has an entirely different code. "There's no consistency," complained an Amish mason. "I could take it if it was the same across the county, but this having different rules everywhere just doesn't make sense."

Second, financial considerations also play a part. Commercially zoned property carries a higher rental cost and thus requires more capitalization for a new business. Because many Amish businesses start on a shoestring, the higher costs of beginning in an industrial park render it impractical. "How can a guy start out if he can't start out at home?" one entrepreneur asked. When you're just starting out, you can't afford to lease a huge building in an industrial park." An Amish plumber, commenting on zoning rules, remarked, "I can see where you can't let things get too large, but why not let a business start out wherever it is and then if it gets too big, say, 'Ok, it's time for you to go rent somewhere else.' But let them start small at home. You can't go out and rent at first."

The third and most important reason for the resistance is the fear that zoning will tear home, community, and work asunder. Zoning controversies entail far more than economics—they are in many ways a clash of cultural values. The Amish place a high value on family- and neighborhood-centered work, which zoning ordinances sometimes thwart. The Amish originally opted for small businesses instead of factory labor in order to keep their work in the context of kin and neighbor. Separating work from home threatens the very core of Amish life. In contrast to the larger society, where many employees see their homes as shelters from work, the

Amish see their homes as the best setting for work. Thus, their resistance to zoning often flows from their commitment to keeping businesses family-centered. "What we're trying to do," said one Amishman, "is to keep the family together."

One owner reflected, "We could set up our businesses in industrial parks and hire drivers to pick up all our workers and take them there. But it wouldn't be the same. For an Amishman, his work is his way of life. Our day doesn't start at eight and stop at five so we can go play golf and watch TV. We are more tied to our work. Our families help; we like to be together. We can't jump in the car and go to work; we have to stay there. So we want to work at home or close by." An older Amish farmer who began carpentry in his retirement noted: "It's just not for us to work away like that. We can't and we don't want to." Non-Amish people, he acknowledged, "like to get away from their work. They want to go home when they're done and forget about it until the next day. But that's not our way. We want to work at home." Horse-and-buggy transportation, of course, also helps to tether work near home.

Repeated conflicts with municipal officials have embittered a few businesspeople who felt zoning officers were intentionally vindictive. "The way it is around here," a young shop owner pouted, "if you can get the zoning man as your friend, you'd better not lose him, because if you step over the line one time, they'll nail you, your dad, and your brothers for years." Ironically, some entrepreneurs wish that local government were less infected with cronyism. A quilt shop owner explained his resentment of being told to stay on the "good side" of township officials in order to receive a fair zoning hearing: "There shouldn't be a 'good side.' If it's legal and right, it shouldn't matter whether you're on their 'good side' or not." There's no 'sides' to it. It's either right or wrong by the book." Some non-Amish observers contend, however, that Amish shops too easily slip through the regulatory guidelines because of lax enforcement in some townships.

Entrepreneurs also complain about the time and cost required to maneuver through the maze of zoning ordinances. Several owners noted that even routine paperwork requires hiring a lawyer to interpret the jargon that increasingly fills municipal documents. A man who owns a small business lamented the cost of public hearings and legal fees. "They're not allowing the entrepreneur to work," he fears. "We're losing out if we let this red tape and zoning get out of hand. It's terribly expensive getting a lawyer all the time." A wood products manufacturer predicted: "The ruin of the Lancaster County Amish community will be the local township government." He believes that if Amish families are unable to farm and, due to restrictive zoning, unable to work at home, they will move to other communities. A harness maker complained: "I can't figure out what they [local offi-

◆

The tobacco barn (right) has been converted into a retail tourist store by an Amish family. Nonfarm businesses in rural areas have raised new zoning issues in some townships.

cials] want," he said. "They say they want Amish around here because it builds up the farmland and helps with tourism, but then they harass people who can't farm. Do they want us or not? If not, we don't have a problem with moving. We moved from Switzerland, we can move again if they want us to."

Moving toward Resolution

Although a few Amish have chosen to move to areas with less restrictive zoning, the vast majority have remained at the bargaining table in Lancaster County. During the 1980s conflicts erupted in a number of townships across the settlement. Frustrated by fines, legal fees, and various procedural hassles, some Amish did the unthinkable—they hired private consultants who proposed changes in local zoning codes. Amish farmers and businesspeople approached several townships to petition for small shops on farms or adjacent to them. By this time, some municipalities, tiring of the struggle, were willing to implement the proposed changes.

Eventually, a number of municipalities, following the lead of county planners, established zoning allowances permitting rural and agricultural businesses. Farm shops and related occupations often fit within the new zoning guidelines. "The at-home location of these uses complements the lifestyles of Old Order residents by acknowledging their religious beliefs and relative lack of mobility," one model ordinance noted.[30] Said one government official, "We recognize that farm businesses support farming by supplementing income and providing employment during the off-season." By allowing ancillary businesses on farms, officials hope to boost the farm economy and keep more families engaged in farming. In one case, the Lancaster County Planning Commission rejected the advice of its own staff and endorsed expansion plans for six businesses in an agricultural area.[31]

Another common allowance is the exemption for enterprises that support agriculture. Operations that directly aid and support farming—grain mills, blacksmiths' shops, harness-making shops, and establishments manufacturing or repairing farm machinery—are often permitted in rural and agriculturally zoned areas. Although businesses unrelated to farming, such as woodworking shops or dry goods stores, still face difficulty in some townships, many municipalities have accepted at-home enterprises that employ family members. Some zoning allowances limit the physical size of the business and the number of employees. One township allows up to four thousand square feet of shop space on active farms. Single homeowners, however, have little leeway in establishing new businesses. One township that allows cottage industries limits them to four employees, while another caps the number of nonfamily employees at two. Ironically, public law, in these cases, enforces small-scale Amish values and family involvement. Thus, some progressive entrepreneurs face not only church censorship but legal curbs as well, should they want to expand.

Municipalities that have struggled to create workable ordinances have taken the needs of the Amish community into account when designing new mandates. One model ordinance noted "Supplemental . . . agricultural income has become especially important for many Old Order farm families in Lancaster County. [Farm businesses] provide job opportunities on the farm, thus allowing farm families to continue to work together."[32] Indeed, implementation of the new mandates sometimes reflects Amish advice. Officials in some townships hold informal meetings with Amish leaders to hear their concerns and test possible policies. Explained one official, "Most municipal zoning amendments have been made by Amish constituents making their needs and concerns known. I think most townships make decisions with the collaboration of interested Amish businessmen." A few Amish businesspeople have even served on local planning committees and zoning boards, although at least one stepped down at the request of the church.

Some problems remain with advertising signs. "You just about have to go to the Supreme Court to be able to put up a two-by-four-foot sign by your mailbox these days," complained one gazebo builder. Nevertheless, in the opinion of many onlookers, the tension between Amish businesspeople and local government is on the wane. Said one civil engineer, "The tolerance for Amish businesses is growing. In the past, there was a lot of frustration on all sides. The uncontrolled growth scared local officials, but they didn't want to run small businesses out of the area, either." The informal bargaining between the Amish and local leaders has wrought many constructive agreements. Said one county official, "There are more thought-through regulations and fewer haphazard ordinances. There's been a lot more negotiation. The government has become much more educated about the needs and importance of Amish businesses. At the same time, there's more appreciation on the side of the Old Order communities that we are trying to meet their legitimate needs."

Indeed, some of the once-frustrated shop owners have mellowed and now endorse the idea of zoning and growth management.[33] Said one storage shed builder, "I think the local government has a job to do. They can't have everyone out doing whatever they want or building whatever they want. They have a job to do, and they do pretty well. None of us would like to have a big factory go up next to us. If zoning is reasonable, it's a good thing." An Amish contractor expressed sympathy for the tough situations and questions that zoning thrusts upon local officials. "Where does my right stop for your rights?" he asks thoughtfully. "That's the question. My land is your neighboring land. Zoning is difficult. It really is."

Despite the significant number of conflicts, the majority of Amish entrepreneurs have had little difficulty with local ordinances. A dried-flower shop owner expressed appreciation for local government. "We've had no problems with zoning officers," she reported. "They've always been nice to us. The one township fellow stops by sometimes to see how we're doing!" Even those who dislike zoning speak respectfully of their local officials. After noting some conflicts with local government, an Amish businessman suddenly summarized, "But we can't be thankful enough as Amish for what the government *has* allowed us to do."

Compromising with Caesar

Conflicts between the Amish and the state are a significant part of the Amish story in North America. With the rise of Amish business, tensions with the state have spilled into areas of commerce. When the Amish resist welfare programs, employ their children, and struggle to work at home, they are seeking, above all else, to perpetuate their cultural values in the face of powerful economic forces. These high cultural stakes have pushed them back to the bargaining table again and again.

The Amish have been respectful but firm in their refusal to acquiesce to government demands that would undermine their culture. But they have conceded, in part, their traditional stance of political avoidance. They have sought legal advice and petitioned local governments for relief from zoning codes that would separate work and family. They have attended public meetings and counseled with municipal officials. Keeping a low public profile, they have nevertheless become more entangled in public policy. In exchange for greater civic participation, the church hopes to safeguard its own destiny.

For their part, the Amish have been granted most of their requests. They have won the right to care for their own members without participating in Social Security and Workers' Compensation. In many instances, they have also received clearance to keep their work near home and family. The Amish cherish these economic and cultural freedoms. And should they dissolve, entrepreneurship would not only be less inviting, but it might also become a means of dismantling Amish culture.

12. Failure and Success

*The huge wealth created by Amish businesses in recent years
is simply staggering.*

— FINANCIAL OFFICER

 ## Small-Scale Failures

The story of Amish enterprise is largely a story of success, with only scattered tarnishes of failure. The default rate among small business in general is rather sobering, however. Nearly one-quarter of new American firms fold within two years, and some 63 percent close their doors within six years. During the 1980s, the rate of business failures nearly matched that of the Great Depression.[1] The Amish launched more than 40 percent of their business ventures in the 1980s, but surprisingly, fewer than 5 percent of the Amish operations failed.[2]

Most Amish enterprises avoid the pitfalls that lead to closure in several ways. When starting up, they typically begin with little or no initial debt. Their use of family labor and their at-home location offer flexibility during the first years of operation. Amish shops typically control the rate of growth, thus eluding over-expansion, which, at times, leads to failure. The thick ethnic network of family and friends provides ample sources of free counsel and advice

Nevertheless, some businesses do run aground. In the past when farmers faced financial stress, the church appointed trustees to manage the operation toward profitability. The same practice has been applied to business. Fellow entrepreneurs, acting as church-appointed trustees, guide a faltering firm toward recovery and profitability. The church's active role in the financial affairs of members bears testimony to the practice of mutual aid within their community.

The typical procedure with troubled firms involves three church-appointed trustees. The faltering business owner selects one, the local bishop appoints a second one, and then the two appointees select a third one. The three trustees are typically seasoned and successful businessmen. The intensity of their involvement varies from case to case. In some situations, they may serve as consultants and offer informal advice to get the business back on track. In more serious situations, they may assume the power of attorney and execute all financial decisions related to the business, including closing it if necessary.

In some cases financially strapped entrepreneurs have received little help from the church. Their failing enterprises quietly fold, and they find new jobs or start other businesses. Why this apparent gap in mutual aid? Amish leaders suggest two reasons.

Some point to the personality of entrepreneurs. They note that risk-taking business people—even among the Amish—tend to be more individualistic and less submissive. The creative spirit that gives rise to new ventures is not always willing to receive counsel from others. Trustees can only be appointed and operate effectively if the failing business owner is willing to accept their authority. One Amishman explained the difference between farmers and business owners: "Businesses are more prone to go up the spout without help from the church, mostly because they won't take help. If you're in business, let's face it, you have some ideas of your own, and you won't listen to other people telling you how to run it as quick."

Others think the church works harder to save family farms because farming is still a revered way of life. If a business venture collapses, one can find work as a day laborer or begin a new enterprise without the enormous investment required for farming. One entrepreneur says, "The farm is where the family lives. The children are brought up there. With a business, you can always get into something else if that doesn't work out." An Amishwoman who co-owns a bakery agreed: "With the farmer, they would try to save the farm for the family. They live there. . . . I don't think anyone would come in to save a bakery. It's just not that important [to the church]." Sometimes church leaders may be slow to appoint trustees because they assume that an accountant will tell owners if they are "getting in trouble and what to do about it before any outside help has to come in." Nevertheless, the trustee model is frequently used to assist ailing businesses.

Sometimes, when the church appoints trustees to rescue a business, the intervention may come too late. The overseers may counsel a business to liquidate its assets, but unlike their non-Amish competitors, Amish owners do not seek sanctuary in the courts. The Amish view bankruptcy as an unethical skirting of responsibility, and whether engaged in farming or business, they try to make good on all liabilities. It may take years to pay off indebtedness, but full reimbursement must be made. To protect forbearing creditors from greedy ones, a few business owners have asked sympathetic third parties to file involuntary bankruptcy proceedings on their behalf. Unwilling to use bankruptcy as an escape, these owners nonetheless see it as a valid way to ensure orderly repayment.

In the short run, fellow church members may pitch in to cover immediate obligations, freeing the entrepreneur from the control of creditors. Then, after a business has been shut down, the one-time business owner will work at paying off his or her Amish benefactors. In one case, a middle-aged Amish carpenter assumed the crippling debts of a younger church member. The carpenter then hired the one-time entrepreneur, allowing him to work his way out of debt and learn the valuable experience he needed. The two men developed a bond of loyalty, and their combined efforts energized the carpentry operation. Eventually, the owner included the younger man in a joint partnership. This informal arrangement saved an unfortunate beginner from bankruptcy, gave him management experience, and further prospered an already successful business. Despite occasional blunders, the Amish story is marked more by success than by failure.

Amish Success

Success is not a favored word in Amish circles. Among a people who prize humility and diffidence, success opens the door to pride and arrogance. To admit that one's enterprise, farm, or even family garden is noticeably productive opens oneself to the perils of vanity. When queried about their success, Amish entrepreneurs wrap their response in a cloak of modesty. A diffident reply, a long pause, a playing down of their own accomplishments grace their words. Entrepreneurs are more likely to point to a neighboring firm than to their own when describing an exemplary business. Drawing on agricultural imagery, Amish entrepreneurs frequently describe their evolution as slow, organic growth—not quick, explosive expansion. When tracing their growth, they are more likely to cite discipline, hard work, and persistent effort than the more glamorous, individualistic virtues of intelligence, shrewdness, or skill.

Yet despite their reticence to verbalize their commercial success, Amish businesses, by all accounts, are growing, prospering, and thriving. New firms sprout annually, develop new product lines, and offer increasingly competitive services. Although profitability data are not readily available, many firms have annual sales above one million dollars. *Forbes* magazine pegged the sales of an Amish leather shop with broad national distribution at $6 million.[3] According to one financial observer, the top ten Amish businesses have annual sales of $8 to 12 million, and most of them likely net 10 percent in profit.[4] A banking official knowledgeable of Amish finances said, "The huge wealth created by Amish businesses in recent years is simply staggering."

What are the sources of success? The commercial flowering of Amish enterprise is rooted in both external and internal socioeconomic factors. External factors that enhance the vitality of these enterprises include a strong regional economy, positive public perceptions of Amish products, a sizable tourist trade, certain payroll exemptions, and cooperative support from public officials at the state and county levels. Business ventures are also bolstered by the resources of their ethnic culture: a rural heritage of entrepreneurial values, a strong work ethic, religious values of austerity and simplicity, cultural taboos on higher education and on certain forms of technology, extensive involvement of family members, small-scale operations, attention to artisanship and quality, and an informal but effective system of apprenticeship.

External Sources of Success

The Amish settlement in Lancaster County is situated in one of the more productive regional economies of the United States. The county's economy is both diverse and stable. Business leaders point to the trio of agriculture, industry, and tourism as a three-fold guarantee of sustainable growth. Additionally, the county boasts low unemployment figures as well as a sterling reputation for work. A reasonable cost of living and a tradition of amiable labor relations make Lancaster a prime location for many companies.

Demographics also play an important role in the region's economic health. Some sixty million people live within a six-hour drive of Lancaster. Indeed, according to one estimate, 40 percent of the U.S. population and half of the country's personal buying power live within 500 miles of Lancaster.[5] With large and ready markets close at hand, transportation costs shrink. The close proximity of so many people turns Lancaster County into a tourist haven for East Coast urbanites searching for rest and a touch of Amish culture. Visitors bring vacation dollars to fuel the economy as well as a penchant for take-home crafts.

Amish businesses benefit from the mass markets that lie within easy reach of Lancaster County. Firms selling agricultural goods and equipment are in the midst of the eastern agricultural region. When hiring outside their ethnic community, Amish employers can tap a solid pool of labor. The annual visits of millions of tourists provide ready markets for outlets selling Amish products. Travelers in the area sometimes order Amish-produced kitchen cabinets, furniture, or antique carriages before returning home. All of these contextual factors undergird the vitality of Amish business and, in part, bolster its success.

Amish entrepreneurs recognize the importance of the surrounding economy. Said one shop owner, "Lancaster is very aggressive business-wise and farm-wise. And I like that about this area. People get out there and hustle. They work, and they look for the next customer." An Amish building contractor noted the competitive atmosphere of the regional economy as well. "Competition keeps the sloppy work out," he remarked, suggesting that Amish firms have to be efficient in order to survive.

Occasionally the tight competition hinders those who strive to operate low-profile, small-scale shops. The aggressive nature of Lancaster's commercial atmosphere wins approval from most Amish entrepreneurs, but some consider it problematic. "Sometimes I see it as a bad thing," one owner cautioned. "It can get too aggressive that way. It can be too competitive, and it's hard to run a business in an Amish way—in a Christian way—when it gets too tight. You can't let it get out of control." Yet most believe that Lancaster's favorable business climate has fertilized their productivity.

Some Amish entrepreneurs realize that their own establishments might

◆

Public demand for Amish products has boosted the profitability of retail shops.
The Amishwoman who owns this shop is permitted by the church to have
electric lights because she rents the building.

TABLE 12.1

Public Perception of Amish Products Relative to Non-Amish Products

Attribute of Products	Lower than Non-Amish Product	Similar to Non-Amish Product	Higher than Non-Amish Products
Value	0	9	91
Artisanship	0	12	88
Quality	0	14	86
Uniqueness	0	27	73
Cost	5	84	11

Source: Product Perception Survey (*N* = 200).
Note: See appendix D for methodological details. Perceptions were rated on a seven-point scale where 1–2 = lower, 3–5 = similar, and 6–7 = higher.

be less profitable if they lived elsewhere. "If you picked us up and put us down in some county in western Pennsylvania where things don't look so bright, I don't think we'd be able to make it like we do here," said one cabinetmaker.[6] Others play down the Lancaster environment and suggest that their ventures have developed independent of the larger economy. The success of Amish firms that sell to an Amish clientele is linked, of course, more directly to the size and growth of the Amish settlement itself than to the wider commercial climate. Many entrepreneurs who deal with non-Amish wholesalers and dealers, however, believe that outsiders come to Lancaster County because of its reputation for quality and high-value products.

A significant factor in the strength of Amish commerce is the favorable public perception of Amish products. Indeed, Amish products carry a public mystique that enhances their marketability. Many tourists view Amish products as handcrafted, of high quality, and individually unique. As shown in table 12.1, 88 percent of public respondents rate the artisanship of Amish products as "higher or much higher" than similar non-Amish products, and 86 percent perceive Amish products to be of higher quality. Some 91 percent of those interviewed rated the overall value (what you get for what you pay) of Amish products as "higher or much higher" than that of other products. Moreover, even without a purchase, the public carries a favorable perception of Amish products.

A few Amish, trying to capitalize on the favorable mystique of Amish identity, have included horse-and-buggy silhouettes on their business cards or outdoor advertisements. A few print "made locally by the Amish" on their promotional literature. It is the non-Amish entrepreneurs, however, who make far more use of Amish images in advertising and promotion. In fact, most Amish businesspeople shy away from associating Amish images with their advertising. One Amish manufacturer said, "I don't like to stick the Amish name on anything. Quality and good service is what brings the people back." Another Amish merchant agreed: "I don't like the name—Amish Farmers' Market. I don't like to play that off. I always say—Pennsylvania Dutch Market. That takes in more of eastern Pennsylvania, and I don't want to point to myself." Happily for them, the Amish have not had to point to themselves. Media images, public perceptions, and satisfied customers point the way to Amish doors and help to boost the profits of Amish operations.

Other external factors that have aided Amish enterprises include exemptions from Social Security and, within Pennsylvania, from Workers' Compensation. As noted in chapter 11, the Amish object to participation in public welfare and insurance programs. Self-employed Amish persons and ethnic employees who work for Amish employers receive federal exemption from Social Security and state exemption from Workers' Compensation. The payroll savings Amish employers realize from these exemptions boost the profitability of their firms.

A few non-Amish business owners contend that such exemptions discriminate. These non-Amish competitors argue that exemptions should remain on the farm when the Amish enter the public arena of commerce. In the words of one non-Amish masonry contractor, "When the Amish were on the farm, the exemptions were no problem. But now they're out competing with the work force. It's different now—they're working for other people and hiring other people, but they're still exempt." Other businesspeople argue that payroll exemptions give Amish contractors an unfair advantage in the marketplace. Yet the wider Lancaster County business community has benignly tolerated the exemptions, knowing that Amish employers and employees do not draw on state or federal welfare coffers or Social Security programs. Moreover, some non-Amish general contractors actually benefit, albeit indirectly, from the church's payroll exemptions. These firms are able to lower their own costs by hiring Amish subcontractors at lower hourly rates. State legislators living in the local area support the exemptions, as do most business leaders in the larger non-Amish world.

External factors bolstering Lancaster's Amish enterprises:
a strong and stable regional economy
access to sizable markets in the eastern megalopolis
a large tourist market in Lancaster County
positive public perceptions of Amish products
exemption from Social Security and Workers' Compensation
positive relations with state and county government officials
Amish visibility in national and regional media

Amish employers contend that their cultural ethos contributes more to their success than external factors like product perceptions and payroll exemptions. Entrepreneurs are most likely to cite hard work, service, integrity, and a simple, low-overhead approach to business when explaining their entrepreneurial growth. Outside the Amish community, business leaders cite the same factors when asked to assess the roots of Amish prosperity. Said a non-Amish business leader, "The Amish are specialized, but ingenious and able to experiment and try new things. They are definitely skilled. I'd say that's a pretty widespread opinion in the larger business community here." Whatever the factors, Amish businesses have proven remarkably resilient and healthy—features that have embellished the financial stability of their ethnic community.

Internal Resources for Success

Although Amish entrepreneurs may debate their reliance on the host economy, it is clear that internal cultural resources have also contributed significantly to their success. In the first place, the Amish continue to champion the traditional work ethic rooted in their farming background. Shop owners and employees work long, hard hours, take few breaks, and rarely go on vacations or extended holiday trips. "If I worked from nine to four and then watched TV the rest of the evening, I wouldn't make it on what I get an hour," noted an Amish furniture maker. He suggested that long hours and a substantial investment of his own time in addition to that of his employees accounted for his business's growth. The Amish value hard work and censure idleness. Laziness is still considered the vestibule of the devil's workshop.

The entrepreneurial skills of independence, problem solving, and ingenuity, also cultivated on the farm, have been critical assets in the growth of Amish enterprise. Bringing a bushel of agrarian values along from their pastoral past, Amish entrepreneurs have applied the thrift, self-sufficiency, and sheer stamina of their heritage to their work. The results have been profitable.

Profitability is also boosted by the lack of excessive trappings and corporate accoutrements that keep Amish shops cost effective and trim. Simple, unadorned offices slash overhead costs and hold capital expenses down. Without air conditioning, wall-to-wall carpeting, office computerization, or utility bills, Amish businesses avoid many of the expenses that non-Amish firms may take for granted. Modest showrooms and simple display areas are functional but not showy. Hand-lettered signs, sensible brochures, or descriptive cards explain products. And by contracting or leasing vehicle service, Amish businesses are able to pay for the exact transportation they need without incurring the added costs of purchasing, insuring, and maintaining a vehicle. As reported in table 12.2, when asked to compare their operations with non-Amish enterprises, 68 percent of the owners thought their overhead was lower, and 69 percent estimated that they did less advertising than their non-Amish counterparts.

Few businesses hire full-time clerical staff. Frequently the entrepreneur or another family member does the bookkeeping during the early morning or evening hours. Some shop owners even belittle the idea of fancy bookkeeping equipment. Said one gazebo manufacturer, "Some people think they need computers so they can check to see at any given minute whether they just lost a nickel or made a dime. I can usually tell pretty well where I'm at without a computer printout. At the end of the year when we total it all up, I'm never surprised."

Low overhead costs are coupled with rather austere lifestyles. Although many material distinctions exist within Amish society, business owners live much more simply than their non-Amish counterparts. Modest lifestyles have allowed Amish shopkeepers to plow more earnings back into their businesses. When asked why few Amish businesses fail, one church member and machine shop owner remarked, "One of the clear reasons in my mind is that we live a simpler life. It doesn't take as much for us to live. . . . I could live on $10,000 right now with six children if I had to. How many other people could do that today? It would take more than that for most [non-Amish] people. Now the Amish have to 'keep up with the Jones,' too, so to speak, among our own people—we're human too. But we don't have as many things to keep up with. Take a car, for example. That's a real expense. And a lot of people trade one every four years. Our buggies never go out of style. They wear out. That's a savings."

Subtract the cost of college education, expensive vacations, tennis camps, fashionable furniture, electronic accessories, designer clothes, cable TV, and dozens of other modern "necessities," and the Amish lifestyle appears rather frugal. The church's emphasis on a family-centered, slower-paced life trims household budgets and frees businesspeople from having to bring home professional-size salaries. Comparing his own lifestyle with one of his non-Amish employees, a shop owner chuckles, "He's got something going every night of the week. That's expensive—to be running around all the time. People don't think about it that way, but it's a cost. Leading a simpler life and staying at home more and having fewer things make a big difference in business."

Compensation factors also cut costs for Amish entrepreneurs and add to their success. As shown in table 12.2, about 40 percent of the entrepreneurs surveyed think their labor costs are lower than those of non-Amish operations. Moreover, 71 percent think their employees are more depend-

TABLE 12.2

Amish Entrepreneurs' Perception of Amish Enterprises Relative to Non-Amish Enterprises

| | Percentage of Respondents | | |
Attribute of Enterprise	Lower than Non-Amish	Similar to Non-Amish	Higher than Non-Amish
Dependability of employees	0	29	71
Productivity of employees	0	39	61
Quality of artisanship	0	41	59
Quality of products	0	52	48
Customer service	0	59	41
Overhead	68	21	11
Price of product	44	44	12
Cost of labor	42	54	4
Amount of advertising	69	31	0

Source: Entrepreneur Survey (*N* = 35).

able than those in nonethnic firms. Amish firms save on labor costs in a number of ways. Amish business owners hire little clerical help, and they work alongside their employees, contributing directly to productivity. Family members supply valuable labor, with spouses and children contributing many hours of work without remuneration. "Most of our businesses are family run" one entrepreneur stated. "Each member of the family puts a lot into it and doesn't take much out."

Grandparents also provide cost-saving labor for family businesses. Although generally paid, such individuals do not command the high wages of workers who support large families. Wages themselves, although commensurate with comparative non-Amish firms, do not approach those found in urban or unionized plants. In addition, fringe benefits are slim. Few businesses provide paid holidays, health insurance, or medical benefits. Virtually no Amish-owned businesses provide pension plans, because extended families bear the responsibility of caring for aging relatives. These and other payroll savings, as discussed above, add increased profitability to Amish businesses.

Another element of success is a well-established commitment to producing quality products and services. A reputation for providing overall value and unique artisanship has increased sales and loyal customers. Many Amish entrepreneurs cite their commitment to service as one of the primary reasons their businesses thrive. Said one entrepreneur, "Service is the key. Quality service gives you the edge. That's what people who come to me want. We're in a very competitive world. Customers shop around and they want price, but mostly they want quality. Do it right and do it right the first time." An Amish contractor agreed: "The customer doesn't want to be in the back seat. You've got to keep him out front." Indeed, 41 percent of the owners thought their customer service was higher than that of non-Amish firms, and none thought it was lower, as reported in table 12.2.

Quality and service often count more than price. "We have a higher price," one fencing supplier admitted, "but we still get the job because the customer knows we have it in stock. We have a large inventory, and we'll have what they want, when they want it." An Amish harness maker agreed. "Price is about the third thing we look at. It's not our top priority. Quality and the market are the two most important. You have to keep your prices in line, of course, but quality and the demand that's out there are more important than price."

Produce stand holders have found that fresh, quality produce has earned them an enviable reputation. In one case, a non-Amish competitor opened a roadside produce stand beside an established Amish merchant. Although the competitor offered a wider and less expensive array of shipped produce, he closed within two weeks. Customers preferred the locally grown, though more expensive, offerings at the Amish stand.

Likewise, a leading voice in Lancaster's wider non-Amish business community described the relation between the Amish commitment to quality and their commercial success: "In the business world they are very respected. They've gained that respect over the years. If they tell you that a job is finished and done right, you know that it's finished and done right— that's it. We talk a lot about 'quality initiative' now and making sure that the quality standard is based on the customer's perceptions. The Amish have been doing that for years."

Finally, both Amish and non-Amish members of the business community cite the trust and integrity Amish entrepreneurs bring to their jobs as a significant factor in their success. Non-Amish contractors and customers respect the honesty and sensibility they find in working with Amish businesspeople. One private contractor, who works with a number of Amish firms, explained his high regard for Amish businesspeople and his desire to work with them: "They pay on time. . . . I've done jobs ranging from $1,000 to $40,000 for them, and I never need a down payment or deposit or contract. I've always been paid. It's their word to you."

An attorney who works closely with Amish businesses knows of no suits against them for bad debts. A credit officer who loans millions of dollars annually to the Amish has "never had to foreclose on a bad loan." Another banker said, "I never lost a dime lending to the Amish" in over fifteen years with a loan portfolio averaging $30 million.

Amish entrepreneurs realize that they have acquired a reputation for honesty and fairness, and they hope to uphold it. In fact, some business owners see their people's commitment to integrity as their most significant

The storage area of this Amish owned food store illustrates the scale of a successful retail business.

mark in the business world. Said one Amish merchant, "We have to try harder, there's no doubt about that. If we would ever cheat anyone, that would be it. We would be finished." In his eyes, the success of his business is linked to his reputation for honesty and integrity.

Internal factors bolstering Lancaster's Amish enterprises:
a heritage of entrepreneurial values rooted in agriculture
an unwavering commitment to a strenuous work ethic
an austerity that minimizes overhead costs
a frugal lifestyle that rejects excessive consumerism
extensive use of family members as a source of labor
access to an ethnic labor pool with a strong work ethic
a tradition of occupational apprenticeship
educational taboos that funnel creative minds into business
small-scale operations that spread entrepreneurship across the settlement
informal operations that minimize overhead, hierarchy, and alienation
technological taboos that encourage innovation and invention
attention to product quality and value
uniqueness and variety of product lines
mutual aid, which reduces the cost of health care and retirement plans
a flexible Ordnung that permits innovative technology

Ironically, even the cultural restraints, discussed at length in earlier chapters, factor into the calculus of Amish success. The lid on education channels many of the brighter minds toward business and undergirds the tradition of apprenticeship that has served the Amish community so well. Technological taboos encourage innovation and ingenuity. The limits on size have spread entrepreneurial energies widely across the settlement, increasing the ratio of entrepreneurs to day laborers, minimizing alienation in shops, keeping work lodged at or near home, which encourages large families, which in turn, provide an ample pool of ethnic labor. The large families supported by this diffused pattern of entrepreneurship also do their share to expand the ethnic market for Amish products. In all of these ways, some of the restraints of Amish culture have inadvertently enhanced the viability of Amish enterprise.

The restrictive harness of Amish culture is the Ordnung itself. And although it appears constraining to outsiders, the Ordnung of the Lancaster area is one of the more flexible ones in Amish communities across North America. In particular, its tolerance of telephones, air and hydraulic power, electrical inverters, and forklifts, as well as the hiring of motor vehicles, has boosted the productivity of Amish shops.[7] The permitted use of electrical welders in shops and electrical power tools at construction sites has helped to enhance the profitability of Lancaster's firms. Entrepreneurs who rent market or retail space may use electrical lights and appliances provided by the owner of the space. The widespread acceptance of inverters permits greater use of small electrical tools—cash registers, digital scales, typewriters, copy machines, and special purpose lights.

One shop owner attributed the productive output of Lancaster's Amish shops to a tolerant church: "Thanks to our church leaders for permitting forklifts and telephones close to the shop."[8] The economic forces of the marketplace have stretched the traditional guidelines of the Ordnung, but the adaptability of church leaders has also aided business success. On the other hand, an Amish leader in another community lamented the flexibility of Lancaster's Ordnung: "The rise of businesses was so sudden, so unexpected, and so widespread that the bishops and congregations in Lancaster County were caught unawares; thus the Ordnung for business is not as plainly stated or as clear as it is for farming, which saw changes evolve much more slowly."[9] Indeed, as noted in chapter 7, Amish farmers complain that church leaders have not given them enough flexibility.

The entrepreneurial success of Amish enterprise rides on favorable external conditions as well as on the rich resources of its ethnic heritage. Even cultural restraints, sometimes in ironic ways, aid the vitality of Amish productivity. Refuting much of the conventional wisdom about the ingredients of business success—education, state-of-the-art technology, marketing research, and strategic planning—Amish enterprise has enjoyed prosperity. Indeed, it is the growing prosperity that troubles some Amish sages, who worry that in the long run prosperity will ruin the church. "Persecution hurt the church in the past," said one elder, "but today, it's prosperity."

PART FIVE

The Transformation of
Amish Society

13. The Fate of a Traditional People

You shouldn't be in business if you're married.
— AN AMISHWOMAN

Gender Roles in Transition

What will be the fate of a traditional people who are enjoying the fruit of their productive labor as they move into a market economy? The rise of ethnic enterprise has brought the most significant changes in the life of Lancaster's Amish community in the past two centuries. Throughout this book, we have argued that microenterprises are a negotiated outcome produced by the countervailing forces of cultural resources and restraints within the Amish heritage. Once established, however, the microenterprises act back upon and revise the very cultural values and forces that gave birth to them in the first place. The move toward a market economy will surely transform the total fabric of Amish society—gender roles, child-rearing practices, attitudes toward leisure, church life, class structure, the distribution of power, traditional values, relations with outsiders, and indeed the Amish worldview itself.[1]

Entrepreneurial developments are quietly touching the traditional roles of Amish men and women in this particular society. "We're to be mutually submissive," an Amish deacon explained, "but if it really comes down to not seeing eye-to-eye on something serious, the man must bear the responsibility to make the decision alone." Amishwomen have always played a key part in farming operations—often handling household and gardening responsibilities in tandem with fieldwork, milking, and sometimes record keeping. Yet such work was always performed within the context of the family. Although women were not strangers to work, they rarely owned or managed self-made enterprises.[2]

Today, more than half of all single Amishwomen engage in full-time work outside the home—typically as domestic help, restaurant staff, retail clerks, or teachers.[3] Single women enjoy some measure of autonomy in their work. Married women, however, rarely work full-time away from home. With the arrival of children, a woman is expected to devote full attention to her home. One Amish writer warned that, as "keeper at home," a mother should not divide her energies and seek "fulfillment in a 'career.'"[4]

The arrival of entrepreneurship has pushed some homekeepers beyond traditional borders. The first foray of women into business was largely under the umbrellas of their husbands—handling paperwork, payroll, inventory, and accounting for a family business. If located near the home, females might also help with nonclerical functions including production—running belt sanders and operating engines. Women, however, do not work on construction crews or engage in heavy manufacturing—even in shops operated by their husbands. The involvement of women in business often mirrors life on the farm, where various family members work together.

Although many women continue to assist their husbands, some have established their own enterprises. Females operate nearly 20 percent of the Amish-owned shops in the Lancaster settlement.[5] About 6 percent of Amish women (aged 25–65) own a business.[6] Single women have opened some of these businesses, but married women operate others. Some ventures are small-scale cottage industries that produce jellies, relishes, horseradish, and pies for wholesale distribution. Larger retail stores sell crafts, health foods, or dry goods. Women entrepreneurs typically follow traditional gender roles—making food products, selling quilts and fabrics, and making handcrafts of all sorts, but not selling farm equipment, managing plumbing operations, or traveling with construction crews.

Married women have engaged in entrepreneurial pursuits for a number of reasons. Some admit a natural interest in business. Said one female storeowner: "In think some people are just born with it. . . . I have this love of selling and working with fabrics." Financial need has pushed other women into the marketplace. Without health insurance and despite church aid, high medical bills have forced some families toward business. For others, the lure of more spending money motivates them. Farm wives often earn extra funds by selling eggs or vegetables, and now wives of shop owners or day laborers are also increasingly seeking independent incomes.

In some cases, the entry into business grows out of a new division of labor as families leave the farm. Because nonagricultural work is less family-centered and more male-dominated, wives are less able to contribute to their household's financial well-being than on the farm. As a result, some seek to supplement their household purse. The owner of a quilt business, describing why she began her shop, said, "I felt guilty spending my husband's money. . . . I needed things, and I felt guilty using it." She went on to confess how she feels with a thriving operation: "Now I don't feel as guilty. . . . I tell myself, 'You're making some money. You can afford it.' If I need something, I'll buy it."[7]

Although most female-run shops remain relatively small, several have evolved into larger establishments—topping annual sales of a half million dollars. In several instances, a woman's business has grown so large that her husband dropped outside employment to work for his wife. One husband left carpentry to work full-time in his wife's home-based quilt and craft business. The woman manages the business but spends little time in the store, choosing instead to remain at home to handle orders and attend to housework. Her husband waits on customers and operates the cash register. If a woman's business eventually provides employment for her husband, it typically operates under both names—or even under the husband's name alone—so as to maintain the propriety of patriarchy. Nevertheless, within the community everyone knows who began the business.

Such propriety is critical because married women in business occupy a delicate position in Amish society. Despite the rise of female entrepreneurs, full-time businesswomen sometimes feel the stigma of tradition. Socialized in a culture that frowns on independent careers for married women, older females, especially, sense disapproval. After several of her children were born with a serous disability, one woman started a fabric business to stave off crippling medical costs. Despite her virtuous motive, she felt tinges of disapproval. "It's hard," she admitted. "People say, 'You shouldn't be in business if you're married.' And it does make me feel guilty sometimes." She worries that she does not devote enough time to her children and her husband.

Role conflicts plague women entrepreneurs of all ages as their work splits into rival roles: "How can you be a businesswoman and a wife?" one storeowner asks. "How can you do everything you're supposed to? The woman should be at home, but she should be at the store. And working [out of] your home isn't the answer, because you still have to answer, Which comes first—the children or the customers? And if the customers are there, you feel you must help them, but yet the children are always there, and you know you should be with them."

Another businesswoman and quilt shop owner sounded a similar note. "Sometimes I feel guilty and wonder, 'Did I put too much into the business and not enough into the family?' Did I discipline enough? . . . When I had a customer, it seemed that [the children] were always there and had to know something right away. I don't know if it was because they knew I'd say 'yes' sooner, to get them out of the way and not make a fuss in front of the customers."

An older businesswoman advises young entrepreneurs: "You need to spend time with your family. The mother needs to be with her children. They have to be taken care of or they'll rebel." From the perspective of Amish parents, raising children who join the church is a far greater measure of success than handsome profits. Married women without children are somewhat freer to pursue their business ventures. Said a craft shop owner, "If we had children, we couldn't do this. It would be too much. I would have to spend a lot more time in the house." Single women, of course, do not face the conflicts of management and motherhood.

Amish women are moving into uncharted territory as they blaze new paths between traditional gender roles and business ownership.[8] As work leaves the farm, gender roles become more sharply defined and differentiated. Striving to keep marital roles integrated and negotiating new understandings can be exhausting. Reflecting on nearly three decades in business, an Amish grandmother and businesswoman summed up her bittersweet struggle: "It's been successful," she says simply, "but it's not been nice."

Changes in Child Rearing

The development of cottage industries provides work for children and supports larger families more readily than does factory employment. Nevertheless, the size of Amish families is shrinking somewhat. One business owner's daughter has a two-year-old child. When asked when she will have another baby, she said, "Not for awhile yet." The grandfather noted that in the past "they would have already had a second one!" Families of five or six children are becoming more typical than those of eight or nine, which were common in decades past. There are likely several reasons for the decrease. The greater use of technology in shops eliminates the demand for human labor. The demographic crisis created by decreasing land and a growing Amish population is also a likely factor. And greater familiarity with medical services and advice from health professionals possibly encourages some forms of birth control. Nevertheless, traditional Amish family values and the important contribution of child labor in ethnic business will likely keep Amish families large by middle-class America standards.

The exodus from the farm is also reshaping the role of children in the economy of Amish society. Participation in family-related work is not easy when fathers work away from home on mobile crews or in the larger shops. Labor laws also limit the involvement of children in certain types of work. Beyond legal barriers, some shop work is simply too heavy or dangerous for Amish youngsters. Commercial work also differs from farming in its margin of acceptable error. Children can be allowed errors when they

◆

This dried flower shop, established by an Amishwoman, provides employment for her husband as well. The shop and attached horse barn are located behind the owner's home.

practice harrowing the family field, but quality control cannot be jeopardized when industrial contracts carry detailed specifications.

Adjustments loom large for children whose fathers leave their plows to work away from home. Such children not only lose extensive contact with their father but are also isolated from his habits and attitudes toward work. Church leaders worry that without work to keep them busy, the children will more likely get into mischief. When father works away from home, one businessman asserted, "children come home from school and don't know what to do."

Removing the father from the home also splits parenting responsibilities—weakening the father as a role model and laying a greater burden on the wife and mother. When "the father works away and the mother is home all day with the children underfoot," warned one young Amishwoman, "there's nothing for the children to do." Moreover, children may face divided parental authority. In her words, "The father's not there to discipline. When he comes home he's tired, and when he is here he doesn't want to reprimand the whole time. It's a problem. Actually, it's the same problem the world faces when the husband works away." Said one Amishman sadly, "I worked away and my wife did very good raising the children on her own. But it's not like farming with them, not like working with them yourself."

Worried by these changes, many Amish families, especially those with home-based businesses, make special efforts to include their children in their work. Indeed, that is a major reason many shops are lodged at or near the home. In some cases, children perform simple cleaning chores on a daily basis, developing a sense of responsibility at an early age. Explained a fencing manufacturer: "With a business like this at home, my two boys come home from school and they go out to the shop to clean up. They clean up every day. It's not a lot, but it's something for them to do."

Home businesses also encourage parent-child interactions in the context of work. One shop owner described his son and daughters' participation in the business: "Children are involved [here] from little on up. From the time they could stand on a five-gallon bucket, they're up looking and watching what you're doing." So successful was this owner in socializing his son into work that at seventeen the young man began managing the woodworking shop by himself, accepting major contracts and handling personnel matters.

Amish parents believe that children should be taught to work when they are young. A common adage reiterates the wisdom: "It's too late to teach children to work after they're through school." A manufacturer spoke for many Amish parents when he said: "Often a six-year-old child can do the same work a regular adult worker can do. A child certainly can't do it all day, of course. A child has to play. But for an hour or two a child can do most anything an adult can—well, except things like run a table saw, that's too dangerous. But within reason, you know, if you put children to work a little bit at a time, they'll soon learn. And when they are old enough to work a full day, they'll know what they're doing, and they'll be good workers."

Home businesses permit parents not only to teach their children the skills required to operate a successful establishment but also to socialize them into the work ethic that is engrained in Amish culture. Being able to work alongside parents and grandparents and to develop emotional ownership of the work at an early age is critical to passing on a love of work to the next generation. Few Amish businesses formally employ school-age children, but youngsters participate in dozens of informal ways and absorb the values of a thriving work ethic.

Some parents and church leaders, however, worry that despite the best of intentions, some Amish children are being left behind in the pursuit of profits. The church is sharply critical of the few cases in which both Amish parents work away from home in a retail store or market stand. During the summer months the children may accompany their parents, but when school begins, they come home to a parentless house—though rarely an empty one: older siblings, extended family, and grandparents are usually nearby. Even so, the Amish assessment is blunt: "The children come home from school and there's no one there. It's terrible."

Some parents also fear that children will become too comfortable with the technology of the workplace. Power tools, cash registers, and other equipment may be run with pneumatic power or shop-generated electricity. Such gadgetry has traditionally been barred from the home in an effort to insulate family life from the tentacles of technology. With more and more businesses operating in or adjacent to the home, technology inches ever closer to the heart of the family. Children growing up in technology-filled surroundings may push for greater automation in the years to come, a push that may accelerate the rate of social change in Amish life.

Home businesses also expose children to frequent interaction with outsiders. Although traditional farm families had regular dealings with milk haulers, veterinarians, and sales people, such contact was limited and controlled. Most interactions with outsiders took place on non-Amish turf—at stores and auctions—thus maintaining a symbolic boundary between the haven of home and temptations beyond. The advent of Amish enterprises in or near the home redrew the lines of demarcation between church and world. As families open retail shops to non-Amish customers and tourists, they expose themselves and their children to frequent interaction with the larger outside world. Indeed, they invite outsiders to interact with them *inside* the Amish world, and the very success of their business depends on it. Retail shops are certainly front-stage platforms of social interaction; nevertheless, they make it more likely that some outsiders will slip backstage into kitchens, living rooms, and basements.[9] Whereas Amish children formerly grew up having few non-Amish friends, a good number of youngsters now meet outsiders on a regular basis, subtly blurring the lines of separation.

Frequent interaction with outsiders will surely affect children in a number of ways. Greater social intercourse will likely soften the strict separatism of traditional Amish life. Children now receive firsthand exposure to the dress, speech, attitudes, and personal habits of worldly outsiders. The business motto "The Customer Is Always Right," also on Amish lips, may further erode the barricades of sectarianism. Involvement in businesses with significant numbers of non-Amish suppliers and customers will surely dilute, if not diminish, the Pennsylvania German dialect, as children become more comfortable using English.

The individualistic values so central to entrepreneurship will likely mold the personal attitudes and deportment of children, making them less reserved and less willing to yield to traditional authority. Some children have begun to develop an uncharacteristically Amish confidence when dealing with outsiders on a regular basis. Interchange with outsiders teaches children "to deal with people, and talk with people," one father said with approval. "It teaches them not to be ashamed of themselves, it gives them some self-esteem." In short, it builds self-confidence and verbal expertise that fly in the face of traditional Amish humility.

But in other cases, interaction with outsiders may serve as a social inoculation that galvanizes cultural separatism and Amish fears of the outside world. An entrepreneur attending a bankruptcy hearing for a non-Amish enterprise that owed him money arrived home in time for the evening meal at an Amish wedding. Reflecting on the sharp contrast, he remarked to his wife, "Other people have no idea how good we have it here." Said one market stand holder, "I think that being out in the world makes me appreciate my way of life more. I mean, some of the things I've seen have been a real eye-opener. Seeing what's involved in the outside world, I appreciate our church more. I think I might even see more clearly what we've got as a church than a farmer might." Other Amish leaders are less optimistic, fearing that working "out in the world" will eventually lower the fences of cultural separation for their children.

Although farming often left a legacy of land, implements, and buildings, some businesses leave an inheritance of cash for children.[10] Such easily disposable capital, some businesspeople worry, could impair the church. Access to "loose," unearned money might encourage young adults to tamper with the moral boundaries of Amish life, to hanker after more worldly conveniences, or even to leave the church. Some entrepreneurs fear that the risk is too great, and they limit their business growth so they will have less to turn over to their children. Some have invested cash in real estate to shield their heirs from the lure of easy money. One couple explained their decision to avoid stowing away a cash inheritance: "We asked ourselves why we would have all this money here for our children. When we got married, we had to work our way through. We didn't get handed a big amount of money. It's better for them if there's not a big pile of money waiting for them. We shouldn't have a fortune for our kids. That's the way we feel."

Changes in Church Life

The entry into business has affected local church districts in a number of ways. Two of the most obvious results have been an increase in population density and a decrease in the geographic size of church districts. No longer separated from one another by acres of farmland, many families now live on small adjacent plots. Entrepreneurs and day laborers often reside on small parcels along country roads or in crossroad towns, nearby fellow ethnics. Because people are living closer together, the geographic size of church districts is shrinking.

Today, the households in an average district cover half as much land as they did forty years ago. One fifty-year-old businessman noted that the church district in which he was raised covered the land area of four present-day districts. Smaller church districts facilitate social interaction and horse-and-buggy travel. Members can more easily travel to a nearby home for Sunday morning worship. Indeed, many are able to walk to services. In recent years, church services in some districts begin and end a half-hour earlier than they did forty years ago because members have shorter distances to travel. Thus, the rise of shops has reinforced and increased the social solidarity of local churches.

Although businesses have opened their doors to outsiders, the move off the farm has boosted interaction within the Amish fold. Many members work with or for coethnics, increasing daily contact beyond the old neighborly patterns on the farm. Newly established Amish stores and businesses also supply services once provided by outsiders. Amish grocery and dry goods stores, scattered throughout Lancaster County, provide merchandise and services that were previously purchased in non-Amish stores—often in Lancaster City. An Amish grandmother living on the eastern edge of the county remembers traveling with her husband to the city almost weekly years ago. Now, with Amish stores nearby, she treks to the city but once a year.

The move off the farm has also touched leadership roles. Bishops, ministers, and deacons in the Amish church are self-supported. Traditionally, only farmers were considered prospective candidates for ordination. Farming represented the ideals of the church, and leaders were selected who best modeled those values. Agriculture minimized interaction with the world and brought fewer technological temptations. Farmers were also closely tied to the soil and less likely to move away and leave their congregation with a leadership void. Recently, however, with the number of farmers dipping low in some districts, the church has begun to ordain businesspeople.

Some church members fear, however, that innovative entrepreneurs will permit too many innovations in the church if they become leaders.

Younger members often express fewer concerns about having a bishop who runs a business. Said one young woman, "To me it [the hesitation to ordain businessmen] just doesn't make sense. There are businessmen who are perfectly good speakers." She predicts a growing number of ordained businessmen: "There just won't be enough farmers!" As more shop owners become church leaders, the church will face new challenges. Bishops and ministers, expected to model cultural virtues, will need to limit the size of their enterprises, but ordained leaders who own a business might be more likely to tolerate technological change. They may, for example, be more lenient with the use of cell phones and computers.

The growing involvement in business also affects education.[11] The Amish church opened its first private school in the Lancaster settlement in 1938. Today more than 160 one-room schools dot the countryside and provide instruction for students in grades one through eight. Teachers are typically single Amishwomen, often in their late teens or early twenties, who graduated from Amish schools. Some teach for only a few years before marriage; others spend much of their lives in the classroom. Uncertified by the state, they are selected for their academic ability and their commitment to core cultural values.

In years past, teaching was one of the few occupational avenues open to young unmarried women outside the home. However, new job opportunities for young women in business have diminished the lure of teaching. Whereas at one time school boards had a half-dozen applicants for a vacancy, now fewer candidates come forward. More and more single women are working in businesses of one type or another. Parents are less likely to encourage a daughter to leave home to take a teaching job. Salary has become another consideration. Younger women may be able to earn as much going to market two days a week as they can teaching for a whole week. One father admitted that teacher salaries would have to rise if schools hope to continue to attract bright young women.

On a more substantive level, the needs of future entrepreneurs might challenge the traditional curriculum of the schools. Greater involvement in business may require greater proficiency in math or writing. When the Amish won the blessing of the U.S. Supreme Court for their educational program in 1972, they argued that their educational efforts were adequate for a rural people of the land. With the spiraling rise of business, however, the traditional education offered by Amish schools may not suffice. Will youth sporting an eighth-grade diploma be prepared to compete in the commercial world over several generations? Will apprenticeships in shops provide an adequate education for aspiring Amish entrepreneurs?

Church leaders view the present school curriculum as adequate and contemplate few, if any, instructional changes. The school system also provides church leaders with a subtle means of regulating business. By limiting academic subjects, the church puts an early damper on curiosity about such things as science and computers. Moreover, the eight-grade cap prevents youth from straying into undesirable careers. By controlling their educational system, the ethnic community inadvertently limits the type and scope of commercial endeavors. Meanwhile, dozens of entrepreneurs with an eighth-grade diploma operate very successful, thriving firms. Thus, outside voices of reform must bear the burden of proof for any need to tamper with the curriculum in Amish schools.

New Social Classes

Because the foray into business is a recent phenomenon, the role and place of the entrepreneur in Amish society is still evolving. Historically, Amish society had been rather flat without the typical American gradations of social class. Uniformity of occupation and education led to equality in wealth and social standing. Although certain families possessed greater means than others, when compared with the larger American society Amish life had few class distinctions. Individual members of the church received esteem by virtue of their age and wisdom, not their educational credentials, salaries, or prestigious positions. The primary status one could obtain was through ordination to church leadership. Yet even here it was primarily God's choice and did not involve personal initiative, because leaders were selected through a congregational process that involved the drawing of lots.[12]

With the flowering of enterprises, however, the egalitarian ethos of Amish society is eroding. By its very nature entrepreneurial creativity thrives on individualism and personal achievement. The recent success in business is producing greater financial disparity among members. While farmers and wage laborers may have similar disposable incomes, some business owners have the means to earn significantly more than their neighbors. One entrepreneur noted that "anyone who has a fine eye can detect a clear difference between farmers and business owners. The businesspeople have finer clothing—the same color and style but better material. They buy a new carriage every three or four years and have a high-quality horse." An Amish quilt dealer observed that the entrepreneurs "try hard to conceal their wealth, but some of their new homes almost look like beach houses." Indeed, some of the newly rich, mocking traditional standards of Amish modesty, are building well-landscaped homes that cost upwards of $250,000.

◆

*A new shop and home under construction. The small "Grossdaadi" house on
the left serves as a retirement home for grandparents. New wealth has
encouraged the construction of new shops and larger homes.*

A few homegrown cottage industries would hardly disturb the balance
of Amish society, but the ramifications of multimillion-dollar manufacturing operations are a different story. "The old graybeards have no idea
how much money is flowing around in this community," remarked one
banker. The more successful entrepreneurs earn several hundred thousand dollars a year. One business owner paid $117,000 on personal taxes
alone. In one year, a furniture shop owner cleared $340,000 in profit. Con-
struction foremen may earn $65,000 a year, while their Amish boss tops
$200,000. Meanwhile, shop workers and farmers may be earning $35,000.

These numbers reflect not only growing economic disparities within the
community but also an enormous flow of new wealth. In the words of one
credit officer, "The wealth generated in the Amish community in the last
ten years is just fantastic; it's phenomenal." *Forbes, Fortune 500,* and the
Wall Street Journal have all featured stories on Amish millionaires and the
new wealth in the Amish community.[13] Moreover, a new bank, initiated by
Amish leaders but owned mostly by outsiders, serves many businesses in
the plain community.[14] A financial advisor to the Amish has more than 750
Amish clients who invest in mutual funds on a monthly basis. Some save
only a few dollars a month, but some shop owners save thousands on a
monthly basis. All of these indicators underscore the flow of new wealth
in Amish society.

Although the church tries to regulate growth, a well-established business is difficult to bridle. Will the church be able to limit the wealth and

influence of successful entrepreneurs over the generations? Some business leaders have already become private loan brokers of sorts, lending money to fellow church members and providing start-up capital for new commercial ventures. Although a noble and concrete form of mutual aid, such a role can add to the status and power of entrepreneurs. Might the financially powerful, by virtue of their business acumen, exercise undue influence across the community?

More broadly, will the growth of small-business capitalism disturb the social equilibrium of Amish life? In a society that values age and wisdom, will those who master the mechanics of marketing become the new sages? Although Amish businesspeople forgo some technological wonders, they still operate with more sophisticated technology than farmers. Some owners, working closely with computer-literate accountants, gain a measure of electronic literacy. Armed with expertise and worldly connections, they might tip the delicate balance of power preserved by years of rural life. One church district, for example, is informally known by the name of its leading entrepreneur rather than by the name of its resident bishop—the traditional means of identifying a district.

Contact with outside suppliers, dealers, and customers puts some entrepreneurs in regular contact with the ethical values of the larger world. Will scientific and financial knowledge become more important than the bestowed wisdom from previous generations? As entrepreneurs come to rely more on professionals and outside consultants, will they give greater deference to diplomas and Fortune 500 mentalities? Equally important, will the church itself ascribe status to younger businesspeople simply because they are successful—giving more credence to their opinions than to elderly members seasoned with age?

Some church members believe that entrepreneurs are naturally more progressive in their outlook. "The businessmen are more liberal in what they do and think," a young woman commented, reflecting a rather widely held belief. Although many entrepreneurs resent the progressive label and work diligently to operate within the Ordnung, the popular image persists—sometimes for good reason. The broader use of technology and exposure to outside contacts fuels the notion that entrepreneurs are less conservative than farmers. Will the liberal label eventually discredit their influence? Or might their rising status hasten the emergence of a distinctive entrepreneurial class in Amish society? The conduct of businesspeople and the response of the church will determine whether the entrepreneurs become the gatekeepers of progress or the ignoble examples to which church leaders point in warning.

The role of the entrepreneur remains ambiguous. Entrepreneurs do not yet receive the public acclaim that typically comes with financial success, but they walk a careful line, balancing their activity in the marketplace with their role in a changing but still traditional culture. Although the deacons still collect alms money and officially function as caretakers of the needy, the business community has taken the lead in lending money and securing loans. Businesspeople have also assumed new positions as coordinators of mutual aid activities in some districts.

Just as entrepreneurs assist fellow ethnics in getting started in business, they also help young farmers buy land, which helps to preserve the agricultural heritage of their people. Indeed, one of the surprises of the story is that many times only well-to-do entrepreneurs have the resources to buy expensive farmland when it comes on public auction. Farmers may not have the finances to compete against developers or may not be able to pay off a farm with a farmer's income. Thus, in an ironic twist, it is often the successful entrepreneurs who are able to preserve farmland and keep at least a remnant of Amish on the land.

Entrepreneurs, of course, have employees. And at first blush there may seem to be many benefits for those who have found hourly work within ethnic boundaries. Large factories quickly lose their lure when compared with the satisfactions of working in an Amish shop or store. Entrepreneurship has provided the Amish with an escape from their demographic

◆

Some retired business owners spend time each winter in a small Amish village near Sarasota, Florida. Shuffleboard is a favorite wintertime sport of the "snowbirds" coming from various areas of the country, including Lancaster County.

squeeze, yet the nonfarm employment that came in the wake of burgeoning businesses contains the seeds of a three-class society consisting of farmers, entrepreneurs, and day laborers.

Hourly employees may find themselves locked into a day-laborer status in a three-tiered community. Although farmers bank on the security of increasing land values, and business owners count on a steady cash flow, permanent hourly workers constitute a new, wage-earning lower class in Amish society. Without the resources to begin their own firms, some young Amish will likely work as day laborers for years to come.

As Amish businesses acquire more employees, successful entrepreneurs quietly—often unintentionally—tend to build a base of support within the church. Workers beholden to a fellow church member for their economic survival may, in a moment of conflict, support their boss rather than listen to the voice of the church. Might employers be able to overstep church bounds, knowing that they have enough church members on their payroll to snuff out serious opposition? If a business moves against the commonly accepted Ordnung, employees could find themselves caught in the precarious middle, wanting to stand with the church but also trying to carry out the wishes of their employer. Although it is difficult to predict how a three-tiered class structure will shape Amish life over the years, it is clear that many cultural realignments will follow on the tails of entrepreneurial success.

A New Worldview

The appearance of commercial enterprises has severely pressed Amish taboos on technology; indeed, it has revised them in recent years. A variety of cultural taboos have conceded to the economic pressures exerted by commercial involvement. Although tapping electricity from public utility lines for use in homes and shops is still prohibited, mobile work crews are permitted its use at public work sites. Entrepreneurs using rented buildings have considerable freedom to use electricity from public utility lines. Generators and inverters, now widely used, enable shop owners to make 110-volt electricity to power copy machines, coffeepots, cash registers, electric typewriters, and electric lights for special purposes. Clearly, the old cultural limits on electrical usage are undergoing revision.

A variety of other arrangements have also been negotiated to access more technology. Along with growing access to computer technology and Web sites via third-party vendors, motor vehicle use is on the upswing, as is the practice of leasing vehicles. As noted earlier, telephones are also inching closer to shops and homes—and in some cases, into pockets. Portable beepers for fire alarms and emergency medical teams have become standard equipment in some church districts. Battery-operated calculators are widely used everywhere. Nevertheless, the growing distinction between use and ownership permits access to certain technologies while still keeping them harnessed to some extent.

The widespread acceptance of air and hydraulic equipment has paved the way for the use of large and sophisticated manufacturing equipment. All of these negotiated cultural agreements have enabled the Amish to harvest some of the fruits of scientific progress while still honoring their ethnic heritage. The wider use of technology, however, reflects a deeper change in the structure of Amish values—a transformation of the Amish worldview. "There is a whole new group of young shop owners who think some of the traditional distinctions are foolish!" said the young owner of a retail store.

At the outset, we suggested that the modern world abounds with individuation, rationality, efficiency, and control—values at odds with many cherished Amish virtues. Business ventures are indeed transforming many of the cultural sentiments that have regulated Amish life over the generations and that gave birth to Amish enterprise in the first place. Individuation is clearly on the rise. Personal names are appearing more frequently on business cards, in business names, and on advertising trinkets. And unlike farming, failure or success in business points much more directly to the personal ability of an entrepreneur to conquer the harsh competition of the marketplace.

Our discussions with entrepreneurs and the stories written by shop owners and storekeepers in *The Diary* testify to the growing influence of market forces and the need for efficient production. One shop owner, writing about "wasted motion," calculated that if eight shop workers waste several seconds with each move, it adds up to a $5,760 yearly loss for the owner. He concluded by noting that "if you avoid needless moves, your profits will increase."[15] The pursuit of profit ushers in a whole new world—a world quite at odds with the modest pace of plodding horses pulling old-fashioned plows. The world of Amish entrepreneurs is driven by calculation, competition, specialization, and individuation—it is in short, a modern world.

Entrepreneurs who straddle the worlds of tradition and modernity often feel pulled in conflicting directions. Always tempted to use more and more advanced technology, they also realize that the restraints of their culture have bestowed on them a satisfying way of life. One successful entrepreneur, who at times has faced the censure of the church for stepping across the boundaries of the Ordnung, summed it up this way: "Sometimes I think of leaving the church, but why should I leave when I know there are millions of people out there who would just love to have this way of life."

Lancaster's Amish have negotiated a workable settlement with the forces of modernity. Forced to leave the farms of their past, they have refused to enter the alien culture of corporate America. Their embrace of micro-enterprises represents a tenuous cultural agreement—a midway point between their pastoral past and the world of high-tech industry. They have, indeed, relinquished their grip on the plow as well as on some aspects of their family-centered living, shaped by three centuries of tilling the soil. But they have yielded neither their right to manage their own time and resources nor their control of technology. Acting rather judiciously, the Amish have held the terms and conditions of their work within the religious boundaries of their ethnic community. Their move toward entrepreneurship marks a pivotal moment in their history—a most significant adjustment to the modern world. They have struck a bargain that nourishes their economic health without conceding their cultural soul—a bargain that appears to be working in their favor for the moment. But in time the byproducts of that bargain may, in fact, transform the very cultural values that gave birth to it in the first place.

14. National Patterns of Amish Work

High-paying factory jobs force us to pay higher wages in our shops.
— INDIANA AMISH SHOP OWNER

Regional Differences

In the dim light of early morning an Amish man living near Nappanee, Indiana, hops on his bicycle and rides a mile and a half to a large factory. He works an eight-hour shift on an assembly line alongside scores of Amish and non-Amish men outfitting recreational motor homes for dealers across the country. In northwestern Ohio's Williams County, members of an Amish household begin the day in their family's sawmill business. They build rough pallets for commercial shippers rather than construct fine cabinets that undoubtedly would yield wider profit margins. Near Arthur, Illinois, a van leaves an Amish homestead after picking up the eighth member of a mixed Amish and non-Amish carpentry crew. The men will spend the day building an addition to a large home sixty miles to the west on the outskirts of Springfield.

Like the Lancaster, Pennsylvania, settlement, these midwestern Amish communities have undergone notable economic, social, and cultural shifts as they have entered nonagricultural work. Indeed, despite the wide variety in history, custom, and practice among Amish across the United States, the growing nonfarm economy of Amish communities is remarkably similar. In large and small settlements, in old communities and recently established "daughter" settlements, and in remote rural areas and suburbanizing regions, the Amish are abandoning their plows for other occupations.[1]

The specific shape and implications of this common development, however, vary from place to place, highlighting the importance of local context in shaping Amish interaction with the larger society and underscoring the interactive role of cultural resources and restraints in the process of social change. A comparative look at the shift to nonfarm work in an array of Amish settlements shows how Amish enterprises emerge as a negotiated outcome of the mixing of cultural resources and restraints within settings that shape and are shaped by them. Indeed, the diversity of economic experience testifies to the vitality of Amish culture.

Cultural values expressed and regulated by church Ordnung are both a resource and a restraint that vary considerably from place to place. Unlike the Lancaster community, where bishops seek to maintain a common Ordnung, many Amish settlements do not have a uniform Ordnung. In places like Holmes and Wayne Counties, Ohio, distinct Amish affiliations each maintain a discrete Ordnung, resulting in different practices within a single settlement. Indiana's Elkhart-LaGrange settlement, along with many other midwestern communities, is highly congregational, lacking both a settlement-wide Ordnung and Ohio-type affiliations. In such places the Ordnung can vary from district to neighboring district, creating a patchwork of practices that are hard to generalize and forming a context in which multiple factors manage the pressures of progress. Ordnung surrounding technology, for example, may limit or expand the range of entrepreneurial options from one district to another.

But Ordnung does more than draw lines of restraint at different places; it seeks to check change as a way of promoting and preserving a community ideal—an ideal that also varies from place to place. Some churches regard at-home businesses as the next-best thing to family-centered farming, while those in other places may see the presence of microenterprises in the home as downright threatening because they carry the temptation to introduce technological change and customer interaction into the very heart of family life itself. Where such views prevail, the preferred occupational outcome may well take the father away from home—as part of a mobile construction crew, for example—so that the concrete effects of entrepreneurial change are held at bay from the family's sacred center. Thus, the same desire to protect the family drives Amish household heads in some communities to work away from home, while it encourages those in other places to cultivate home-based businesses.

Meanwhile, local geographic context also shapes the direction and limits the possibilities of Amish off-farm work. Proximity to major markets or interstate highways, as well as the historical tradition of particular Amish settlements, may promote or discourage certain types of business. Long-term relationships with non-Amish neighbors stretching back for generations could help develop customer bases, employee pools, and product perception. Moreover, the local presence of industrial jobs or the absence of tourist traffic may open some economic doors while closing others.

Yet social, environmental, and economic contexts do not serve just as the setting in which cultural resources and cultural restraints play against one another. Rather, context itself becomes one of the players as it interacts with ethnic facilitation and resistance. For example, the mere presence of industrial employment opportunities in rural communities is not enough to ensure that the Amish will find them attractive. Amish objections to labor union membership or union contracts that require the hiring of high school graduates may limit the appeal of industry. Amish men in north central Indiana and in Geauga County, Ohio, are heavily involved in factory work because nonunion shops are common in those places and because non-Amish employers waive company preferences for high school graduates. In contrast, industrial jobs abound in the factory town of Kokomo, Indiana, but the Amish there have avoided factory work because Kokomo industries are unionized and insist on high school credentials.

Moving Off the Midwestern Farm

Like their fellow Amish in eastern Pennsylvania, Amish communities in other parts of the country find themselves deeply involved in nonfarm work. Some of the elements that precipitated this shift were familiar everywhere: large families that pushed church population upward, shrinking land availability and affordability, and the financial pressures of the American farm economy that squeezed all family farms in the late twentieth century. Other factors were uneven in their impact. For example, suburbanization and rising non-Amish populations affected some areas more than others.

Amish in the Midwest, especially, had long dealt with the tension between land and population pressures through migration. If the Lancaster Amish used a strategy of migration only sparingly—launching a few new settlements in the 1960s and 1970s, and none during the 1980s when they faced demographic pressures most acutely—the midwestern Amish pattern was one of remarkable mobility.[2] Since the nineteenth century, setting up new settlements in states such as North Dakota, Oregon, Nebraska, or Michigan was a typical response to economic pressures in older Amish settlements. New farmland might be just over the next valley or even in another state; nevertheless, moving was one way of staying on the farm.

All that began to change with the onset of the Great Depression. Newer settlements, often established on marginal land to begin with, folded up.[3] Some families began moving back to traditional hearths after absences of a couple years or a couple generations, and they brought with them the message—spoken or implied—that the choice to preserve a particular way of life elsewhere might not be viable. Perhaps it was better to stay in historic Amish communities and explore other occupational options. During the 1930s, then, some Amish men in older settlements began taking off-farm jobs. Anecdotal evidence points to carpentry or factory work, employment in feed mills, and even working as delivery truck drivers in a few cases where the church approved a driver's license if driving was limited to work.[4] In rare cases, household heads in communities especially hard-hit by the Depression took government-sponsored jobs through the Works Progress Administration.[5]

In 1940 a church census seeking information on Amish men liable for the military draft documented a small but undeniable number of men working in industry or the building trades on a regular basis.[6] The growth in such work continued in the decades that followed. By 1980—when the Lancaster settlement was just beginning to wrestle with the implications of putting aside its plows—off-farm employment for midwestern men was an established reality, and in some cases had been for several generations, as the number of farmers dwindled.

Not that Amish families eagerly surrendered fieldwork for lunch pails and time clocks. In many places communities experimented with ways to sustain the family farm. In the 1940s the Kalona, Iowa, and Kokomo, Indiana, settlements adopted tractor farming in an effort to boost the viability of agriculture. By the 1970s the Arthur, Illinois, Amish community had moved toward a more specialized agricultural economy that combined smaller acreage with large laying hen, hog finishing, or drylot cattle feeding operations.[7] That approach initially worked until volatile commodity prices and environmental regulation of animal waste rendered it as problematic as traditional small-scale farming.

Moreover, in a number of places a conservative-minded Ordnung resisted modification in these and other ways. For example, many Amish in New York, Delaware, and the Midwest resisted installing bulk milk tanks as their Lancaster brethren did in 1969 to boost their farm income. In these other places, new milking technology often came later—indeed, after many farmers had left their farms for other work.[8] In the Allen County, Indiana, settlement, for example, church districts endorsed automatic milkers only in the 1990s, but by then few farmers were left to benefit. In a handful of places, such as the Nappanee, Indiana, settlement, Amish farm families who carried lunch pails to nearby industrial jobs began renting their land to non-Amish tractor farmers in the 1960s. To be sure, in some locations creativity, coupled with opportunity, birthed new ventures in cheese making or organic produce production that gave farming a second wind.[9] But the trend in virtually every community was away from the timeworn path of the plow.

Thus, the move toward nonfarm jobs took place in contexts marked not only by a shrinking land base and surging Amish populations but also in an unsteady farm economy and often with an inflexible Ordnung govern-ing traditions central to Amish identity such as farming. In some places, in fact, the relative rigidity of the Ordnung on farming issues helped to push Amish people into new occupations that were less threatening than revis-ing the rules for farming.

The depth of this reorientation is demonstrated by the many newer Amish settlements founded in the later twentieth century where families moved from crowded communities to more rural locations with no inten-tion of farming. If the desire to be free of traffic congestion and oppressive real estate prices drove households to more isolated or sparsely settled areas in western Pennsylvania, New York, and the Midwest, these settlers often founded communities with as few or fewer farmers as the older settlements they had left behind. Shops and mobile carpentry crews abound in newer communities that, while rural, are often not known for productive soils.

Yet amid this dynamic Amish occupational panoply, patterns do emerge. Across the country three major clusters of alternatives to agriculture have surfaced: microenterprises, industrial employment, and mobile work crews. Very often one of the three dominates a given settlement, and the prefer-ence stems from an interactive mix of church Ordnung and outlook as well as contextual factors: geographic location, employment opportunities, the nature of customer or client bases, and access to markets and materials. Amish leaders are generally able to articulate why they believe the non-farm occupational choices they have made are preferable and what they gain from them. Typically, they also can identify some negative influences these choices brought as well as undesirable changes other types of non-farm work might bring. In each case, ethnic resources and restraints play an important role in the promotion and limitation of Amish enterprise.

The Shape of Small Shops

If the Lancaster Amish find small businesses attractive, they are not alone. Microenterprises have sprung up in most settlements across the country—though they are more common in some places than in others. Such firms tend to mushroom where the mix of cultural resources and local context is right. They have been the occupational choice of many in the Holmes and Wayne Counties in Ohio for the same reasons they have thrived in south-eastern Pennsylvania.[10] Even in new midwestern Amish communities, ostensibly established by migrants looking for available farmland, many households quickly established small businesses.

Some small shops in Ohio, Illinois, Indiana, and elsewhere seem much like their Lancaster counterparts profiled in previous chapters, producing a wide range of wholesale and retail goods for Amish and non-Amish clients—from dry goods stores and welding shops to traditional leather trades and furniture making. They involve male and female entrepreneurs, children, and older adults.[11] Typically limited in size to a dozen or fewer employees, these shops use adaptive technology and relatively convenient telephone service to compete successfully in the modern marketplace. Other Amish shops are strikingly different from these progressive cousins and emerge from churches with more restrictive Ordnungs that severely bridle the size and technology of their operations. Prohibitions on electric generators in the Dover, Delaware, settlement, for example, have eliminated machine and metal fabrication shops, channeling Amish enterprise into woodworking establishments that do not require electric welding technology.[12] And in some communities, additional constraints come from the particularities of local markets and materials.

For the most part, the cultural resources for entrepreneurship are similar across Amish settlements: an ample pool of ethnic labor, frugality that minimizes overhead costs, a rigorous work ethic, and an entrepreneurial heritage rooted in farming, to name a few. But other factors that might be seen as cultural resources in one place function more as restraints in another. For example, a flexible Ordnung in the Lancaster settlement allows hydraulic and pneumatic power and relatively convenient telephone access. In more tradition-minded settlements, these things are off-limits, restricting power sources in many cases to a small engine that drives a spinning line shaft to operate belt-driven machines. Coupled with prohibitions on electric inverters and in some cases even battery-powered calculators, these cultural limitations funnel the energy of conservative shops into crafts where intensive handwork rather than volume production is an advantage—for example, making hickory rockers. Similarly, making and retailing wooden baskets is common among the ultraconservative Swartzentruber Amish, where technology restrictions severely narrow the range of possible products.

Even such restrictions, though, can become ethnic resources that play up product distinctions in the marketplace. An innovative precision machine shop near Fort Wayne, Indiana, makes brass fittings and couplings for major industrial clients as well as decorative trinkets for gift shops across the country. It has a glossy catalogue without a phone number. Noting its Amish ownership, the catalog clearly states: "Traditionally, normal telephone service is not available, please respond by mail"—thus abiding by the local Ordnung while adding cachet for customers looking for product uniqueness. Nor have the limits on power sources seriously hindered production. The entire operation runs on an under-the-floor line shaft instead of hydraulic power that might be used in Amish facilities in LaGrange County not far to the northwest.

◆

*This Amish furniture shop in Ohio is one of dozens that make high-quality
household furniture that is distributed in several states. The equipment is
hydraulic powered.*

Indeed, a highly restrictive Ordnung can also be an ethnic resource for
channeling nonfarm work into microenterprises of a special sort. Ultraconservative communities such as those in Paoli, Indiana, or Williams
County, Ohio, discourage married men from working away from home,
leaving nonfarmers only one alternative: establish home-based businesses
that require no more labor than the immediate family can supply.[13] Restrictive rules on technology push these firms into a narrow range of services, including rough-cut lumber and pallet production.

At the other end of the spectrum, shops among the so-called New Order
Amish have freer reign to install hydraulic power or battery inverters as
well as to advertise telephone numbers for in-shop phones. Yet the small
size of many New Order settlements and a preference for hiring their own
members caps their labor pool and helps keep their shops relatively small.[14]

In addition to Ordnung, geographic, social, and ecological contexts
shape the entrepreneurial energy of Amish business people. The Amish
settlement in western Pennsylvania's Indiana County—founded in 1962 by
arrivals from Ohio and later augmented by newcomers from Delaware and
other places—is awash in microenterprises. A conservative Ordnung prohibits pneumatic power sources, battery calculators, and phones near shops,
thus limiting the size and diversity of businesses in Indiana County.[15] But

these cultural factors alone do not explain the economic landscape. Instead, the literal landscape—coupled with the contours of the regional economy—plays a decisive role. Farmland of marginal productivity and a regional business climate that fosters wood-related enterprise encouraged more than 70 percent of Amish businesses into furniture, lumber, or lathe work. A regional economy oriented toward forestry and connected to dealers and suppliers of wood products provides effective wholesale outlets for this relatively remote area that is distant from large retail markets or a sizeable tourist trade.

In some places contextual factors also militate against small businesses. Proximity to market networks and the history of wholesale connections can hinder as much as help would-be entrepreneurs. Amish from eastern and central Pennsylvania moving to Wayne County, Indiana, for example, found that Amish-built gazeboes and lawn furniture were popular in the Midwest. But retailers there already had access to large-volume Amish suppliers in the huge Lancaster and Holmes County settlements. Indiana retailers were reluctant to buy products from infant Amish shops even if they were nearby.

Similarly, in locations offering the possibility of factory employment, the urge to build small businesses is less pronounced since entrepreneurship involves start-up costs and financial risk, while factory work requires only an investment in a lunch box. In Indiana's Elkhart-LaGrange settlement, where factory work predominates, advocates of home-based businesses in 1995 organized a revolving loan fund known as Bruder-Hand to supply seed money for microenterprise ventures.[16] The aim, one supporter said, was "getting fathers established at home so they wouldn't have to work away." Rooted in Amish traditions of mutual aid and modeled on church-based plans for mortgage funds, fire coverage, and product liability, the Bruder-Hand testifies not only to these enduring Amish values but also to the fact that concerns about industrial jobs may spur structured financial support for entrepreneurs.[17]

Industrial Amish

In some communities, industrial employment is an option for nonfarmers. It is the most common line of work in northern Indiana's Elkhart-LaGrange and Nappanee settlements as well as in Geauga County, Ohio. In these communities, Amish hands assemble recreational vehicles or prefabricated homes, labor with hot rubber extruding equipment, or construct mass-produced furniture and cabinets. In the Geauga community, about a third of working-age Amish men are involved in factory work—more than any other job category—while in northern Indiana, such employment is actually the majority pursuit. In 2001 and 2002, 53 percent of household heads age 65 and younger in the Elkhart-LaGrange settlement worked in industry, as did 55 percent of the same cohort in Nappanee. A few Amish near Decatur, Indiana, also work in factories, and an industrial plant near Yoder, Kansas, that manufactures cabinetry for corporate jets also employs Amish. Some household heads in the Holmes County, Ohio, settlement spend their days in cabinet shops large enough to qualify as factories even if they are not located in an industrial park and do not bear other marks of heavy manufacturing.[18]

Unlike home-based microenterprises, factory work is almost exclusively the domain of traditional working-age Amish males. The few Amish women working in factories in northern Indiana leave upon marriage. While adult men of various ages punch industrial time clocks, younger men—those age 35 and under—are more firmly ensconced in industry, with a full 71 percent of that cohort in northern Indiana drawing factory paychecks. Those numbers reflect the growth of factory employment in these settlements and the fact that such work requires no up-front financial investment on the part of young men. Then too, some men in their 50s exit the factory for what they perceive to be less stressful jobs in small shops, leaving industry positions to those with greater stamina.

Amish workers find employment in different types of industrial work. Some work in factories that produce components for other plants; others staff assembly lines making finished products. Line work is more demanding, more stressful, and higher paying. Working in component construction is less rigorous but sometimes more tedious, and it almost always brings lower wages. Rarely do the Amish comprise the entire labor force within a single plant. In one fairly cosmopolitan environment in northern Indiana, Amish, Mexican, and Yemenite workers staff a Japanese-managed firm.

The Amish bring more to the factory floor than their lunch pails; they also carry cultural resources that make them a steady, stable, and reliable workforce that makes few demands and exhibits a strenuous work ethic. A tradition of woodworking and cabinetry among the Amish—coupled with a positive public perception of their products—channels the Amish toward construction and assembly line jobs.

Amish in the Elkhart-LaGrange and Nappanee settlements, moreover, have a slimmer ritual calendar than their fellow church members in Lancaster, Pennsylvania, and thus can more easily accommodate industrial production schedules without compromising churchly duties. For example, weddings occur throughout the year and often fall on Saturdays (in contrast to Lancaster's November weekdays); and Pentecost Monday and Ascension Day may involve only evening rather than daylong visiting.

In some ways, the Amish predilection for separation from the world also serves as a resource for successful industrial work. The factory makes no demands of off-duty workers. Amish employees, then, need not find their identity in paid positions but can view their work as a means to an end, a way to make a living. Amish factory workers typically speak Pennsylvania Dutch more than English on the job. While eating lunch and taking breaks, Amish co-workers use the dialect to discuss their off-work Amish lives.

Cultural factors also guide Amish employment choices. Rather than taking industrial jobs randomly, workers gravitate toward employers who offer attractive benefits. For example, the ability to work a 5:30 A.M. to 1:30 P.M. shift that leaves one free to help on a family farm, is more important than a flexible savings accounts for child care.[19] Thus, Amish values guide employment choices, which increases the number of Amish in a given factory and creates an ethnic subculture on the job. Lack of a high school education also limits their involvement in some factories and keeps them out of top management positions.

In most places, factory work is not an option for Amish job seekers simply because there are few large manufacturing concerns in many rural communities. Some Amish cite the regimented, compartmentalized nature of factory work as antithetical to their values. However, the Amish may choose industrial employment in settings where local industrial employers bend to Amish interests, the church has a flexible ritual calendar, and large numbers of ethnic employees are able to create an Amish subculture on the factory floor.

Workers on the Move

Mobile work crews—typically involved in carpentry, excavation, roofing, and other building trades—engage in the third major cluster of nonfarm occupations. Such crews take on the wide range of commercial and residential jobs, from new construction to remodeling. They build, finish, or contribute to single-family homes, apartment complexes, restaurants, and stores—even structures associated with Amish-theme tourism. At times these jobs are local, while in other cases work crews commute two or more hours one way. Occasionally workers will stay overnight in a local motel rather than return home each evening. Mobile crews are entirely male and appeal to a wide age spectrum, though many men take less physically demanding jobs as they age.

Construction work is not the first choice of many Amish people who resist traveling far from home. Furthermore, many small settlements in remote areas cannot compete for construction contracts. Still, such employment is present to some degree almost everywhere, and it is the over-whelming choice in some settlements. In the Berne area of eastern Indiana, for example, mobile work crews provide employment for a large majority of household heads—perhaps as many as 80 percent. In some midwestern daughter settlements stemming from the Lancaster, Pennsylvania, community, carpentry work is also common, though these contractors prefer jobs close to home.

In certain ways, mobile workers share characteristics with employees of both at-home shops and factories. While some Amish carpenters and trades-men work for non-Amish contractors, many are part of Amish crews or mixed partnerships where at least some of the management is Amish. They labor in an Amish work environment, and the Amish entrepreneurs who own or co-own the businesses face many of the same issues as owners of home-based firms. Like factory workers, however, members of work crews spend their days away from home and family.

As in the factory setting, Amish builders bring cultural resources that appeal to non-Amish employers and customers, producing a margin of ethnic advantage. Amish employees provide general contractors with a stable and reliable workforce, ready to work long hours and often with the requisite skills and an eagerness to learn. Moreover, Amish employees do not unionize, which some employers find appealing.

For both the Amish and casual onlookers, construction work is an un-surprising alternative to farming because of its perceived (and often real) link to traditional Amish trades such as carpentry. In past generations many farmers did some carpentry work of their own, and it was not uncommon for retired farmers to engage in woodworking. Any such knowledge handed down along these lines—as well as positive public perceptions of skills and attention to quality—function as cultural resources.

At the same time, an obvious cultural restraint on mobile work crews is the Amish taboo on motor vehicle ownership. For some ultraconservative Amish craftsmen, including members of the Swartzentruber affiliation, construction work must stay within buggy-driving distance of home. Most mobile construction crews, however, include at least one non-Amish em-ployee or co-owner who supplies transportation. In a rather exceptional sit-uation, Amish carpenters in the Arthur, Illinois, community began in the mid-1950s to acquire driver's licenses and drive trucks for work-related jobs while using buggies for personal trips. By 1970 so many men were driv-ing for work-related activities that local bishops began strongly to counsel against it. Thirty years later only about a dozen men still drive on the job, the rest having either turned the keys over to a non-Amish co-worker or left carpentry for home-based work.

In many cases taboos on technology are less of a limitation for contrac-

◆

*An Amish family in New York assembles nylon nets for the ends of lacrosse
sticks for a non-Amish distributor. Working in the main room of their home,
members of this conservative Swartzentruber Amish affiliation can assemble
about 1,000 nets a week.*

tors than for shop owners, precisely because mobile work crews perform
their jobs away from home. Like the factory employee, the carpenter or
subcontractor works on admittedly alien turf, very often for a non-Amish
customer (though Amish contractors will, of course, build homes for Amish
families). By separating their work from their home, most Amish trades-
men are freer to use an array of innovative tools that are not permitted at
home.

In fact, this understanding is what makes mobile work crews so popular in communities with a restrictive Ordnung, such as many of the so-
called Swiss Amish settlements scattered in Indiana, Missouri, Ohio, New
York, and Pennsylvania. As farming became less viable in these places, a
move toward at-home shops was not immediately appealing because Ordnung restrictions on power sources and near-the-house telephones seemed
to limit business effectiveness. However, by working away from home and
for outsiders, entrepreneurs could employ the tools of the trade and not
overstep the protective parameters that guarded the family. In short, because the mobile crew took work away from the home, it was freer from
cultural restraints. In some places this logic does not prevail, yet it has not

short-circuited the entrepreneurial spirit. In the Dover, Delaware, settlement, where contractors cannot use electric tools even on non-Amish job sites, the Amish have developed a recognized specialty in masonry instead of carpentry.[20]

Restraints can, of course, also become resources that provide an ethnic margin of difference. Amish church-based mutual aid and a reluctance to participate in mandatory Workers' Compensation programs, for example, lower Amish labor costs. Only Kentucky, Pennsylvania, and Wisconsin exempt the Amish from Workers' Compensation participation, but Amish in other states maintain their own medical aid plans. Thus, Amish contractors can carry the legally required coverage without ever submitting claims, thereby keeping their insurance rates quite low. Church aid plans cover injury claims fully without the administrative overhead of traditional Workers' Compensation programs. The net result is reduced operating costs for Amish contractors—a benefit born of a coolness to commercial insurance and a churchly commitment to bearing one another's burdens.

Similarly, Amish dress standards, which restrict the members' freedom of choice, also publicly announce the presence of Amish work crews on the

◆

Web sites owned by non-Amish distributors market Amish products around the world.

Amish.Net is America's first website devoted to Amish Country information, products and tourism services. Here you'll learn about the Amish people and history, the Amish culture, and its best-known icon, the horse-drawn Amish buggy. Browse online stores featuring handcrafted Amish quilts, Amish furniture, dolls and other crafts. Sample Amish foods and recipes. Better yet, plan your visit to Amish Country here. See Amish farmers working their fields, savor the aroma of home-cooked Amish noodles, and relax to the clip-clop sounds of a

Visiting The Amish | Amish Lifestyle | The Amish Buggy | Amish Life FAQ's | Free Listing | Advertising | Terms of Use

DIRECTORY

Search the Amish.Net Directory
[   ] [Search]

Amish Country Tourist Bureaus
OHIO , Holmes County , Loudonville-Mohican , Tuscarawas County , Wayne County , PENNSYLVANIA , Lancaster County , Indiana County , INDIANA
Shipshewana/LaGrange County , Elkhart County , Grabill (Allen County) , Berne , Illinois , Arcola , Arthur , Tuscola , Iowa , Bloomfield , Buchanan County , Kalona , Delaware , Wilmington , Dover/Kent County , Wisconsin , Michigan , Mio , River Country , New York , Heuvelton , Minnesota , Missouri , Jamesport , Kentucky , Tennessee , Maryland , Virginia , Florida , Kansas , Oklahoma , Montana , Ontario, Canada
Amish/Mennonite Information Centers
Mennonite Information Center (PA) , Menno Hof (IN) , Behalt (OH) , Amish History , About Amish , Amish Schooling Court Case
Amish Remedies
Unkerssalve.com
Books, Calendars, Jigsaw Puzzles, Videos and Artwork
Amish Jigsaw Puzzles , Book Stores , Coffee Table Books , Cook Books , Travel Guide Books , Calendars , Photography , Videos , Artwork and Paintings , Publishers
Attractions and Special Events

Quilts
Amish Owned Quilt Stores , Ready Made Quilts , Made to Order Quilts , Quilting Service , Quilts Kits , Quilt Clubs/News/Information , Quilt Auctions
Crafts and Gift Shops
Gift Shops , Souvenir Shops , Amish Dolls, Baskets, Candles and Clocks , Bird Feeders and Houses , Wooden Crafts , Wrought Iron
Furniture
Amish Made Hickory Rockers , Beds, Cribs, China Cabinets, Tables, Chairs, Rockers, Desks , Chests, Armoires and Quilt Racks , Patio and Lawn Furniture
Lodging
Lancaster Area & Pennsylvania , Western Pennsylvania & New Wilmington , Holmes County & Ohio , Shipshewana, Elkhart, Goshen & Indiana , Kalona & Iowa , Arcola, Arthur & Illinois , Cashton & Wisconsin , Harmony & Minnesota , Jamesport & Missouri , New York , Michigan , Other States , Ontario , Farm Stays , Campgrounds
Restaurants
Amish Family Style Menu , American Style Menu , Buffet
Amish Country Tours/Packages
Vacation Packages , Extended Bus Tours , Local Bus/Van Tours , Step On Guided Tours , Horseback Rides and Tours ,

job. The federal Occupational Safety and Health Administration's exemption of the Amish from hardhat rules not only frees Amish men from unwanted state interference with church tradition but also allows contractors to capitalize on the public perception of Amish craftsmanship that is visually apparent in the headgear of their construction crews. Ethnic garb, in short, provides on-site, no-cost advertising.

Continuity and Change in Amish Work

The economic and occupational changes in Amish communities in recent decades have transformed Amish society in ways even casual observers can appreciate. Increasingly common are church districts with no farmers, vanloads of men working on construction sites many miles from the nearest Amish settlement, and shops advertising sometimes in aggressive ways that challenge traditional humility. Amish products are now marketed around the world. A Google search on the Internet for "Amish furniture," for example, will generate more than 100,000 hits.

Yet in some ways, occupational change has not altered key components of Amish life. New employment venues have not lured the Amish into high school or college, and the Amish continue to observe a clear line between automobile use and ownership, reinforcing the significance of their horse culture. Indeed, for those Amish working in industry or on construction sites for non-Amish clients, using the latest technology may actually cement, rather than dilute, their notions of Amish separateness, since encounters with the fruits of modernity occur on clearly alien turf.

Likewise, the shifting patterns of work do not automatically undercut central aspects of Amish identity such as their use of Pennsylvania Dutch. Linguist Steve Hartman Keiser's comparison of the Kalona, Iowa, and Holmes County, Ohio, Amish demonstrated greater convergence toward English in Kalona, even though a majority of the men in the Iowa community still worked on the farm, and only 31 percent did so in Holmes County in 1995.[21]

Nor is the family—that central component of Amish society—necessarily turned upside down by changing work habits. Sociologist Thomas J. Meyers has shown that there is no statistically significant difference in the number of children in the families of northern Indiana farmers, factory workers, and shop owners. Indeed, there seem to be greater differences between major settlements than between occupational segments within a settlement.[22]

Significantly, in that same northern Indiana Elkhart-LaGrange settlement, Amish children raised in homes headed by farmers, factory workers, and shop owners joined the church in equal rates. There was not a higher defection rate among nonfarm children. Remarkably, in the Geauga County, Ohio, settlement, which is tilted toward factory and construction work, researchers Lawrence Greksa and Jill Korbin discovered that farm families had slightly *higher* rates of defection for their children than did households employed in lumber yards, shops, factories, or construction.[23] Factors such as gender, attendance of public versus parochial schools, proximity to town, and a local church's understanding of Ordnung are more important in influencing Amish teens' choices for or against church membership than their father's occupation.[24]

Yet economic shifts do have important implications for Amish life, including use of time, family relationships, access to capital and consumer goods, interaction with the wider world, and even one's worldview and sense of self. While none of the new occupational venues signals the end of Amish society, they will bring changes. But even here the implications vary in ways that betray the particular resources, restraints, and regional contexts at play. Each of the alternatives to farming holds its own set of potential problems and possibilities. The Amish understand this, aware that the choices they make preserve some aspects of their traditional ways while opening others to risk.

Outsiders may see factory employment as strikingly un-Amish since it places Amish in a rationalized bureaucratic culture—not to mention involvement in the production of products that may fall outside the sacred boundaries of the Ordnung. However, whatever tension Amish employees feel likely surfaces in areas of life other than the work day itself because Amish people do not find personal identity in a career in the way most middle-class North Americans do. Instead, the Amish see industrial jobs as a means to an end: a way to make a living in forty hours so they otherwise can live Amish lives.

Amish life outside the factory is undergoing significant change, however. A major consequence of factory work, for example, is leisure time. Unlike farming or small business ownership, manufacturing jobs are limited to certain hours five days of the week. Indeed, such labor is attractive to some Amish employees because they can easily separate factory life from home and church. Nevertheless, life outside the factory is altered by the presence of discretionary time. Relatively new leisure-time activities, such as fishing, boating, eating in restaurants, or shopping at the local Wal-Mart, are all more likely for the factory-employed Amish person, no matter his or her age. Free time for the children of these employees is also an issue, since work is removed from the home. Observers speak of Amish "factory homes"—small houses with a horse stable and tiny pasture and, in some cases, not even enough room for a garden to occupy young hands. Idleness, many elders worry, can lead to mischief.

Another byproduct of industrial employment is disposable wealth. Especially during the 1990s when the national economy was strong, frequent overtime produced hefty paychecks. Unlike small business owners who often need to plow some of their profits back into their business, Amish wage earners have disposable income. Ordnung and community concerns guide the spending of some of that money—channeling some of it into creative land trust accounts for newly married Amish couples' first mortgages—but the dollars are also used for landscaping, concrete driveways, second buggies or "run-around" carts, hunting trips, and motor boats.

Traditional notions of church-based mutual aid may also face an uncertain future in communities with heavy factory employment because Amish employees in non-Amish businesses must pay into the Social Security system. While the church discourages them from later collecting any benefits from the government, they are legally free to do so, and anecdotal evidence suggests that some retired factory workers do collect. Indeed, in 1999 the Social Security Administration communicated to the National Amish Steering Committee its surprise at the number of Amish factory workers who wished to collect benefits.[25] While the mere presence of Social Security payments does not spell an end to traditional practices of mutual aid, it does signal a trend toward greater personal financial planning in some communities.

Microenterprises induce different sources of social change. Small business ownership may lessen the lure of free time by keeping all hands from several generations busy at home. Indeed, one entrepreneur with a thriving firm reported: "We're busier than we were on the farm." Small shops, however, bring their own set of challenges to Amish tradition. By establishing a business at home, Amish entrepreneurs place the pressure for technological change and strategic innovation right in the sacred center of Amish life. For example, small businesses typically desire telephone service, and home businesses bring that temptation—among others—into the normal routine of home life for children and adults. In fact, the seriousness with which some Amish communities regard this threat underlies their strict shop-related Ordnungs that keep small businesses remarkably small or even discourage them altogether.

Especially if the enterprise is a retail business catering mostly to non-Amish customers, more of the day's activity may be carried on in English than would be the case for a farmer or a factory worker. Moreover, business owners may be involved in product liability issues that employees of non-Amish firms avoid. In some cases indemnity may come through church-sponsored aid plans, but sometimes commercial coverage is needed or preferred.

Additionally, the very strategic nature of entrepreneurship promotes a

◆

*A propane gas lamp illuminates the office of this Indiana Amish engineer and
inventor. A battery-powered calculator sits on the desk.*

sort of critical thinking that may be less common for the tradition-guided
farmer or the factory hand following supervisors' orders. Developing new
products, creating greater production efficiencies, and marketing new
products encourages a rational mindset that may challenge traditional
practices. Consciously trying to please the customer or thinking about how
to make one's product or sales space more accessible to others is the sum
and substance of successful entrepreneurship.[26]

Small businesses also hold the potential of generating significant amounts
of wealth. While it may not be conspicuously on display, given the lack of
free time to exploit it, wealth nevertheless produces inequality within
Amish society. In some places the church has bridled the growth of Amish
businesses by forcing owners to sell to non-Amish outsiders when firms
grew too large. But the end result, ironically, might be a former owner with
now even more money (from the sale of the business) and newly acquired
free time to use it creatively.

For their part, Amish households with members on mobile work crews
experience some of the same challenges faced by families of factory workers. Fathers are separated from families, and work is disconnected from
children's daily routines. In addition, however, mobile work crews often
take men out of the local community itself. It is not uncommon for contractors to take employees thirty miles or more from home and perhaps
even stay overnight for distant jobs. These arrangements introduce even

greater differences between the lives of working men and their wives and children. Especially since mobile work crews are often common in settlements with conservative Ordnungs, the employee's travel, workday meals in restaurants, or even accommodations in motels are not matched by travel, eating out, or similar activities for the household members tethered at home.

A Public Face in the Larger World

If the move away from farming has changed Amish society from within, it also holds the real possibility of reshaping its relations with the larger world of neighbors, local government, media, and public opinion. As in Lancaster County, conflicts with local government over zoning regulations are one area of concern, particularly as home-based manufacturing shops outgrow rural zoning limits. County authorities have shared some information from place to place. For example, officials from Fort Wayne, Indiana, and Lancaster, Pennsylvania, have compared notes on so-called Heritage Preservation zoning models as they seek to draft meaningful and relevant ordinances.[27] In 2002 when LaGrange County, Indiana, launched a new county master plan initiative and held a series of "town meetings" to gather citizen input, they organized two meetings specifically for Amish residents. Everyone was pleased when several hundred Amish showed up at each gathering.

That same year a number of Amish businessmen had a series of informal meetings with zoning officers and county commissioners in Elkhart County, Indiana, illustrating a growing concern among both Amish and civic leaders to address potential conflicts proactively and preemptively.[28] At the same time, the desire to escape close government regulation of business has been a motivating factor in the establishment of some new settlements. Households have left older Amish communities in suburbanizing America for less-populated places without zoning codes and where locals welcome the Amish presence as a force for economic revitalization.

Occasionally, Amish entrepreneurs have initiated various types of political action. In some states, Amish leaders have quietly worked with state legislators to gain exemption from state Workers' Compensation requirements in favor of their own church-backed plans. To date these efforts have failed in Ohio and Indiana.[29] Some settlements have replicated the Product Liability Aid Plan pioneered in Lancaster and described in chapter 10. In 1999 a "Shop Support Committee" in Ohio's Holmes-Wayne Counties settlement approved such a plan for churches in that community. The Support Committee also facilitates meetings for Amish small business owners such as a seminar on torch and gas safety for welding shop employees.

Examples of conflict and compromise with the state, though, are a small part of the measurable impact of the growing Amish economy. The bigger footprint that such activity leaves on the entrepreneurial and wage-labor landscape is the presence of Amish employees and employers in rural economies that often lack robust business sectors. The fact that Amish firms create jobs and turn out taxable products is not lost on business and civic leaders. If rural shops create zoning headaches, they happily do not demand government start-up loans or other public perks. In some depressed areas, new Amish settlements have pumped up land values in addition to raising taxes and introducing new businesses. In all of these ways, nonfarming Amish have gained a reputation as an economic asset almost everywhere.

Business leaders rarely worry that an Amish workforce will drag down their local economy or that new industries might refuse to locate where a sizable segment of the workforce has no high school credentials. Because some lucrative contracts involve international trade protocols that demand the employment of high school graduates, lone voices have called for the Amish to participate in higher education as a part of local economic development schemes, but such ideas have not gained any significant following.[30] Indeed, if anything, Amish success in the modern world of work has helped to cement their claim that avoiding the lures of high school and college will not leave them destitute.

More often, however, the move toward the economic mainstream has been a boon to Amish community relations, as non-Amish customers have come to identify certain products and high quality standards with Amish firms. Members of new Amish settlements report that often the first things neighbors say when they hear that Amish are moving into the area is, "Good! When will you open a chair shop, start a bakery, or launch a tack shop?" In some areas Amish businesses are closely tied to tourism, which also pleases local commercial interests. Although non-Amish economic interests dominate tourism in all areas, Amish entrepreneurs are often a vital, if small, piece of the puzzle.[31]

Separation and Integration

The occupational changes rippling across the Amish communities of North America are changing their culture in interesting and sometimes surprising ways. The rise of nonfarm employment may, at first glance, suggest that these separatists have assimilated into American society and lost their cultural soul. Indeed, they are no longer heretics tortured and executed for their beliefs as was the fate of their ancestors in sixteenth-century Europe. Nor are many of them barefoot farmers walking behind handheld plows, who, like Luddites, scorn advances in technology.

Their stunning success in entrepreneurship, construction, and factory work has pulled many Amish into the mainstream economy like never before in their history. These developments are bringing changes to their traditional way of life that will reverberate across the generations. The convergence of Amish convictions and contemporary culture has produced a wide array of creative cultural bargains as the Amish have negotiated new ethnic spaces and new ethnic identities in the face of massive social, economic, and technological pressures. Regardless of the outcome, the enduring myth of the Amish as backward, withdrawn farmers is just that—a myth.

Clearly, nothing unmasks the myth of Amish isolation like an examination of their economic involvement in the surrounding society. But nothing also better illustrates the resilient and dynamic character of Amish culture in the face of alien pressure. Amish enterprises demonstrate the interplay of continuity and change that mark Amish success in the modern world. Willing to adapt to changing times, they are also keenly committed to drawing lines of distinction and making choices based on cultural criteria, not simply on cost analysis.

No matter how the Amish negotiate their way through the transformative and sometimes turbulent economic worlds of the twenty-first century—in home-based business, at a job site, or on the factory floor—they will be bargaining with the resources of their cultural capital in hand. New and different contexts will continue to call forth different ethnic resources and induce new cultural restraints, combining in ways that will allow Amish communities to remain separate from the world without withdrawing from it. Indeed, their ability to reconstruct and renegotiate new identities in the midst of social change is one of the keys to their survival and success.

APPENDIXES
Research Methods and Data Sources

The data reported in the revised edition come from four sources: (1) a Settlement Profile, (2) an Enterprise Profile, (3) an Entrepreneur Profile, and (4) a Product Perception Survey, all of which are described below.

Appendix A: Settlement Profile

The Settlement Profile gathered occupational information on 888 individuals, age 16 years and older, living in 10 church districts in the spring of 2000. The sample of 10 districts from a settlement total of 131 was purposely selected to represent the distribution of districts across the settlement regarding their location, size, and age. In addition to these survey data, face-to-face interviews were conducted with more than a dozen entrepreneurs in 2002.

Appendix B: Enterprise Profile

The Enterprise Profile gathered data from a purposeful sample of 13 church districts in 1993. The sample was representative in regard to: (1) geographical location, (2) relationship to tourist sites, (3) size, and (4) age of the districts.

Within each district, an Amish informant identified the number of district households and enterprises with an estimated annual sales volume of above $1,000. An interviewer contacted the owner of each enterprise to validate its existence and gather basic information about the business. Three criteria were used to determine an enterprise's eligibility for the study: (1) annual sales volume above $1,000, (2) the owner's intention to operate an enterprise, and (3) public evidence of an enterprise (signs, business cards, letterheads, etc.).

Enterprises that met all three criteria were included in the study. A few businesses that did not have public signs but clearly met the first two criteria were included. Small, informal enterprises were not included. Seasonal produce stands, as well as informal sales of milk, eggs, and garden produce to neighbors with annual sales of less than $1,000, were excluded. Interviewers identified 118 enterprises that met the criteria in the sample of 13 church districts.

One hundred and fourteen owners agreed to participate in the survey. In several cases, a participating entrepreneur did not answer every question—either because a question did not apply, or because the owner did not know the answer or refused to give the information. Interviewers considered a questionnaire complete if the owner supplied information for more than half the questions. An overwhelming majority provided complete information. The overall participation rate for the Enterprise Profile was 96.6 percent (114/118). A fuller report of the research methods and the project appears in Smith et al. (1994).

Although the interviews for the Enterprise Profile were conducted between 1 February and 15 May 1993, the data reflect business activity during 1992. Interviewers spoke with owners in a private settling to avoid asking questions in the presence of customers or employees. The interviews generally took about thirty minutes, depending on the type of business. Younger entrepreneurs were typically more interested in the survey and more talkative than older ones. Reflecting he Amish emphasis on humil-

TABLE A.I

Households and Enterprises in the Enterprise Profile Sample, by Church Districts

District Name	Number of Households[a]	Number of Enterprises[b]	Percentage of Households with an Enterprise
East Centerville	23	11	48
Mechanicsburg	37	16	43
North Soudersburg	35	14	40
Southwest Groffdale	30	10	33
Lower Pequea Millwood	42	13	31
Upper Millcreek	32	10	28
Upper Pequea	25	7	28
Southeast Lower Millcreek	22	6	27
Greenland	45	10	22
Northeast Georgetown	36	7	19
North White Horse	28	5	18
Fairmont	24	4	17
Steelville	40	5	13
TOTAL	419	118	28

Note: Average households per district = 32.2; average enterprises per district = 9.1.
[a]Includes households of retired persons.
[b]The owner lives in the household, but the enterprise may or may not be located at the household.

ity, virtually all participants tried to play down the success, size, and sales volume of their businesses. Occasionally, interviewers had to press participants to talk about a new product, service, or market because the entrepreneurs did not want to call attention to their "success."

The church district with the fewest enterprises had 4, and the most industrious had 16. The average number of enterprises per district was 9.1. On the whole, 28 percent of the households in the sample had a member who owned an enterprise. Based on the data from the sample of 13 church districts, we estimate that in 1992 the Lancaster Amish settlement had 3,320 households and 937 enterprises in 103 districts.

Appendix C: Entrepreneur Profile

In an attempt to gather more in-depth information about the attitudes and experiences of shop owners, personal interviews were conducted with thirty-five selected entrepreneurs in the Lancaster settlement. The purpose of the Entrepreneur Profile was not to project generalizations about the Lancaster County settlement as a whole, but to gain a deeper understanding of the characteristics of Amish enterprises and entrepreneurs. The businesses in the Entrepreneur Profile tended to be larger than average and involved entrepreneurs who were willing to discuss their work at length with the interviewer. A structured format was used to gather data for a questionnaire, which was completed by the interviewer. Most of the interviews were two or three hours in length. The selected entrepreneurs were cooperative and helpful.

Appendix D: Product Perception Survey

The data regarding public perceptions of Amish products were gathered in interviews conducted at the Mennonite Information Center, Lancaster, Pennsylvania, during a two-week period in the summer of 1993. Two hundred personal interviews were completed with visitors who came to the Mennonite Information Center seeking information on Amish and Mennonites. The Mennonite Information Center provides interpretative information on Anabaptist groups for tourists who come to Lancaster County. Only 6 percent of the respondents lived within 50 miles of the Mennonite Information Center. Twenty-one percent had traveled 51 to 100 miles, 17 percent had traveled 101 to 250 miles, 12 percent had traveled 251 to 500 miles, 14 percent had traveled 501 to 1,000 miles, and 19 percent had traveled 1,001 to 3,000 miles. About 10 percent came from outside the United States. One-fifth (22 percent) of the respondents lived in Pennsylvania. The remainder came from twenty-five other states and four countries outside the United States. Fifty-three percent of the respondents were female, and 47 percent were male. One percent were under thirty years of age, 16 percent were thirty to thirty-nine years of age, 19 percent were forty to forty-nine years of age, and 64 percent were fifty years of age or older. Respondents were asked if they had ever purchased an Amish product. Of the 200 respondents, 74 percent said that they had purchased an Amish product sometime in the past.

Appendix E: Estimates of the Number of Amish Enterprises

Based on the data gathered in the Enterprise Profile in 1993, we estimated some 937 businesses (9.1 x 103 districts) in the Lancaster settlement based on the sample of 13 church districts. By 2003, the number of church districts had expanded to 145 with an estimated 11 businesses per district, yielding a total of nearly 1,600 enterprises across the Lancaster settlement. Increases in the actual number of businesses reflect the growing number of church districts as well as a growing rate of entrepreneurship. The estimates in figure 3.1 in chapter 3 are extrapolated from the historical data of the 13 church districts in the Enterprise Profile as well as from the 2000 Settlement Profile.

NOTES

1. The Roots of Amish Life

1. For introductions to Anabaptist history and thought, consult Dyck (1993), Klaassen (2001), Loewen and Nolt (1996), Snyder (1995), and Weaver (1987). Selected Anabaptist primary sources appear in English in Klaassen (1981). *The Mennonite Encyclopedia* (1955–59, 1990) includes a wide variety of articles related to the Anabaptist movement, its subsequent history, and current expressions.

2. An influential statement of Anabaptist beliefs, the so-called Schleitheim Confession of 1527, appears in J. H. Yoder (1973: 344–54). For a brief and now classic restatement of Anabaptist beliefs, see Bender (1944). Not all Anabaptists in the early decades of the movement rejected violence; indeed, some participated in violent uprisings. But by the second generation, non-violence had become an Anabaptist norm.

3. Braght (1998) authored the *Martyrs Mirror* in Dutch in 1660. The *Ausbund* (1997), first published in 1564, is an Anabaptist hymnbook that includes a number of martyr tales in both ballad and prose. This book is still used by the Lancaster County Amish in their Sunday morning worship services.

4. See Menno Simons (1956) for many of his writings and a brief biographical introduction to his life. For a more recent, in-depth assessment of Menno Simons, see Brunk (1992). The name *Mennonite* was applied to northern German Anabaptists after 1545, (see Menno Simons 1956:20). The south German and Swiss Anabaptists were not known as Mennonites until later, if at all.

5. See Séguy (1980) for a discussion of the emergent differences.

6. The practice of social avoidance or shunning is based on biblical injunctions in Matthew 18:17; Romans 16:17; 1 Corinthians 5:9–11; 2 Thessalonians 3:6, 14, 15; 2 Timothy 3:2–5; and Titus 3:10. The seventeenth article of the Dordrecht Confession, a Dutch Anabaptist statement of faith written in 1632, outlines the practice of and the reasons for shunning. The Amish still regard the Dordrecht Confession as their official statement of doctrinal belief. See Horst (1988) for a modern English translation.

7. At the time of the Amish and Mennonite separation in 1693, the term *Mennonite* was not widely used by Anabaptists living in south Germany and Switzerland. We use the term in the text for literary purposes to distinguish between the two groups. During the controversy that gave rise to the Amish church, numerous letters were sent back and forth between

the participants. Roth (1993) supplies a modern critical edition of the correspondence and an overview of the schism. Several extended discussions of the Amish division are found in Hostetler (1993:31–48), Nolt (2003), and E. S. Yoder (1987:43–58). On the derivation of the name Amish, see Luthy (1978).

8. See Nolt (2003) and P. Yoder (1991) for nineteenth-century developments in the Amish church and for its interaction with Mennonites.

9. On religious liberty in Pennsylvania, consult Frost (1990).

10. On eighteenth-century Amish settlements in Pennsylvania, see a series of articles by Joseph F. Beiler entitled "Our Fatherland in America," which appeared regularly in *The Diary* beginning in May 1972. For additional discussions, consult Beiler (1976–77), Mac-Master (1985:86–88, 125–27), and G. M. Stoltzfus (1954).

11. The Amish do not compile membership statistics. Estimates of membership can be calculated by multiplying the known size of church districts in some settlements with the total number of districts in the settlement. Raber (1970) offers annual listings of Amish settlements and church districts. Luthy (1974, 1985, 1992, 1994a, and 2003) also provides data on the distribution of Amish settlements in North America. For a turn-of-the-century listing of all Amish congregations by state, see Kraybill and Hostetter (2001).

12. For a discussion of Amish growth, migration, and settlement patterns see Luthy (2003).

13. Hostetler (1993) and Kraybill (2001b) provide extensive discussions of the culture and social organization of Amish society.

14. A brief history of the New Order Amish movement in the Lancaster settlement is provided by A. Beiler (n.d.). E. S. Yoder (1987) details Beachy Amish history.

15. For a definition and description of the meaning and role of the Ordnung by an Amish minister, consult J. F. Beiler (1982).

16. Those who are not baptized and leave the community are not shunned. Church members who break their baptismal vows and leave the Amish church for another group or Amish affiliation will face shunning. The Old Order Amish of the Lancaster settlement, along with some other Old Order Amish groups, maintain lifelong shunning against those who leave the church. However, some other Old Order Amish groups lift the ban after several years if a shunned member leaves the church and becomes a member "in good standing" in another Anabaptist-related group.

17. The seminal work on *Gelassenheit* was done by Cronk (1977). Kraybill (2001:29–38) provides an extended discussion of its role and significance in the life of Old Order communities.

18. An introduction to Weber's ideas can be found in Weber (1947). Ritzer (1996) provides an engaging application of Weber's thought in *The McDonaldization of Society*. Appling (1975:239) analyzes the economic ethic of the Amish from a Weberian perspective and argues that Amish doctrines have "anticapitalistic consequences."

19. For a brief discussion of the meaning of this metaphor in Amish life, see the preface to Kraybill and Olshan (1994:vii).

20. Our interpretative model of entrepreneurship emphasizes the significant role of ethnic culture in creating and regulating patterns of entrepreneurship. The seminal work of Brigitte Berger (1991a) and the collection of essays that she edited underscore the singular influence of culture in shaping distinctive expressions of entrepreneurship. This conceptualization of our model is also indebted to the work of Light and Bonacich (1991), Waldinger, Aldrich, and Ward (1990b), and Ward and Jenkins (1984), all of whom emphasize the importance of mobilizing the resources of ethnic culture in the formation of ethnic enterprises. While building on the work of these scholars, we have added the significant

component of cultural restraint, missing from previous research, which the Amish have marshaled to limit the freedom of entrepreneurs.

Another way of viewing ethnic resources for entrepreneurship is to conceptualize them as forms of cultural and social capital. Cultural capital refers to the values, beliefs, and levels of trust in the Amish community; whereas social capital focuses on the social networks, rituals, and organizational patterns of Amish society. Cultural and social capital typically blend together in the actual practice of Amish entrepreneurship. The productivity of Amish shops benefits from an ethnic labor pool that values hard work (cultural capital) and is easily accessible through extended family networks (social capital). Recent discussions of social and cultural capital can be found in Fukuyama (1995), Portes (1998), Putnam (2000), Tan (1998), and Woolcock (1998a, 1998b).

21. Our approach to the study of Amish entrepreneurship is grounded in the growing sociological tradition of cultural analysis, which stresses the bona fide role of culture in shaping and regulating social organization. For an introduction to this approach, consult Hall and Neitz (1993), Hunter (1991), Hunter and Ainlay (1986), Wuthnow (1987), and Wuthnow et al. (1984).

22. The Amish church does not strictly speaking prohibit interaction with the outside world, but its teaching on separation from the world does limit and regulate interaction and forbid marriage to outsiders.

23. An ethnic group is one whose members share a common religious, racial, or national background, a sense of peoplehood, and a memory of a common past. The social symbols and membership boundaries of an ethnic group give it a visible public identity recognized by insiders and outsiders alike. The bulk of the literature on ethnic business and entrepreneurial activity underscores the important role of cultural resources. The Amish story is unique in the way in which cultural restraints have also been marshaled to obstruct and regulate business activity. The formation of business enterprises in the Amish ethnic context is a negotiated outcome produced by these two countervailing cultural forces.

24. Ethnic facilitation and resistance refer to the active social processes that are used to mobilize the resources and restraints that are embedded in the culture of an ethnic heritage. Our approach illustrates the ways in which the cultural and social capital of a community contributes to entrepreneurial success.

25. Although the Amish themselves would not use the word *negotiation* to describe this process, we find it a useful analytical concept that enhances our understanding of the sociocultural dynamics that gave rise to microenterprises in the Amish context.

2. From Plows to Profits

Epigraph: The words of an Amish entrepreneur reported in *Forbes,* 9 March 1998, 140.

1. During the nineteenth century, successful wheat and tobacco crops tied local agriculture to the larger American marketplace. By 1900, the Lancaster stockyards sold some six thousand head of cattle each year, making it the largest livestock auction east of Chicago. Lancaster also developed robust industry and commerce. At the turn of the century, sizable firms manufactured everything from cork and silk to candy and bricks. In 1909, Lancaster City was Pennsylvania's fourth-largest industrial producer. Other towns within the county, such as Manheim and Terre Hill, were also engaged in manufacturing. Lancaster's economy never rested on a single, dominant industry but included meat packing, beer brewing, cigar making, and watch and clock production, along with banking and other commercial businesses (Loose 1978:105–17, 128–32).

2. Lancaster County Planning Commission documents, 2002.

3. These characteristics of Lancaster County are described in the promotional materials of the Lancaster Chamber of Commerce and Industry.

4. The agricultural data were obtained from Lancaster County Chamber of Commerce and Industry documents and the Pennsylvania Agricultural Statistics Service for 2001. Detailed reports of the country's agricultural productivity for 2001 appeared in the *Lancaster New Era*, 18 October 2002 and the *Intelligencer Journal*, 31 October 2002.

5. Lancaster Chamber of Commerce and Industry documents, 2002. The success of Lancaster's farmland preservation efforts was celebrated in 2002 when it topped the 50,000-acre mark. This story appeared in the *Intelligencer Journal*, 9 October 2002.

6. The Pennsylvania Dutch Convention and Visitors Bureau supplied these figures and estimates in 2002. For more information, visit their Web site, www.padutchcountry.com.

7. Jones (2002:397–98).

8. The long-standing Amish and Mennonite agricultural tradition is described by Correll (1991), Deeben (1992), Hostetler (1993:114–44), and Séguy (1973). The Amish are descendants of the Anabaptists, whose economic and entrepreneurial patterns have received little scrutiny and analysis. A notable exception is the work of Klassen (1964). For more recent scholarship on the economic and entrepreneurial patterns of Mennonite groups see Kreider (1980), Nafziger (1965 and 1986, esp. chap. 12), and more recently Redekop, Krahn, and Steiner (1994) and Redekop, Ainlay, and Siemens (1995).

9. In his extensive monograph on Lancaster's Amish community in the early 1940s, Kollmorgen (1942) describes their traditional agricultural practices. Amishman Gideon Fisher (1978) offers his view of Amish farming in his book *Farm Life and Its Changes*.

10. *Directory* (1977:ii).

11. For an excellent historical overview of development issues and pressures in Lancaster County, see the six-day series by Ed Klimuska in the *Lancaster New Era*, 27 June–2 July 1988.

12. The Lancaster Chamber of Commerce and Industry formed a Tourism Committee in 1957. The committee evolved into the Pennsylvania Dutch Visitors Bureau, acquired property, and built a visitor's center in 1967. It became organizationally independent from the chamber in 1972. Although its current name is the Pennsylvania Dutch Convention and Visitors Bureau, it is still incorporated under its old name. The history of tourism in Lancaster County is told by Louise Stoltzfus (2000).

13. David Luthy (1994c) provides an interesting history of the development of Amish-related tourism in Lancaster County. David Walbert (2002) describes how Lancaster has marketed rural nostalgia and Amish images to lure tourists. In a creative analysis of the Amish in the American imagination, David Weaver-Zercher (2001) discusses some of the images and perceptions that tourists hold of the Amish. See Kraybill (2001b:287–94) for an analysis of the interplay between tourism and the Amish of Lancaster.

14. John H. Hostetler (1989) chronicles the loss of farmland and pleads for its preservation. See Testa (1992) for an impassioned critique of development in Lancaster County.

15. Kauffman, Petersheim, and Beiler (1992) tell the story of the expansion into southern Lancaster County. The expansion into Lebanon County and later Dauphin County is told by King (1993).

16. Kollmorgen (1942:29).

17. *Directory* (1977:iii).

18. This is reported by Kollmorgen (1942).

19. *Lancaster New Era*, 30 November 1970.

20. *Lancaster New Era*, 8 April 1975.

21. A discussion of the Amish fear of factory work can be found in the Amish publica-

tion *Family Life* (July 1972). Scholarly articles by Ericksen, Ericksen, and Hostetler (1980) and Martineau and MacQueen (1977) discuss nonfarm work among the Amish. Local newspapers also reported the trend to nonfarm employment in the Lancaster area *(Intelligencer Journal,* 7 April 1975 and 8 April 1975, and *Lancaster New Era,* 30 July 1987 and 31 July 1987). Olshan (1994a) discusses the significant shift of Amish society to the outside culture because of their involvement in small business. Amish concerns about the future of farming can be found in two issues of *Family Life* (October 1993 and June 1994).

22. In a 1987 survey of one Amish district, a member reported that among the married men who had not retired, 37 percent were day workers, 19 percent owned their own business, 11 percent farmed and had a shop, and 33 percent were full-time farmers *(Die Botschaft,* 15 September 1987).

23. The story of the growth of Amish schools in the Lancaster settlement is chronicled in *Pennsylvania School History* (1991), a book compiled by some Amish educational leaders. It is also described in Kraybill (2001b:161–87).

24. The small business option was not negotiated in a literal fashion, of course, and the Amish would not describe it that way. But from an analytical perspective, the rise of microenterprises represented a sociocultural compromise at several levels.

25. In some other settlements, the Amish have accepted factory work. See Meyers (1994a) for a discussion of the Elkhart-LaGrange, Indiana settlement, where industrial employment is the most common form of work. See also chapter 14 of this book for more details of nonfarm work in other settlements.

26. The Amish choice is clarified by noting the response of other groups. The Groffdale Conference of Old Order Mennonites in Lancaster County is similar to the Amish in some ways—especially in its rejection of motor vehicles. But unlike the Amish, these horse-and-buggy Mennonites use tractors to pull machinery in their fields. The Groffdale Conference members have been more willing to migrate to other states in search of farmland and less likely to enter business than the Amish. In other settlements, the Old Order Amish have entered factory employment or have been more willing to migrate in search of farmland. Both of these alternative responses underscore the element of choice in the Amish response to the demographic crisis in the Lancaster settlement.

27. Although this was the choice of Lancaster's Amish, it was not the strategy in the Elkhart-LaGrange settlement of Indiana, where 54 percent of the Amishmen were working in factories by 1995. See chapter 14 of this book and Meyers (1994a). Earlier, Meyers (1983) had studied stress in nonfarm occupations in Indiana and found few stress-related differences between Amish farmers and Amish factory workers. The proportion of Amish men working in modern non-Amish factories varies considerably by settlement. Foster (1984) found that more than two-thirds of the Amish males in the Geauga County area of Ohio were working off the farm by 1982. By 1993, some 83 percent there were in nonfarm work according to Greksa and Korbin (2002).

28. Various shop directories have been produced that list many of the shops and their products. See, for example *Directory* (1977, 1988, 1989). The editor of the 1988 Amish directory of Lancaster County describes the evolution of shops in the introduction (*Amish Directory,* 1988). A monthly Amish newspaper, *Plain Communities Business Exchange,* is devoted to small business. The emergence of this paper in the fall of 1993 reflects growing interest and activity in the evolution of shops. In 1993 and 1994, *The Diary,* a monthly Amish magazine, began carrying a number of monthly diaries related to microenterprises—the "Shopworker's Diary," The "Storekeeper's Diary," the "Attorney's Diary," and the "Greenhouse Diary." These columns underscore the interest and growing attention being given to commercial enterprises.

29. The literature on ethnic industries has conceptualized three general types of commercial activity: the ethnic economy, the middleman minority, and the ethnic enclave. Light and Bonacich (1991), in the preface to the paperback edition of *Immigrant Entrepreneurs,* provide a helpful discussion of the differences between the three conceptual types. The ethnic enclave is the most segregated type of ethnic economy and parallels what we call a *segregated enterprise*. Light and Bonacich's conceptualization of an ethnic economy parallels what we call an *integrated enterprise* because it is primarily integrated into the larger economy and its only tie to the ethnic community is ownership and, usually, the employment of coethnics. The concept of a *middleman minority* refers to an immigrant ethnic group that has historically operated in certain service industries. Such entrepreneurs have also functioned as a middleman between powerful classes and oppressed minorities other than their own group. The concept of a middleman minority is not relevant to the Amish experience because they are not sojourners, nor are they involved in service industries or in catering to oppressed minority groups. For an additional discussion of middleman minorities, consult Waldinger, McEvoy, and Aldrich (1990:119–22).

30. For an extended discussion of the negotiation model in Amish culture, see Kraybill (2001b:23–26 and 295–318, and 2003:18–20). Once again, we must emphasize that negotiation is an analytical concept rather than a literal term on Amish lips or a formal process in Amish interaction with the outside world.

3. A Profile of Amish Enterprises

1. The numerical data undergirding this book were gathered in personal interviews with more than 170 Amish business owners as described in the appendix. In addition, a series of interviews with non-Amish business and community leaders as well as local government officials rounded out our data collection. A description of the research procedures appears in the appendix as well as in Smith et al. (1994), which contains the final technical report of the project. The *Lancaster New Era* carried a major story on 24 June 1994 based on our research, and applauded development of small businesses on its editorial page on 28 June 1994. Additional data gathered in 2000 and 2002 were used to update the revised edition of the book.

2. The rise of Amish businesses plotted in figure 3.1 are estimates based on a sample of 13 church districts in 1993 and a sample of 10 church districts in 2000. For a more complete discussion of these data sources, see the last section of the appendix, Estimates of the Number of Amish Enterprises.

3. Sam Stoltzfus, in a booklet titled *17th Annual Woodworkers Get Together,* 6 June 1998, 6, 26.

4. These numbers are reported in the "Shopworker's Diary" in *The Diary,* February 1994.

5. For a discussion of the "putting out" system of labor in early American life, consult Clark (1990), especially pages 176–91, which provide interesting parallels to the Amish system of quilt production.

6. The figures for American business patterns reported in this section are cited in Scarborough and Zimmerer (1993).

7. Although the Amish have generally refused to participate in the federal Social Security program, some individuals do occasionally tap benefits they may have acquired by working for a non-Amish employer at some time in their life. The church discourages receiving Social Security benefits, but it does occasionally happen on the sly. For discussion of Amish attitudes toward Social Security, consult Ferrara (2003) and Kraybill (2001b: 276–80).

8. Although popular in the early 1980s, this strategy proved problematic. Although these partnerships were legal on paper, tax auditors found irregularities in the contrived arrangements. Moreover, with each employee turnover, firms had to organize themselves anew. Eventually many Amish and non-Amish accountants, wary of the legal and tax implications, refused to assist the "paper" partnerships.

9. The story of this successful shop was reported in the April 1984 issue of *The Coleman Lite*. It was also described in the November 1984 issue of the *Central Pennsylvania Business Journal*.

10. There are not exact limits to growth in terms of sales or number of employees in Amish society. The determination often rests with local church leaders who may consider the attitude and behavior of the owner as well as the public perception of the size of the business. Sometimes owners may grow weary of their business responsibilities and voluntarily sell it off to a non-Amish buyer without pressure from the church.

11. An informal loan agency within the Amish community provides funds for church members buying a property or setting up a business. Begun originally in the Midwest, the network, known as Helping Hand, was established in the Lancaster settlement in 1998.

12. The story of Lapp's Coach Shop was featured in the *Intelligencer Journal's* "Business Monday," 26 July 1993.

13. Ed Klimuska's excellent five-part series on the dramatic growth of the quilting industry in Lancaster County appeared in the *Lancaster New Era,* 9–13 March 1987, and was reprinted in 1987 in a booklet entitled *Lancaster County: Quilt Capital USA*.

14. The "Problem Corner" of the July 1992 issue of *Family Life* carried a discussion of the use of the Amish name to market products and services. Several readers responded by strongly arguing against using the word "Amish" to identify products and services. Luthy (1994b) identifies many of the ways in which non-Amish retailers have used the Amish name to market their products.

4. Homespun Entrepreneurs

1. The conceptual definition of entrepreneurship has been widely debated in the scholarly literature. For a sampling of the discussions, consult Carland et al. (1984), Cochran (1967), and Woo, Cooper, and Dunkelberg (1991). Following Light and Bonacich (1991: 157–58) and others, we have defined the owner-managers of Amish businesses as entrepreneurs. It is conceptually possible that second- and third-generation managers who assume control of existing firms may lack many of the entrepreneurial characteristics of entrepreneurs who establish their own business. In the Amish case, virtually all the owner-managers are first-generation entrepreneurs who have actually established their own firms. Moreover, the small size of even the few second-generation firms requires an entrepreneurial style to remain solvent.

2. National Federation of Independent Businesses figures cited in Scarborough and Zimmerer (1993:15).

3. The estimates of farms owned and purchased by the Amish are based on a study conducted by Conrad L. Kanagy, "Comprehensive Study of Farms Owned by Plain Groups in Lancaster County, PA, 1999." The unpublished report is available from the author. The estimate of 1,500 farms is based on the Settlement Profile 2000, which found an average of twelve farms per district (12 x 114 in Lancaster County = 1,368).

4. These quotes come from the January 2002 and March 2002 issues of the Amish magazine *Family Life*. Numerous readers responded to an essay by a woman in the January 2002 issue that described her husband's nonfarm employment. See the November 2001

issue of *Family Life* for an essay by a shop owner-farmer who worries about "Where we are headed" with the proliferation of shops.

5. The story of the harness shop was briefly told in the *Lancaster Sunday News*, 1 March 1994 and in the *Lancaster New Era*, 22 March 1999.

6. Hostetler and Huntington (1992), Huntington (1994), and Kraybill (2001b) address Amish attitudes toward education and the organization of their private schools.

7. These conflicts are detailed by Meyers (2003:87–106). The rise of Amish private schools in the Lancaster settlement is described in Kraybill (2001b:161–187).

8. Keim (1975) provides a helpful summary and analysis of the landmark *Wisconsin v. Yoder* case, which was decided by the U.S. Supreme Court in 1972.

9. In some cases, the further training was of a general nature or was not closely related to their business ventures. A small number of Amish individuals completed ninth grade during the years before church members received exemption from high school.

10. In the early 1980s, an Amish farmer and foundry owner built a significantly improved waterwheel. An ancient source of power, the waterwheel was frequently used on Amish farms to pump water and operate other tools. Traditional wheels produced erratic power, however, because of uneven speeds. The new product used a lightweight wheel with aluminum paddle blades, a power-take-off assembly, and a drive shaft with universal joints to bolster performance. The improved wheel requires less water and provides more power. Although windmills and waterwheels have been a traditional source of power on Amish farms, in recent years hydraulic and air power are much more widely used to operate equipment and pump water for farms and shops.

11. The complete story of Ivan Stoltzfus' golf course recupper appeared in the *Lancaster Sunday News*, 17 July 1988.

12. The story of Christian Stoltzfus' horse collar clocks is told by Ed Klimuska in the *Lancaster New Era*, 11 February 1993.

13. In some Midwestern communities, notably Indiana and Ohio, the Amish have more readily entered factory employment, as described in chapter 14.

5. Labor and Human Resources

1. The data for these estimates were gathered in 1993 for the Enterprise Profile. Informants suggest that many Amish firms in the next decade have increased their number of full-time employees. Thus, it is likely that half or more of the enterprises now have two or more employees.

2. In a discussion of Chinese businesses in Britain, Song (1999) provides an analysis of children's labor in ethnic enterprises, which parallels the Amish experience in many ways.

3. The discussion of desirable employee traits in this section is based on in-depth interviews conducted with thirty-five selected entrepreneurs in our Entrepreneur Profile.

4. Moses B. Glick, "The Shopworker's Diary," in *The Diary*, June 1993, 38.

5. Although exempt from Social Security and Worker's Compensation, Amish wage earners must pay mandatory state unemployment insurance, but they virtually never take advantage of the program's benefits.

6. The quotations in this paragraph and the following one are from *One Thousand and One Questions* (1992:160, 161), a listing of questions and answers in catechismal form released by Pathway Publishers, an Amish publishing house in Aylmer, Ontario.

7. Ibid.

6. The Moral Boundaries of Business

1. About two-thirds of Amish children in the Lancaster settlement are born at home under the supervision of a certified nurse-midwife. The others are born in hospitals or in birthing clinics under the supervision of a physician or certified nurse-midwife.

2. *One Thousand and One Questions* (1992:139).

3. Ibid., 139, 140.

4. From an essay by an anonymous minister in *Family Life,* July 2000, 24.

5. In the highly publicized drug bust, two Amish-raised young adults were arrested for buying cocaine from members of the Pagans motorcycle gang and reselling it to other Amish youth. The two arrested youth worked on Amish construction crews that often traveled out of Lancaster County. This embarrassing incident sobered the Amish community and led to some drug awareness meetings for parents and youth.

6. The literature on ethnic business often cites social discrimination against minorities and immigrants as a prime force prodding the development of minority enterprises. The Amish represent an entirely different twist in this regard because it is their own restrictions on education, factory work, and certain occupations that have propelled them into micro-enterprises.

7. Easter Monday, Pentecost Monday, and second Christmas are not observed in some Amish communities in other states. Other holiday observances also vary from settlement to settlement.

8. *Family Life,* July 2000, 24.

7. Taming the Power of Technology

1. Members sometimes complain that the Ordnung in various settlements grants more freedom to use newer technology to shop owners than to farmers. For various discussions of the impact of nonfarm occupations, see the Amish publication, *Family Life:* April 1982, May 1982, June 1982, April 1987, June 1987, November 2001, January 2002, March 2002, and July 2002.

2. For extended discussions of the process of social change and technological innovation in the Amish community, consult Kraybill (2001b) and Kraybill and Olshan (1994).

3. Kraybill (2001b:188–97) and Umble (1994, 1996) discuss the Amish struggle with the telephone in greater detail.

4. This schism described by Kraybill (2001b:188–90) and E. Yoder (1987:100–12), led to the formation of the Beachy Amish, also known as the Weavertown Amish-Mennonites in Lancaster County.

5. Numerous examples of the specific hours of availability, instructions for leaving messages, and answering service numbers can be found in dozens of ads for Amish firms that appear in the *Lancaster County Business Directory, 2003.*

6. *Wired* magazine carried an article on the Amish use of cell phones in its January 1999 issue.

7. As noted above, the distinction between use and ownership is a critical one in Amish culture. It has emerged in many areas of Amish life as they have struggled with new forms of technology. By forbidding ownership but permitting use, the Amish are able to tap some of the fruits of technology while still keeping it under control and at some distance.

8. In rare cases, entrepreneurs may indirectly own vans or trucks—with special permission from their bishop—by acquiring vehicles in the name of the business. Although the entrepreneur might be the sole owner of such a firm and therefore of the vehicle, the

personal name is not used on the owner's registration. Adding even further symbolic distance, the church requires that a non-Amish employee sign the necessary paperwork on behalf of the business. Thus, occasionally, a businessperson may legally own a motor vehicle without having his or her name associated with it. Some church and business leaders believe that these arrangements are better than leasing vehicles in the entrepreneur's name. Said one contractor whose fictitiously named business owns several trucks, "How could we tell the next generation that cars aren't allowed if we have our names on them now? They have to be company vehicles in the company name, no matter who owns them." The nameless bargain is a constant reminder that the vehicle is intended for business and not for private pleasure.

9. For a more extensive discussion of Amish views toward the use of electricity, consult Kraybill (2001b:197–212) and Scott and Pellman (1990).

10. For a broader discussion of the reservations that plain communities have about the use of computers and electronic media, see Kraybill (1998).

11. Re-Source Lumber is a registered trademark for products distributed by a non-Amish company.

12. The letter, dated 6 March 2002, was signed by dozens of farmers, who felt that church leaders were being too restrictive about forbidding the use of field harvesters to cut green corn for silage. The letter was sent as "an open letter to the Bishops of Lancaster and Chester County concerning the subject of silo filling."

8. Small-Scale Limitations

1. Sale (1980) offers a compelling argument about the significance and consequence of size and scale in human organization. Hurd (1993) discusses Amish attempts to limit size in the social organization of their community life.

2. A lengthy article titled "The Shop that Grew" appeared in the August-September 2002 issue of the Amish magazine, *Family Life*. The story described the detrimental effects of an Old Order businessman who grew his shop too big. In the end his wife is killed in an automobile accident and his adult children leave the church. Eight letters from readers in the November 2002 issue of *Family Life* affirmed the virtues of small-scale operations promoted by the story.

3. The story of Isaac "Ike" Z. Smoker, who invented and manufactured the Smoker Bale Elevator in the 1940s, is often repeated as an example of someone who was forced out of the church because his business became too big. The fact that the story is still told today illustrates the long-term persistence of stories that shape the moral order of the Amish community. Smoker also invented a hay bale loader and a bale thrower and sold the patents to the New Holland Machine Co. The story of Smoker's life is recorded in a family history and genealogy (*Descendants of Isaac Smoker*, 1986).

4. *Family Life*, August-September 2002, 10

5. *Family Life*, November 2002, 15

6. Not every business spin-off is friendly. In the case described above, seven of the eight new businesses were begun with the blessing of the original owner. However, an employee who left the store and took the names of the business's sales representatives and suppliers began a competing store without the owner's blessing.

7. Some of the successful Amish firms that have been sold to outsiders include Beiler Hydraulics, Countryside Wood, Leacock Coleman Center, Mill Creek Manufacturing, and Pequea Machine.

8. These numbers are based on the Entrepreneur Profile (Appendix C) and may not be

representative of all business owners across the settlement because they reflect interviews with well-established, full-time entrepreneurs.

9. Promotion and Professional Networks

1. Olshan (1994a) provides a cogent analysis of Amish cottage industry and its significance in opening Amish society. Another interpretation of separation would suggest that distinctive ethnic practices enable the Amish to maintain a strong ethnic identity and social separation despite their entanglements in the world of commerce. We develop this argument in chapter 14.

2. A software program called "Amish Utilities" featured a barefoot Amish boy—with straw hat and dog—on the display jacket. The promoter of Amish software explained that "the Amish label reflects handcrafted," qualities that were applicable to this carefully crafted software. A description of the Amish software appeared in the *Bay Area Computer Currents,* September 8–21, 1992, 42–43. Amish historian David Luthy (1994b) discusses a number of ways the Amish label has been used to market various products.

3. These observations were made by Joanne Sinclair in an article that appeared in the *Plain Communities Business Exchange,* January 1996, 15.

4. *The Budget* first appeared in Sugarcreek, Ohio, in 1890. Predominantly an Amish-Mennonite paper for its first thirty years, the paper gradually took on more Old Order Amish correspondents (known as scribes) and subscribers. Since about 1920, *The Budget* has been the leading weekly among the Old Order Amish nationwide. After 1970, however, the content of some letters and advertisements from more progressive Amish and Mennonite communities caused concern among certain Old Order Amish leaders. As an alternative, they began publishing *Die Botschaft* in 1975—first in Ohio, but soon bringing the editorial offices and printing to Lancaster, Pennsylvania. The Lancaster County Amish read both papers, although *Die Botschaft* has become more popular.

5. Several editions of an *Old Order Shop and Service Directory* included advertisements from both Amish and Old Order Mennonite businesses across North America. (*Directory* 1977, 1988, 1989). The directories were printed in Lancaster County, Pennsylvania, and had a disproportionate number of firms from that area.

6. The spectacular growth of the *Lancaster County Business Directory* is told in a feature article in the *Lancaster New Era,* 23 October 1998. The DavCo Family Inc. produces the *Directory* and also sells advertising specialties to many Amish businesses.

7. The story of the trade market can be found in the *Lancaster New Era,* 2 April 1996.

8. The Lancaster Chamber of Commerce and Industry originally operated as the Lancaster Board of Trade (Loose 1978:114, 117).

9. This estimate of membership was provided by a spokesperson for the Lancaster Chamber of Commerce in 2002.

10. This estimate of Amish membership was provided by an NFIB spokesperson to Steven M. Nolt in a telephone interview, May 1993.

11. The church does not prohibit voting, and when local issues touch Amish concern, a few Amish persons will vote. Kraybill (2003) provides an extensive discussion of Amish views of the political order and political participation. See also the January and February 1989 issues of *Family Life* for insights into the Amish views of political involvement.

12. The Lancaster Chamber of Commerce and Industry and the Pennsylvania Dutch Convention and Visitors Bureau appoint members to one another's boards of directors and otherwise maintain friendly relations. However, there is no longer an official, organic link between the two groups.

13. The exact number of visitors to Lancaster each year is of course difficult to estimate.

The Pennsylvania Dutch Convention and Visitors Bureau Tourism Fact Sheet in 2002 estimated that "approximately 7 million visitors come to Lancaster County annually."

14. The membership directory for the Pennsylvania Dutch Convention and Visitors Bureau appears on their Web site: www.pdcvb.com.

15. Amish reflections on tourism and a thoughtful discussion of the development of Amish products and stands that cater to tourists can be found in *Family Life,* October 1990. The author asks to what extent the Amish should make products for tourists that the Amish themselves are not permitted to use. See additional Amish comments on tourism in the July 1992 issue of *Family Life.* Kraybill (2001b:287–94) provides an analysis of tourism and its impact on the Amish of Lancaster County.

16. This observation was offered by a spokesperson for the Pennsylvania Dutch Convention and Visitors Bureau in a personal interview with Steven M. Nolt on 15 April 1993.

17. Amish persons with similar interests gather from many states for friendly gatherings and circulate informal newsletters. Amish cancer patients, as well as open-heart surgery patients, have formed interstate groups that circulate letters, sharing local news and updating each other on their surgery, treatment, and recovery. The groups function much like the support groups that hospitals or social service agencies organize for patients in the larger society. Other Amish networks draw participants from across North American for annual fellowship and visiting. Amish persons with various physical and mental disabilities meet for the annual Amish Handicapped Reunion—an extended weekend of visiting in a designated Amish community. Participants from several states attend the long-awaited, annual, family-like affair. Each year the group publishes a directory of the attendees, encouraging ongoing correspondence between both new and longstanding friends.

18. A parallel gathering was established in the mid-1980s. An Indiana accountant organized an annual reunion for Amish accountants across the United States. Held each summer in a different community, the gathering draws participants from Iowa to Pennsylvania. This national meeting functions mostly as a fraternal reunion of accountants, with little discussion of tax law.

19. The events and stories from the annual Horse Progress Days appear in *Rural Heritage,* published six times a year for enthusiasts of horse and mule farming. New machinery and farm implements manufactured by Amish shops are often displayed at these annual events.

10. Coping with Litigation and Liability

1. For an Old Order view of litigation, see the October 1986 issue of *Family Life.* A growing openness to the use of legal resources is indicated by the appearance of an "Attorney's Diary," which began in the December 1993 issue of *The Diary.* The column offers legal advice on a variety of issues, such as tax laws and real estate sales.

2. Yoder (2003) traces Amish attitudes toward the government through the years. The collection of essays in Kraybill (2003) discusses the various ways in which the Amish have negotiated with the state on a wide variety of issues.

3. Discussions of Amish views toward insurance can be found in several issues of *Family Life:* July 1969, May 1970, June 1972, April 1984, December 1989, and February 1990. Despite the church's official rejection of insurance, some business owners have purchased commercial coverage for their properties.

4. *One Thousand and One Questions* (1992:153, 155).

5. For an overview of the mutual aid programs in the Amish church in Lancaster County, see Kraybill (2001b:101–5)

6. G. Fisher (1978:335, 379) gives 1885 as the date of origin. A. Stoltzfus (1984:191–92)

cites what appears to be the same source as Fisher but gives the beginning date as 1875. Stoltzfus is preferred. The Heritage Historical Library, Aylmer, Ontario, has a printed policy for the Amish Aid Insurance Company dated 1879.

7. For an Amishman's stinging critique of liability insurance, see the April 1984 issue of *Family Life.* His views represent those Amish who oppose any type of organized aid other than deacons' (alms) funds or spontaneous mutual care, such as barn raisings.

8. Any national plans for universal health care would stir concern among the Amish. Indeed, when this issue emerged in the 1990s, Senator Harris Wofford of Pennsylvania introduced legislation to exempt the Amish from universal health care, similar to their exemption from Social Security.

9. After 1969, when Amish farmers began storing milk in bulk tanks on their farms, they encountered new liability regulations. With large bulk tanks, the contamination of milk was no longer isolated to a single can. Tainted milk could ruin a whole truckload and make a farmer liable for the losses of other farmers whose milk was on the same truck. An innocent mistake might trigger a loss of thousands of dollars. Thus, in the 1970s, some Amish farmers began buying product liability policies on their milk.

10. From the pamphlet titled, *Regulations and Guidelines for the Old Order Amish Product Liability Aid,* printed in 2000, 2–3.

11. Some non-Amish general contractors do not accept the plan, forcing some Amish subcontractors to carry commercial product liability insurance if they want to obtain subcontract work.

12. *The Diary,* July 2002, 24.

13. *Die Botschaft,* 12 May 1993, 11.

11. Negotiating with Caesar

1. Numerous essays in Kraybill (2003) survey a range of Amish conflicts with government in various states. Kraybill (2001b:161–72, 272–86) examines a number of other instances in which the Lancaster Amish community has gone to the bargaining table with the state.

2. This was the language used by the Old Order Amish School committee in its appeal to the Pennsylvania State Legislature to change public school attendance laws in the 1930s.

3. Kraybill (2001b:16–24).

4. Olshan (1994b, 2003) offers a complete history and analysis of the National Amish Steering Committee. Some of the documents and correspondence related to the work of the Steering Committee on business issues appear in Kinsinger (1997).

5. The Amish conflict with the Social Security Administration is detailed in Ferrara (2003).

6. During the late 1950s, frustrated Internal Revenue Service (IRS) officials foreclosed and sold Amish farms to obtain unpaid Social Security taxes. The government forcibly collected from some 130 Amish households. By 1961, IRS agents were seizing Amish livestock to recover lost revenue. Still the Amish refused to take part in a system they considered detrimental to their family and community life.

7. By the late 1980s, many accountants refused to work for Amish businesses organized as self-employed partnerships. Amish entrepreneurs still felt tied to a system they believed was morally bankrupt because employers and employees who were church members remained liable for the tax. In 1982, an ill-planned and ultimately unsuccessful Amish appeal to the U.S. Supreme Court backfired when the Court upheld the requirement that all employees must pay Social Security taxes. The case, *United States v. Lee* (1982), is described by Ferrara (2003).

8. The Steering Committee and its representatives were actively involved in direct negotiations with members of Congress for the Social Security exemption.

9. The proposed Pitts' bill was described in an Associated Press story published in *Intelligencer Journal* 3 March 2001.

10. Hostetler (1984:45) and Olshan (2003:73).

11. See Song (1999) for a discussion of child labor in ethnic family businesses.

12. In 1996 U.S. Department of Labor investigators fined three Old Order saw mill operators in Pennsylvania for violating child labor laws. Fair labor laws prohibit children under age sixteen from operating power-driven manufacturing equipment and children under fourteen from working in any type of manufacturing facility.

13. The proposed bill, HR 4257, was designed to amend the Fair Labor Standards Act of 1938 so that "certain youth could perform certain work with wood products."

14. Written comments to the House Committee on Education and the Workforce by the chairman of the Old Order Amish Steering Committee, 21 April 1998.

15. *Sunday Patriot News* (8 November 1998). Other accounts of the controversy can be found in *Lancaster New Era* (21 April 1998), *Intelligencer Journal* (22 April and 17 July), *Lancaster Sunday News* (2 August 1998), and *Intelligencer Journal* (29 September, 10 October, 16 November 1998).

16. Hannah B. Lapp, "Labor Department vs. Amish Ways," *Wall Street Journal*, 10 April 1997.

17. The wording is from form LIBC-14 (4–79), Waiver of Workers' Compensation, which must be signed by each Amish employee, notarized, and filed with the Pennsylvania Department of Labor and Industry.

18. "Amish at the Heart of 'Puppy Mill' Debate," *New York Times*, 20 September 1993, A12

19. For more detail on the origins of this controversial issue, see the Associated Press story in the *Intelligencer Journal* (2 October 1993), the *New York Times* (20 September 1993), and the *Philadelphia Inquirer* (10 December 1995).

20. *Intelligencer Journal* (14 August 2000).

21. Some of the extensive regional newspaper coverage can be found in *Lancaster Sunday News* (16 April 2000), *Intelligencer Journal* (12 June 2000), *Lancaster New Era* (27 June 2000), *Intelligencer Journal* (28 June and 6 July 2000), *Lancaster New Era* (13 July 2000), *Sunday Patriot News* (23 July 2000), *Lancaster Sunday News* (23 July 2000), and *Intelligencer Journal* (26 July and 9, 14, and 16 August 2000).

22. *Intelligencer Journal* (28 June 2000).

23. *Intelligencer Journal* (9 August 2000).

24. Elmer S. Yoder's history of the Beachy Amish (1987:94–99) reviews several of these cases.

25. The National Amish Steering Committee followed the case closely and submitted written explanations and opinions to the commission. The story was reported in length by the *Intelligencer Journal* (12 September 1990 and 12 April 1994) and the *Lancaster New Era* (11 September 1990, 12 September 1990, and 12 August 1993). The *Valley News Ledger* (11 August 1993) published a copy of the National Amish Steering Committee's letter to the Pennsylvania Human Relations Commission and excerpts of the commission's fact-finding report. The 15 September 1993 issue of the *Valley News Ledger* reported that Stoltzfoos visited Glick and apologized, apparently encouraged to do so by Amish bishops who were eager to resolve the public dispute. Stoltzfoos reportedly said he would accept cash from Glick but not a check unless it was signed by one of Glick's sons. The 6 April 1994 issue of the *Valley Ledger* reported that both Glick and Stoltzfoos showed conciliatory attitudes.

26. This is the language contained in the Final Order released by the Pennsylvania Human Relations Commission on 27 July 1994. A full account of the stages of the conflict is available in commission dockets P-3412 and P-3544, *Aaron S. Glick v. Valley Hardware* (1994).

27. Quoted in *The Valley News Ledger* (5 October 1990).

28. Place (2003) discusses land use issues and the Amish. For journalistic coverage of the zoning problems related to the Amish, see the *Intelligencer Journal*, 15 August 1987, 18 August 1987, and 3 March 1988.

29. "Lancaster County Comprehensive Plan: Growth Management Plan," January 1992, 28.

30. "Farm-Based Business Model Ordinance Provisions for Lancaster County," April 1990, Lancaster County Planning Commission, Lancaster, Pa., 1.

31. The Planning Commission urged Leacock Township officials to make the exemption, *Intelligencer Journal* (10 September 1996).

32. "Farm-Based Business Model Ordinance," 1.

33. Not all entrepreneurs have mellowed with time. One cantankerous Amish owner of a woodworking shop has been involved in a decades-old battle with township zoning officials since 1970. The controversy continued into 2002. For the recent developments, see *Intelligencer Journal* (12 April 2002).

12. Failure and Success

1. These figures are reported in Scarborough and Zimmerer (1993:28–30).

2. The Enterprise Profile (Appendix B), which covered thirteen church districts, identified 118 functioning enterprises but found only 5 that had failed in those districts in the most recent five years. Reasons for failure included loss of interest on the part of the owner, financial difficulty, competition, and family complications. If the sample is representative of the Lancaster settlement, then approximately 40 Amish businesses, or about 4 percent, failed in the five-year period from 1988 to the end of 1992.

3. *Forbes* magazine, 9 March 1998, 144.

4. A non-Amish financial professional who works closely with many Amish businesses gave this estimate.

5. Economic Development Company of Lancaster County, promotional materials 2002.

6. Members of the Amish community in Indiana County, Pennsylvania, concurred about the importance of the regional economy for the shape and success of Amish businesses (Kraybill and Kanagy 1996).

7. Comparative research in the Amish settlement of Indiana County, Pennsylvania, conducted in tandem with the Lancaster research and reported in Smith et al. (1994), revealed that the Indiana County Ordnung forbids the use of air and hydraulic power as well as telephones and inverters in shops, severely limiting the productivity of certain kinds of enterprises. Large sawmills can easily operate from diesel line shafts and belt power, but smaller shops in the Indiana County settlement are hindered by many restrictions that have been lifted in Lancaster.

8. "Shopworker's Diary," *The Diary*, February 1994. A few other Amish communities, such as the one in Nappanee, Indiana, have an Ordnung that is even more flexible than Lancaster's. Full electrical power, provided by generators, is permitted in Nappanee, for example.

9. Personal correspondence to Donald B. Kraybill, 26 April 1994.

13. The Fate of a Traditional People

1. Applebaum (1984) provides a cogent analysis of the manifold social repercussions that transform traditional societies when they move toward a market economy.

2. Olshan and Schmidt (1994) offer an engaging discussion of Amish women and the feminist conundrum.

3. Kraybill (2001b:244–48).

4. *One Thousand and One Questions* (1992:97).

5. Single women legally own their businesses, but in the case of married women, both husband and wife typically own the enterprise, even though the wife may be the chief entrepreneur.

6. This compares to 30 percent of men in the same age group. See Settlement Profile (Appendix A).

7. Quoted in Tepper and Tepper (1980:68–70).

8. For an extended discussion of the entrepreneurial experience of an Amish woman in another state, see Hawley (1995). Additional information on Amish women in business is provided by Louise Stoltzfus (1994 and 1998). The *Sunday News* of West Chester, Pennsylvania, featured Amish businesswomen in a lengthy article on 24 March 1996.

9. See Kraybill (2001b: 287–94) for a discussion of the way in which roadside tourist stands are dramaturgical sites for Amish interaction with outsiders.

10. Providing work for children in a business is easy enough, but passing one on to the next generation is another matter. Few establishments are more than a generation old. A full 83 percent of the enterprises were begun by the owners themselves. As years pass, however, business owners will increasingly face the challenge of transferring operations to their offspring. Business owners will face the same predicament as farmers with one farm and several children. Some owners suggest that a business can be divided like land, with each heir receiving a share, but others doubt that businesses can be split apart so easily. Generational transfers will likely be solved on a family-by-family basis.

11. Hostetler and Huntington (1992) and Huntington (1994) provide a helpful overview and introduction to Amish schools and education.

12. For an explanation of this process of leadership selection, consult Kraybill (2001b: 128–31).

13. *Fortune 500* magazine did a special feature on Amish millionaires in the June 1995 issue. The *Forbes* story appeared in the 9 March 1998 issue.

14. The new bank formed in 1998 in order to provide financial services to the Plain communities of Lancaster County. Home Town Heritage Bank began through conversations with several Amish leaders and financial experts in the larger community. A few Amish people sit on the board of directors, but most board members are non-Amish. Not all of its clients are Amish, but Hometown Heritage emphasizes "a simpler way of banking," which appeals to Amish customers. Bank officials, sensitive to Amish culture, have adjusted some of their policies to dovetail with Amish values.

15. Moses B. Glick, "Shopworker's Diary," *The Diary,* June 1993, 38.

14. National Patterns of Amish Work

1. Many of the observations in this chapter rely on field work, interviews, and unpublished findings by the authors as part of other projects, including Steven M. Nolt's and Thomas J. Meyer's "Amish and Old Order Groups" project supported by the Lilly Endow-

ment, Inc., and Donald B. Kraybill's and Mark Lacher's "Amish and Technology" project. Publications detailing the results of both studies are forthcoming.

2. On the Lancaster pattern, see chapter 2; on midwestern mobility, see Luthy (1986).

3. Ibid.

4. See some memories in Yoder and Yoder (1998); also information from author interviews.

5. In 1940 Mennonite Central Committee sent a survey to all Amish bishops asking them to report current data, including employment, for conscription-age men in their churches. Though the return rate was incomplete, the results did document that some Amish men were employed in factories, and a handful were in government-funded work jobs. See Peace Section Census, 1940, Questionnaires: Old Order Amish, Indiana, IX-7-1, Box 1, Folder 7, Mennonite Church USA Archives—Goshen, Indiana.

6. Ibid.

7. V. Stoltzfus (1973).

8. In 1972, soon after the Lancaster decision, the Arthur, Illinois, bishops approved the use of bulk milk tanks, but dairying in that settlement continued to decline, and today the community includes very few full-time farmers.

9. An example of Amish efforts to find innovative ways to encourage small-scale dairying is the Deutsch Kase Haus cheese plant near Middlebury, Indiana, which opened in 1979. Instigated by Old Order Amish entrepreneurs who obtained close Ohio Amish advice and counsel, the plant's investors and owners were local Mennonites. The plant accepted milk from Amish and non-Amish farms and marketed its own cheeses. In 2002 it was purchased by Canadian agribusiness Agropur.

It should be noted that some Amish farmers continue to insist on (and for their part, demonstrate) the economic viability of small-scale farming. The notable and unusual spokesman on this score is Holmes County, Ohio, New Order Amish farmer David Kline. See some of his reflections in Kline (1990) and an academic appraisal of his approach in the conclusion of Stoll (2002).

10. A sampling of these firms is found in *Ohio Amish Business Directory* (2001). *Heartland Directory* (2002) includes many small businesses in Indiana, Illinois, and Michigan. Rohrer, Strouse, and Turner (2001) describe the size and scope of Amish-owned wood products manufacturing in Holmes County, Ohio, in the 1990s.

11. Hawley (1995) tells the story of one woman entrepreneur in Missouri.

12. In 2000 one Dover businessman acquired a generator for a welding shop, but the church did not sanction it.

13. The settlements here are not in fellowship with one another. The Williams County settlement stems from the nineteenth-century Amish immigration stream whose heirs are often called "Swiss Amish." The Williams County settlement actually crosses the state line into Steuben County, Indiana. The Paoli church districts (not to be confused with churches of the Swartzentruber Amish affiliation also located near Paoli) are part of a loosely defined ultraconservative network of churches including those near Kenton, Ohio. Their roots are in various midwestern settlements.

14. Exceptions to this pattern emerge in the Holmes County, Ohio, New Order churches where a sizeable population of members provides labor for some fairly large furniture factories.

15. Kraybill and Kanagy (1996).

16. A parallel but organizationally independent program in the Lancaster settlement, known as Helping Hand, was organized in 1998. The Hillsboro, Wisconsin, and Aylmer,

Ontario, settlements have similar initiatives, though they are organized somewhat differently.

17. Another organized effort to promote small business among the Amish in this settlement is the Northern Indiana Woodcrafters Association Furniture Expo, held annually in Elkhart County and drawing some 400 retail and wholesale buyers from all over North America to interact with Amish furniture makers from the region. The expo includes only Amish producers; the association president in Noah Bontrager. For details on the 2003 expo, see Rod Rowe, "Furniture Expo Held in Goshen," *Goshen News,* 8 May 2003, A-7; and Steve Bibler, "Connecting Crafters," [Elkhart] *Truth,* 27 April 2003, C-1.

18. For data and discussion, see Meyers (1994a) on the Elkhart-LaGrange, Indiana settlement; Greksa and Korbin (2002) for Geauga County, Ohio (note that they combine lumber yard and factory work as industrial); and Troyer and Willoughby (1984) for Holmes County, Ohio. Thomas J. Meyers calculated the occupational data for the Nappanee settlement and the Elkhart-LaGrange settlements from the 2001 Nappanee church directory and the 2002 Elkhart-LaGrange church directory. On factory work in Kansas, see David Dinell, "Taking Work to the Labor Pool: Precision Opens Yoder Center," *Wichita Business Journal,* 30 April 1999, 4.

19. Some Amish factory workers own farms and engage in crop farming, which involves seasonal labor. This pattern allows them to keep a family farm in operation without needing to rely on it for income. The more intense labor of dairying or produce farming is much less compatible with factory work. For a profile of one factory that attracts Amish employees with its particular mix of nontraditional "benefits" that appeal to the group, see Scott McGregor, "Amish Pioneering Path from Farms to Factories," *Indianapolis Star,* 1 April 2001, 1.

20. If Dover's Amish contractors are working as subcontractors, they can use electric power tools owned by a general contractor.

21. Keiser (2003).

22. Meyers (1991 and 1994b).

23. Greksa and Korbin (2002). Eriksen, Eriksen, and Hostetler (1980:60–61) stated that children of nonfarmers in the Lancaster, Pennsylvania, settlement were more than five times as likely to leave the church as the children of farmers. Since the data for that study covered the 1970s and earlier when there were few nonfarmers in the settlement, the results cannot be taken as representative of the contemporary situation.

24. Meyers (1994b) and Greska and Korbin (2002).

25. "[Ohio] Shop Support Committee Meeting," minutes, 6 October 1999, citing Steering Committee correspondence.

26. Hawley (1995:321–24) provides a case study of one retail store.

27. "Ind. Weighs Amish Zoning District," *Intelligencer Journal,* 18 February 1995, B-14.

28. One meeting was reported by Marshall V. King, "Amish Businesses Face Zoning Snags," *Mennonite Weekly Review,* 9 December 2002, 7. Other meetings were not reported publicly.

29. An exemption for Workers' Compensation is pending in Missouri. That organized labor has typically been a vocal opponent of such exemption legislation at the state level only confirms Amish distrust of labor unions.

30. The concern is related to ISO 9000 certification—an internationally recognized status granted by the Geneva, Switzerland-based International Organization for Standardization (ISO). ISO 9000 certification is a prerequisite to obtain many major contracts, since industry giants limit their subcontract and supplier relationships to firms with ISO 9000 status. Among the qualifications necessary for ISO 9000 certification is a workforce of

high-school (or GED) graduates. Thus, firms with a high proportion of Amish employees cannot qualify, and some civic leaders fear that businesses already holding ISO 9000 status might hesitate to relocate to an area where a significant portion of the potential workforce is without necessary educational credentials. If in the mid-twentieth century Amish dissent from modern notions of higher education threatened an educational and governmental bureaucracy predicated on certain notions of "progress," these twenty-first-century hiring concerns represent a new round in the Amish refusal to play by modernity's rules that combine education and economics in ways that continue to be threatening in mainstream society.

31. Hawley (1995:319–20) provides one example from rural Missouri.

REFERENCES

This listing includes references cited by the authors in the notes as well as other select works related to the subject. Bibliographic information for some sources—interviews, newsletters, local newspapers—not appearing in this list are provided in the notes.

Aldrich, Howard, Trevor P. Jones, and David McEvoy
    1984   "Ethnic Advantages and Minority Business Development." In *Ethnic Communities in Business: Strategies for Economic Survival*, ed. Robin Ward and Richard Jenkins. New York: Cambridge University Press

Amish Directory of the Lancaster County Family
    1988   Gordonville, Pa.: Pequea Publishers.

Applebaum, Herbert
    1984   Ed. *Work in Non-Market and Transitional Societies.* Albany: State University of New York Press.

Appling, Gregory P.
    1975   "Amish Protestantism and the Spirit of Capitalism." *Cornell Journal of Social Relations* 10(2): 239–50.

Ausbund, Das ist: Etliche schone Christliche Lieder
    1997   Lancaster, Pa.: Lancaster Press. First known edition was 1564.

Auster, Ellen, and Howard Aldrich
    1984   "Small Business Vulnerability, Ethnic Enclaves, and Ethnic Enterprise." In *Ethnic Communities in Business: Strategies for Economic Survival*, ed. Robin Ward and Richard Jenkins. New York: Cambridge University Press.

Beiler, Abner
    N.d.   "A Brief History of the New Order Amish Church, 1966–1976." Lancaster Mennonite Historical Society Library, Lancaster, Pa.

Beiler, Joseph F.
    1976–77   "Eighteenth-Century Amish in Lancaster Community." *Mennonite Research Journal* 17 (October): 37, 46; 18 (January): 1, 10; 19 (April): 16.
    1982   "Ordnung." *Mennonite Quarterly Review* 56 (October): 382–84.
    1983   "A Review of the Founding of the Lancaster County Church Settlement." *The Diary* 15 (December): 17–22.

Bender, Harold S.
    1944   "The Anabaptist Vision." *Church History* 13 (March): 3–24.

Berger, Brigitte
    1991a   Ed. *The Culture of Entrepreneurship.* San Francisco: Institute for Contemporary Studies.
    1991b   "The Culture of Entrepreneurship." In *The Culture of Entrepreneurship.* San Francisco: Institute for Contemporary Studies.
Boissenvain, Jeremy, Jochen Blaschke, Hanneke Grotenbreg, Isaac Joseph, Ivan Light, Marlene Sway, Roger Waldinger, and Pnina Werbner
    1990   "Ethnic Entrepreneurs and Ethnic Strategies." In *Ethnic Entrepreneurs: Immigrant Business in Industrial Societies,* ed. Roger Waldinger, Howard Aldrich, and Robin Ward. Newbury Park, Calif.: Sage Publications.
Bonacich, Edna, and Tae Hwan Jung
    1982   "A Portrait of Korean Small Business in Los Angeles: 1977." In *Koreans in Los Angeles: Prospects and Promises,* ed. Eui-Young Yu, Earl H. Phillips, and Eun Sik Yang. Los Angeles: Center for Korean-American and Korean Studies, California State University.
Bonacich, Edna, and John Modell
    1980   *The Economic Basis of Ethnic Solidarity: Small Business in the Japanese American Community.* Berkeley: University of California Press.
Botschaft, Die
    1975–   Lancaster, Pa.: Brookshire Publications and Printing. Described on its masthead as "a weekly newspaper serving Old Order Amish Communities everywhere."
Braght, Thieleman J. van
    1998   *The Bloody Theater; or Martyrs Mirror of the Defenseless Christians.* Translated by Joseph F. Sohm. Scottdale, Pa.: Herald Press. First edition printed in Dutch at Dordrecht, 1660.
Braverman, Harry
    1975   *Labor and Monopoly Capital: The Degradation of Work in the Twentieth Century.* New York: Monthly Review Press.
Brunk, Gerald R.
    1992   Ed. *Menno Simons: A Reappraisal.* Harrisonburg, Va.: Eastern Mennonite College.
Budget, The
    1890–   Sugarcreek, Ohio: Sugarcreek Budget Publishers. A weekly newspaper serving the Amish and Mennonite communities.
Carland, James W., Frank Hoy, William R. Boulton, and Jo Ann C. Carland
    1984   "Differentiating Entrepreneurs from Small Business Owners: A Conceptualization." *Academy of Management Review* 9:354–59.
Church Directory of the Lancaster County Amish
    2002   Gordonville, Pa.: The Diary. Vols. 1 and 2.
Clark, Christopher
    1990   *The Roots of Rural Capitalism: Western Massachusetts, 1780–1860.* Ithaca, N.Y.: Cornell University Press.
Cobas, José A.
    1987   "Ethnic Enclaves and Middleman Minorities: Alternative Strategies of Immigrant Adaptation?" *Sociological Perspectives* 30 (April): 143–61.
Cochran, Thomas C.
    1967   "Entrepreneurship." In *International Encyclopedia of Social Sciences,* ed. David Sills. New York: Macmillan.

Correll, Ernst H.
    1991   "The Mennonite Agricultural Model in the German Palatinate." Translated by Marion Lois Huffines. *Pennsylvania Mennonite Heritage* 14 (October): 2.

Cronk, Sandra L.
    1977   "Gelassenheit: The Rites of the Redemptive Process in Old Order Amish and Old Order Mennonite Communities." Ph.D. diss., University of Chicago. Excerpts under the same title appear in *Mennonite Quarterly Review* 55 (January 1981): 5–44.

Deeben, John P.
    1992   "Amish Agriculture and Popular Opinion in the Nineteenth and Early Twentieth Centuries." *Pennsylvania Mennonite Heritage* 15 (April): 21–29.

Descendants of Isaac Smoker and Hannah (Zook) Smoker
    1986   Gordonville, Pa.: Gordonville Print Shop.

Diary, The
    1969–   Gordonville, Pa.: Donald V. Carpenter Jr. A monthly periodical devoted to Amish history and genealogy.

Directory, Old Order Shop and Service
    1977   Gordonville, Pa.: Pequea Publishers.
    1988   Lancaster, Pa.: Stemgas Publishers.
    1989   Lancaster, Pa.: Stemgas Publishers.

Dyck, Cornelius J.
    1993   An *Introduction to Mennonite History: A Popular History of the Anabaptists and the Mennonites*. 3rd ed. Scottdale, Pa.: Herald Press.

Ericksen, Eugene P., Julia A. Ericksen, and John A. Hostetler
    1980   "The Cultivation of the Soil as a Moral Directive: Population Growth, Family Ties, and the Maintenance of Community among the Old Order Amish." *Rural Sociology* 45 (Spring): 49–68.

Family Life
    1968–   Aylmer, Ont.: Pathway Publishers. A monthly Amish periodical.

Ferrara, Peter J.
    2003   "Social Security and Taxes." In *The Amish and the State,* rev. ed., ed. Donald B. Kraybill. Baltimore: Johns Hopkins University Press.

Fisher, Gideon L.
    1978   *Farm Life and Its Changes*. Gordonville, Pa.: Pequea Publishers.

Foster, Thomas W.
    1984   "Occupational Differentiation and Change in an Ohio Amish Settlement." *Ohio Journal of Science* 84 (3): 74–81.

Frost, J. William
    1990   *A Perfect Freedom: Religious Liberty in Pennsylvania*. Cambridge: Cambridge University Press.

Fukuyama, Francis
    1995   *Trust: The Social Virtues and the Creation of Prosperity*. New York: Free Press.

Goldscheider, Calvin, and Frances E. Kobrin
    1980   "Ethnic Continuity and the Process of Self-Employment." *Ethnicity* 7: 256–78.

Granovetter, Mark S.
    1984   "Small Is Bountiful: Labor Markets and Establishment Size." *American Sociological Review* 49 (June): 323–34.

Greska, Lawrence P., and Jill E. Korbin
    2002   "Key Decisions in the Lives of the Old Order Amish: Joining the Church
            and Migrating to Another Settlement." *Mennonite Quarterly Review* 76
            (October): 373–98.
Hall, John R., and Mary Jo Neitz
    1993   *Culture: Sociological Perspectives.* Englewood Cliffs, N.J.: Prentice Hall.
Harper, Douglas
    1987   *Working Knowledge: Skill and Community in a Small Shop.* Chicago: Univer-
            sity of Chicago Press.
Hawley, Jana M.
    1995   "Maintaining Business While Maintaining Boundaries: An Amish
            Woman's Entrepreneurial Experience." *Entrepreneurship, Innovation, and
            Change* 4:315– 28.
Heartland Directory of Amish Businesses: Indiana, Illinois, and Michigan, 2002–2003
    2002   Goshen, Ind.: Diamond Design.
Horst, Irvin B.
    1988   Ed. and trans. *Mennonite Confession of Faith.* Lancaster, Pa.: Lancaster
            Mennonite Historical Society. Adopted by the Mennonites at a peace con-
            vention held in Dordrecht, Holland, 1 April 1632.
Hostetler, John A.
    1984   "Silence and Survival Strategies among the New and Old Order Amish."
            In *Internal and External Perspectives on Amish and Mennonite Life,* ed.
            Werner Enninger. Vol. 1. Essen, Germany: Unipress.
    1989   "Toward Responsible Growth and Stewardship of Lancaster County's
            Landscape." *Pennsylvania Mennonite Heritage* 12 (July): 2–10.
    1993   *Amish Society.* 4th ed. Baltimore: John Hopkins University Press.
Hostetler, John A., and Gertrude Enders Huntington
    1992   *Amish Children: Education in the Family, School, and Community,* 2d ed. Fort
            Worth, Tex.: Harcourt Brace Jovanovich.
Hunter, James Davison
    1991   *Culture Wars: The Struggle to Define America.* New York: Basic Books.
Hunter, James Davison, and Stephen C. Ainlay
    1986   Eds. *Making Sense of Modern Times: Peter L. Berger and the Vision of Inter-
            pretive Sociology.* New York: Routledge and Kegan Paul.
Huntington, Gertrude Enders
    1994   "Persistence and Change in Amish Education." In *The Amish Struggle with
            Modernity,* ed. Donald B. Kraybill and Marc A. Olshan. Hanover, N.H.:
            University Press of New England.
Hurd, James P.
    1993   "The Significance of Scale in Amish Society." Paper presented at the
            Amish Tricentennial Conference, July, Elizabethtown College, Elizabeth-
            town, Pa.
Intelligencer Journal
    1794–   Lancaster, Pa.: Lancaster Newspapers.
Jenkins, Richard
    1984   "Ethnic Minorities in Business: A Research Agenda." In *Ethnic Communi-
            ties in Business: Strategies for Economic Survival,* ed. Robin Ward and
            Richard Jenkins. New York: Cambridge University Press.

Jones, Dale E., et al.
    2002   *Religious Congregations and Membership in the United States, 2000: An Enumeration by Region, State, and County*. Nashville, Tenn.: Glenmary Research Center.

Kauffman, John S., Melvin R. Petersheim, and Ira S. Beiler
    1992   Comps. *Amish History of Southern Lancaster County Pennsylvania 1940–1992*. Elverson, Pa.: Olde Springfield Shoppe.

Keim, Albert N.
    1975   Ed. *Compulsory Education and the Amish: The Right Not to Be Modern*. Boston: Beacon Press.

Keiser, Steven Hartman
    2003   "Pennsylvania German and the 'Lunch Pail Threat': Language Shift and Cultural Maintenance in two Amish Communities." In *Perspectives on Language Conflict, Language Competition, and Language Coexistence,* ed. B. Joseph et al. Columbus: Ohio State University Press.

King, David S.
    1993   *Fifty Years in Lebanon County, Pennsylvania*. Elverson, Pa.: Old Springfield Shoppe.

Kinsinger, Andrew S.
    1997   *A Little History of Our Parochial Schools and Steering Committee From 1956–1994*. Gordonville, Pa.: Gordonville Print Shop.

Kilby, Peter
    1971   Ed. *Entrepreneurship and Economic Development*. New York: Free Press.

Klaassen, Walter
    1981   Ed. *Anabaptism in Outline: Selected Primary Sources*. Scottdale, Pa.: Herald Press.
    2001   *Anabaptism: Neither Catholic nor Protestant,* 3rd ed. Kitchener, Ont.: Pandora Press.

Klassen, Peter James
    1964   *The Economics of Anabaptism: 1525–1560*. London: Mouton.

Kline, David
    1990   *Great Possessions: An Amish Farmer's Journal*. San Francisco: North Point Press.

Kollmorgen, Walter M.
    1942   *Culture of a Contemporary Rural Community: The Old Order Amish of Lancaster County, Pennsylvania*. Rural Life Studies 4. Washington, D.C.: U.S. Department of Agriculture.

Kraybill, Donald B.
    1998   "Plain Reservations: Amish and Mennonite Views of Media and Computers." *Journal of Mass Media Ethics* 3:99–110.
    2001a   "Amish Economics: The Interface of Religious Values and Economic Interests." in Donald A. Hay and Alan Kreider, eds., *Christianity and The Culture of Economics*. Cardiff: University of Wales Press.
    2001b   *The Riddle of Amish Culture,* rev. ed. Baltimore: Johns Hopkins University Press.
    2003   Ed. *The Amish and the State,* rev. ed. Baltimore: Johns Hopkins University Press.

Kraybill, Donald B., and C. Nelson Hostetter
    2001   *Anabaptist World USA*. Scottdale, Pa.: Herald Press.

Kraybill, Donald B., and Carl Desportes Bowman

    2001   *On the Backroad to Heaven: Old Order Hutterites, Mennonites, Amish, and Brethren.* Baltimore: Johns Hopkins University Press

Kraybill, Donald B., and Conrad L. Kanagy

    1996   "The Rise of Entrepreneurship in Two Old Order Amish Communities," *Mennonite Quarterly Review* 70 (July): 263–79.

Kraybill, Donald B., and Marc A. Olshan

    1994   Eds. *The Amish Struggle with Modernity,* Hanover: University Press of New England.

Kreider, Carl

    1980   *The Christian Entrepreneur.* Scottdale, Pa.: Herald Press.

Kriedte, Peter, Hans Medick, and Jurgen Schlumbohm

    1981   *Industrialization Before Industrialization: Rural Industry in the Genesis of Capitalism.* New York: Cambridge University Press.

Lancaster County Business Directory

    2003   Gap, Pa.: DavCo Family.

Lancaster New Era

    1877–   Lancaster, Pa.: Lancaster Newspapers.

Lancaster Sunday News

    1923–   Lancaster, Pa.: Lancaster Newspapers.

Light, Ivan

    1972   *Ethnic Enterprise in America: Business and Welfare Among Chinese, Japanese, and Blacks.* Berkeley: University of California Press.

Light, Ivan, and Edna Bonacich

    1991   *Immigrant Entrepreneurs: Koreans in Los Angeles,* 1965–1982. Berkeley: University of California Press.

Loewen, Harry, and Steven M. Nolt

    1996   *Through Fire and Water: An Overview of Mennonite History.* Scottdale, Pa.: Herald Press.

Loose, John W. W.

    1978   *The Heritage of Lancaster.* Woodland Hills, Calif.: Windsor Publications.

Luthy, David

    1974   "Old Order Amish Settlements in 1974." *Family Life* 7 (December): 13–16.

    1978   "Concerning the Name Amish." *Mennonite Historical Bulletin* 39 (April): 5.

    1985   *Amish Settlements Across North America.* Aylmer, Ont.: Pathway Publishers.

    1986   *The Amish in America: Settlements That Failed,* 1840–1960. Aylmer, Ont.: Pathway Publishers.

    1992   "Amish Settlements Across America: 1991." *Family Life* 25 (April): 19–24.

    1994a   "Amish Migration Patterns: 1972–1992." In *The Amish Struggle with Modernity,* ed. Donald B. Kraybill and March A. Olshan. Hanover, N.H.: University Press of New England.

    1994b   "Marketing the Amish." *Family Life* 27 (January): 20–23.

    1994c   "The Origin and Growth of Amish Tourism." In *The Amish Struggle with Modernity,* ed. Donald B. Kraybill and Marc A. Olshan. Hanover, N.H.: University Press of New England.

    2000   *Why Some Amish Communities Fail: Extinct Settlements, 1961–1999.* Aylmer, Ont.: Pathway Publishers.

    2003   "Amish Settlements across America: 2003." *Family Life* 27 (October): 17–23.

MacMaster, Richard K.
    1985   *Land, Piety, Peoplehood: The Establishment of Mennonite Communities in America, 1683–1790.* Scottdale, Pa.: Herald Press.
Martin, David
    1991   "The Economic Fruits of the Spirit." In *The Culture of Entrepreneurship,* ed. Brigitte Berger. San Francisco: Institute for Cultural Studies.
Martineau, William H., and Rhonda S. MacQueen
    1977   "Occupational Differentiation among the Old Order Amish." *Rural Sociology* 42:383–97.
Menno Simons
    1956   *The Complete Writings of Menno Simons,* c. 1496–1561. Edited by John C. Wenger, Scottdale, Pa.: Herald Press.
The Mennonite Encyclopedia: A Comprehensive Reference Work on the Anabaptist-Mennonite Movement.
    1955–59   Vols. 1–4, Hillsboro, Kans.: Mennonite Brethren Publishing House; Newton, Kans.: Mennonite Publication Office; Scottdale, Pa.: Mennonite Publishing House.
    1990   Vol. 5, Scottdale, Pa.: Herald Press.
Meyers, Thomas J.
    1983   "Stress and the Amish Community in Transition." Ph.D. diss., Boston University.
    1991   "Population Growth and Its Consequences in the Elkhart-LaGrange Old Order Amish Settlement," *Mennonite Quarterly Review* 65 (July): 308–21.
    1994a   "Lunch Pails and Factories." In *The Amish Struggle with Modernity,* ed. Donald B. Kraybill and Mark H. Olshan. Hanover, N.H.: University Press of New England.
    1994b   "The Old Order Amish: To Remain in the Faith or to Leave." *Mennonite Quarterly Review* 68 (July): 378–95.
    2003   "Education and Schooling." In *The Amish and the State,* rev. ed., ed. Donald B. Kraybill. Baltimore: Johns Hopkins University Press.
Nafziger, Estel Wayne
    1965   "The Mennonite Ethic in the Weberian Framework," *Explorations in Entrepreneurial History* 2:187–204.
    1986   *Entrepreneurship, Equity, and Economic Development.* Greenwich, Conn.: JAI Press.
Nolt, Steven M.
    2003   *A History of the Amish,* rev. ed. Intercourse, Pa: Good Books.
Ohio Amish Business Directory, 2001–2002
    2001   Charm, Ohio: Countryside Connections.
Olshan, Marc A.
    1994a   "Amish Cottage Industries as Trojan Horse." In *The Amish Struggle with Modernity,* ed. Donald B. Kraybill and Marc A. Olshan. Hanover, N.H.: University Press of New England.
    1994b   "Homespun Bureaucracies: A Case Study in Organizational Evolution." In *The Amish Struggle with Modernity,* ed. Donald B. Kraybill and Marc A. Olshan. Hanover, N.H.: University Press of New England.
    2003   "The National Amish Steering Committee." In *The Amish and the State,* rev. ed., ed. Donald B. Kraybill. Baltimore: Johns Hopkins University Press.

Olshan, Marc A., and Kimberly Schmidt

    1994   "Amish Women and the Feminist Conundrum." In *The Amish Struggle with Modernity,* ed. Donald B. Kraybill and Marc A. Olshan. Hanover, N.H.: University Press of New England.

One Thousand and One Questions and Answers on the Christian Life

    1992   Aylmer, Ont.: Pathway Publishers.

Pennsylvania School History 1690–1990

    1991   Elverson, Pa.: Olde Springfield Shoppe.

Place, Elizabeth

    2003   "Land Use." In *The Amish and the State,* rev. ed., ed. Donald B. Kraybill. Baltimore: Johns Hopkins University Press.

Plain Communities Business Exchange

    1993–   Lampeter, Pa.: Moses B. Glick.

Portes, Alejandro

    1998   "Social Capital: Its Origins and Applications in Modern Sociology." *Annual Review of Sociology* 24:1–24.

Putnam, Robert D.

    2000   *Bowling Alone: The Collapse and Revival of American Community.* New York: Simon and Schuster.

Raber, Ben J.

    1970–   Comp. *The New American Almanac.* Baltic, Ohio: Ben J. Raber. The Almanac's German edition, *Der Neue Amerikanisch Kalender,* began publication in 1930.

Redekop, Calvin W., Stephen C. Ainlay, and Robert Siemens

    1995   *Mennonite Entrepreneurs.* Baltimore: Johns Hopkins University Press.

Redekop, Calvin W., Victor A. Krahn, and Samuel J. Steiner

    1994   Eds. *Anabaptist/Mennonite Faith and Economics.* Lanham, Md.: University Press of America.

Ritzer, George

    1996   *The McDonaldization of Society,* rev. ed. Newbury Park, Calif.: Pine Forge Press.

Rohrer, John D., Sharon Strouse, and Cassie Turner

    2001   "Importance of Furniture Manufacturing in the Amish Community of Eastern Holmes County," unpublished paper, Ohio State University Extension, Community Development, Columbus, Ohio.

Roth, John D.

    1993   Ed. and trans. *Letters of the Amish Division: A Source Book.* Goshen, Ind.: Mennonite Historical Society.

Sale, Kirkpatrick

    1980   *Human Scale.* New York: Coward, McCann, and Geoghegan.

Scarborough, Norman N., and Thomas W. Zimmerer

    1993   *Effective Small Business Management,* 4th ed. New York: Macmillan.

Scott, Stephen E., and Kenneth Pellman

    1990   *Living without Electricity.* Intercourse, Pa.: Good Books.

Séguy, Jean

    1973   "Religion and Agricultural Success: The Vocational Life of the French Anabaptists from the Seventeenth to the Nineteenth Centuries." *Mennonite Quarterly Review* 47 (July): 179–224.

    1980   "The Bernese Anabaptists in Sainte-Marie-aux-Mines." Translated by Mervin Smucker, *Pennsylvania Mennonite Heritage* 3 (July): 2–9.

Smith, Stephen M., Jill L. Findeis, Donald B. Kraybill, Steven M. Nolt, Conrad L. Kanagy, and Michele L. Kozimor

    1994   "Amish Micro-Enterprises: Models for Rural Development, Final Report." State College, Pa.: Pennsylvania State University, Department of Agricultural Economics and Rural Sociology.

Snyder, C. Arnold

    1995   *Anabaptist History and Theology: An Introduction.* Kitchener, Ont.: Pandora Press.

Song, Miri

    1999   *Helping Out: Children's Labor in Ethnic Businesses.* Philadelphia: Temple University Press.

Stoll, Steven

    2002   *Larding the Lean Earth: Soil and Society in Nineteenth-Century America.* New York: Hill and Wang.

Stoltzfus, Amos J.

    1984   *Golden Memories.* Gordonville, Pa.: Pequea Publishers.

Stoltzfus, Grant M.

    1954   "History of the First Amish Mennonite Communities in America." *Mennonite Quarterly Review* 28 (October): 235–62.

Stoltzfus, Louise

    1994   *Amish Women: Lives and Stories.* Intercourse, Pa.: Good Books.

    1998   *Traces of Wisdom: Amish Women and the Pursuit of Life's Simple Pleasures.* N.Y.: Hyperion

    2000   *The Story of Tourism in Lancaster County, PA.* Lancaster, Pa.: Pennsylvania Dutch Convention and Visitors Bureau.

Stoltzfus, Victor E.

    1973   "Amish Agriculture: Adaptive Strategies for Economic Survival of Community Life," *Rural Sociology* 38 (Summer): 196–206.

Tan, Tay Keong

    1998   "Silence, Sacrifice and Shoofly Pies: An Inquiry into Social Capital and Organizational Strategies of the Amish Community in Lancaster County, Pennsylvania." Ph.D. diss., John F. Kennedy School of Government, Harvard University.

Tepper, Terri P., and Nona Dawe Tepper

    1980   "Naomi Fisher: Designer, Manufacturer, and Retailer of Quilts." In *The New Entrepreneurs: Women Working from Home.* New York: Universe.

Testa, Randy-Michael

    1992   *After the Fire: The Destruction of the Lancaster County Amish.* Hanover, N.H.: University Press of New England.

Troyer, Henry, and Lee Willoughby

    1984   "Changing Occupational Patterns in the Holmes County, Ohio, Amish Community." In *Internal and External Perspectives on Amish and Mennonite Life,* ed. Werner Enninger, 52–80. Essen, Germany: Unipress.

Umble, Diane Zimmerman

    1994   "Amish on the Line: The Telephone Debates." In *The Amish Struggle with Modernity,* ed. Donald B. Kraybill and Marc A. Olshan. Hanover, N.H.: University Press of New England.

    1996   *Holding the Line: The Telephone in Old Order Mennonite and Amish Life.* Baltimore: Johns Hopkins University Press.

Walbert, David

    2002   *Garden Spot: Lancaster County, The Old Order Amish, and the Selling of Rural America.* New York: Oxford University Press.

Waldinger, Roger, Howard Aldrich, and Robin Ward

    1990a   Eds. *Ethnic Entrepreneurs: Immigrant Business in Industrial Societies.* Newbury Park, Calif.: Sage Publications.

    1990b   "Opportunities, Group Characteristics, and Strategies." In *Ethnic Entrepreneurs: Immigrant Business in Industrial Societies.* Newbury Park, Calif.: Sage Publications.

Waldinger, Roger, David McEvoy, and Howard Aldrich

    1990   "Spatial Dimensions of Opportunity Structures." In *Ethnic Entrepreneurs: Immigrant Business in Industrial Societies,* ed. Roger Waldinger, Howard Aldrich, and Robin Ward. Newbury Park, Calif.: Sage Publications.

Ward, Robin, and Richard Jenkins

    1984   Eds. *Ethnic Communities in Business: Strategies for Economic Survival.* New York: Cambridge University Press.

Weaver, J. Denny

    1987   *Becoming Anabaptist: The Origin and Significance of Sixteenth-Century Anabaptism.* Scottdale, Pa.: Herald Press.

Weaver-Zercher, David

    2001   *The Amish in the American Imagination.* Baltimore: Johns Hopkins University Press.

Weber, Max

    1947   *Max Weber: The Theory of Social and Economic Organization.* Edited by Talcott Parsons, translated by A. M. Henderson and Talcott Parsons. New York: Free Press.

Woo, Carolyn Y., Arnold C. Cooper, and William C. Dunkelberg

    1991   "The Development and Interpretation of Entrepreneurial Typologies." *Journal of Business Venturing* 6:93–114.

Woolcock, Michael

    1998a   "Social Capital: Its Origins and Applications in Modern Sociology." *Annual Review of Sociology.* Palo Alto, Calif.: Annual Reviews Inc.

    1998b   "Social Capital and Economic Development: Toward a Theoretical Syntheses and Policy Framework." *Theory and Society* 27:151–208.

Wuthnow, Robert

    1987   *Meaning and Moral Order: Exploration in Cultural Analysis.* Berkeley: University of California Press.

Wuthnow, Robert, James Davison Hunter, Albert Bergesen, and Edith Kurzweil

    1984   *Cultural Analysis: The Work of Peter L. Berger, Mary Douglas, Michel Foucault, and Jürgen Habermas.* Boston: Routledge and Kegan Paul.

Yoder, Elmer S.

    1987   *The Beachy Amish Mennonite Fellowship Churches.* Hartville, Ohio: Diakonia Ministries.

Yoder, Freeman L., and Lizzie Yoder

    1998   comps. *Echoes of the Past: Experiences of the Plain People 1920's through 1940's, during the Depression Years and More.* Middlebury, Ind.: F. L. and L. Yoder.

Yoder, John Howard

    1973   Ed. and trans. *The Legacy of Michael Sattler.* Scottdale, Pa.: Herald Press.

Yoder, Paton
1991   *Tradition and Transition: Amish Mennonites and Old Order Amish, 1800–1900.*
Scottdale, Pa.: Herald Press.
2003   "The Amish View of the State." In *The Amish and the State,* rev. ed., ed.
Donald B. Kraybill. Baltimore: Johns Hopkins University Press.
Yu, Eui-Young, Earl H. Phillips, and Eun Sik Yang
1982   *Koreans in Los Angeles: Prospects and Promises.* Los Angeles: Center for
Korean-American and Korean Studies, California State University.
Zimmer, Catherine, and Howard Aldrich
1987   "Resource Mobilization through Ethnic Networks: Kinship and Friendship Ties of Shopkeepers in England." *Sociological Perspectives* 30 (October): 422–45.

INDEX

About the Authors

Donald B. Kraybill
is a senior fellow at the Young Center for Anabaptist and Pietist Studies at Elizabethtown College (PA). He is the author and editor of numerous books on Anabaptist groups, including *Anabaptist World USA* (Herald Press, 2001), *The Riddle of Amish Culture* (Johns Hopkins, 1989; rev. ed., 2001), *On the Backroad to Heaven: Old Order Hutterites, Mennonites, Amish and Brethren*, with Carl Desportes Bowman (Johns Hopkins, 2001), and *The Amish and the State* (Johns Hopkins, 1993; 2nd ed., 2003).

Steven M. Nolt
is associate professor of history at Goshen College (IN). He is the author of numerous scholarly articles on Anabaptist groups as well as several books, including *A History of the Amish* (Good Books, 1992; rev. ed., 2003) and *Foreigners in Their Own Land: Pennsylvania Germans in the Early Republic* (Penn State University Press, 2002).

Center Books in Anabaptist Studies

Carl F. Bowman, *Brethren Society: The Cultural Transformation of a "Peculiar People"*

Perry Bush, *Two Kingdoms, Two Loyalties: Mennonite Pacifism in Modern America*

John A. Hostetler, ed., *Amish Roots: A Treasury of History, Wisdom, and Lore*

Julia Kasdorf, *The Body and the Book: Writing from a Mennonite Life*

Donald B. Kraybill, *The Riddle of Amish Culture*, rev. ed.

Donald B. Kraybill, ed., *The Amish and the State*, 2d edition

Donald B. Kraybill and Carl Desportes Bowman, *On the Backroad to Heaven: Old Order Hutterites, Mennonites, Amish, and Brethren*

Donald B. Kraybill and Steven M. Nolt, *Amish Enterprise: From Plows to Profits*, 2d edition

Werner O. Packull, *Hutterite Beginnings: Communitarian Experiments during the Reformation*

Benjamin W. Redekop and Calvin W. Redekop, eds., *Power, Authority, and the Anabaptist Tradition*

Calvin Redekop, Stephen C. Ainlay, and Robert Siemens, *Mennonite Entrepreneurs*

Calvin Redekop, ed., *Creation and the Environment: An Anabaptist Perspective on a Sustainable World*

Steven D. Reschly, *The Amish on the Iowa Prairie, 1840 to 1910*

Kimberly D. Schmidt, Diane Zimmerman Umble, and Steven D. Reschly, *Strangers at Home: Amish and Mennonite Women in History*

Diane Zimmerman Umble, *Holding the Line: The Telephone in Old Order Mennonite and Amish Life*

David Weaver-Zercher, *The Amish in the American Imagination*